# THE U.S. SENATE: FROM DELIBERATION TO DYSFUNCTION

D0074570

# THE U.S. SENATE:
# FROM DELIBERATION
# TO DYSFUNCTION

Editor
## Burdett A. Loomis

Los Angeles | London | New Delhi
Singapore | Washington DC

CQ Press
2300 N Street, NW, Suite 800
Washington, DC 20037

Phone: 202-729-1900; toll-free, 1-866-4CQ-PRESS (1-866-427-7737)
Web: www.cqpress.com

Copyright ©2012 by CQ Press, a division of SAGE. CQ Press is a registered trademark of Congressional Quarterly Inc.

All rights reserved. No part of this publication may be reproduced or transmitted in any form or by any means, electronic or mechanical, including photocopy, recording, or any information storage and retrieval system, without permission in writing from the publisher.

Cover design: Auburn Associates, Inc., Baltimore, Maryland
Composition: C&M Digitals (P) Ltd.

♾ The paper used in this publication exceeds the requirements of the American National Standard for Information Sciences—Permanence of Paper for Printed Library Materials, ANSI Z39.48-1992.

Printed and bound in the United States of America
15   14   13   12   11        1   2   3   4   5

**Library of Congress Cataloging-in-Publication Data**

The U.S. Senate: from deliberation to dysfunction/Burdett A. Loomis, editor.
   p. cm.
  Includes index.
  ISBN 978-1-60871-727-9 (alk. paper)
  1. United States. Congress. Senate. 2. United States—Politics and government.
I. Loomis, Burdett A., 1945-
  JK1161.U53 2012
  328.73′071—dc23

                                         2011026290

# Contents

# Tables and Figures

**Figures**

## Tables

# Acknowledgments

As Don Matthews finished reading the proofs for *U.S. Senators and their World* in 1960, county attorney Bob Dole was preparing to run against an incumbent Republican congressman in the far northwest corner of Kansas. Thirty-six years later, Dole would leave the Senate, after serving more than 27 years, to become a full-time, if ultimately unsuccessful, presidential candidate. In the wake of that race, the University of Kansas created the Robert J. Dole Institute of Politics, largely dedicated to encouraging the understanding of and participation in American political life. And although Bob Dole's presidential bid was certainly noteworthy, it is as a Senate leader that he truly made his mark on American political life.

In March, 2010, the Dole Institute played host to a two-day conference on the evolution of the Senate over the past fifty years. Institute Director Bill Lacy supported this project from its inception, and the Institute provided the major source of funding for the conference: "Changing the 'Slow Institution': The U.S. Senate, 1960–2010. The Kansas Humanities Commission also provided valuable financial support, which allowed for a wider dissemination of the presentations. In particular, Dan Carey-Whalen was most constructive and encouraging in his backing for the conference. At the Dole Institute, Maggie Mahoney made everything click like clockwork, with the help of Cori Ast and Emily Sherwood. The Lawrence Public Library provided an additional venue for a talk, and I'm most grateful to Bruce Flanders and Maria Butler.

Above all, I'm pleased to have had the opportunity to work with such a terrific group of scholars, both at the conference and book stages. Beyond the authors represented here, I'd like to thank Nate Monroe and Michael Lynch for chairing panel sessions at the conference. Over the years it's been a great pleasure to work within the legislative studies field, where civility and productivity have gone hand in hand for fifty years. The Senate might well take note. This project has confirmed all my positive predispositions toward those who study legislatures, and especially the U.S. Senate. It's just been great fun. Finally, I want to thank CQ Press, and especially Charisse Kiino, for committing to this book early on, and getting it into print in a most timely fashion.

From the moment I began soliciting support on this project to the very end of the publication process, I've never had a more positive and gratifying scholarly experience. I want to thank everyone involved.

This book is dedicated to Don Matthews, Dick Fenno, and the late Senator Paul Simon, for whom I worked as a congressional fellow. All three have contributed to our understanding of the perplexing and singular U.S. Senate.

Burdett Loomis
Lawrence, Kansas

# Contributors

Participants in the Robert F. Dole Institute of Politics Symposium: Changing the "Slow" Institution: The U.S. Senate, 1960–2010

**Alan I. Abramowitz** is the Alben W. Barkley Professor of Political Science at Emory University. He has published widely in electoral politics, including *The Disappearing Center* and *Senate Elections.* He has been an active and influential blogger on electoral politics.

**Ross K. Baker** is professor of political science at Rutgers University. His books include *Friend and Foe in the U.S. Senate* (1980, and 1999), *The New Fat Cats* (1989), *House and Senate* (1989, 1995, and 2000). He is a regular contributor to the editorial pages of the *Los Angeles Times* and *Newsday*, and a frequent presence on NPR.

**Sarah Binder** is professor of political science at George Washington Univeristy and a senior fellow at the Brookings Institution. Among her several books are *Stalemate* and *Politics or Principle: Filibustering in the United States Senate*, with Steven Smith.

**Gregory Koger** is an assistant professor of political science at the University of Miami. His book, *Filibustering: A Political History of Obstruction in the House and Senate* was published in 2010 to considerable acclaim. He has appeared on NPR and has been widely quoted on contemporary filibuster politics.

**Frances E. Lee** is an associate professor of political science at the University of Maryland. Among her publications are the Fenno Prize-winning *Beyond Ideology: Politics, Principles and Partisanship in the U.S. Senate* and *Sizing Up the Senate* (with Bruce I. Oppenheimer).

**James M. Lindsay** serves as the senior Vice-President, Director of Studies, and Maurice R. Greenberg Chair at the Council on Foreign Relations. His books include: *America Unbound: The Bush Revolution in Foreign Policy and Congress* and *The Politics of U.S. Foreign Policy.*

**Burdett Loomis** is professor of political science at the University of Kansas. He edited and contributed to *Esteemed Colleagues: Civility in the U.S. Senate* and is the author of *The New American Politician.*

**Bruce I. Oppenheimer** is professor of political science at Vanderbilt University. He is the co-author of *Sizing Up the Senate* and the editor of *Senate Exceptionalism*. He co-edits *Congress Reconsidered*, the leader reader on Congress.

**David W. Rohde** is Ernestine Friedl Professor of Political Science at Duke University. Among many books and articles, he has written *Parties and Leaders in the Postreform House*, along with many volumes of *Continuity and Change in American Elections* since 1980.

**Eric Schickler** is professor of political science at the University of California-Berkeley. He is the author of the prize-winning volumes: *Disjointed Pluralism* and *Filibuster: Obstruction and Lawmaking in the U.S. Senate* (with Greg Wawro)

**Barbara Sinclair** is Marvin Hoffenberg Professor of American Politics at University of California, Los Angeles. Among her many books are *The Transformation of the U.S.Senate, Legislators, Leaders and Lawmaking: The U.S. House of Representatives in the Postreform Era, Unorthodox Lawmaking: New Legislative Processes in the U.S. Congress* and *Party Wars: Polarization and the Politics of National Policy Making*.

**Steven S. Smith** is the director of the Weidenbaum Center on the Economy, Government, and Public Policy, the Kate M. Gregg Professor of Social Sciences, and professor of political science at Washington University in St. Louis. He has written extensively on procedures, committees, and parties in the U.S. Congress, including *Call to Order: Floor Politics in the House and Senate* and *Politics or Principle: Filibustering in the United States Senate*, (with Sarah Binder).

# THE U.S. SENATE:
# FROM DELIBERATION TO
# DYSFUNCTION

# Introduction

## "The Senate Goes On" – Changing the Slow Institution, 1960 – 2010

> The following January the Capitol, abandoned for several months to the tourists, comes to life again. The senators reappear. Along with them come the throngs of journalists, lobbyists, and staff assistants, and administrators who live on the fringe of power . . . the defeated move out, the old timers move up to better offices, and the newcomers move into whatever is left. The bell rings again. The Senate goes on.
>
> Donald R. Matthews, *U.S. Senators and Their World* (1960)

Thus does Don Matthews conclude the initial book of modern scholarship on the Congress, U.S. Senators and Their World. In the fifty years since its publication, congressional scholarship has evolved and matured, and yet the Senate, that singular body, remains something of a mystery. While the House of Representatives has received an immense amount of scholarly attentions, Senate analyses have been spotty at best. Indeed, only with Barbara Sinclair's 1989 The Transformation of the U.S. Senate was there a broad-brush empirical portrait to match Matthews's 1960 volume. Sinclair's work remains the last such effort, even as the chamber has built on the trends of growing partisanship and individualism that she identified in Transformation and subsequent scholarship (Sinclair 2001, 2006, for example). In addition, in 1989 Ken Shepsle published the brief, but highly influential, article "The Changing Textbook Congress," which provided a powerful label for the Congress of the 1950s. That same year, Call to Order: Floor Politics in the House and Senate, Steven Smith offered a detailed look at Senate procedures as they had evolved.

Even absent definitive conclusions, Sinclair and Shepsle did identify central trends that were still emerging in 1989, especially the growing strength of partisanship in the upper house. Although Sinclair (2006, among others) and Frances Lee (2009) have explored aspects of the Senate's increasing partisanship, no single volume has fully assessed this development in conjunction with the sharply greater willingness of minority–party senators to push the use of Senate rules toward the breaking point – or from a different perspective, to protect the Republic from immeasurable harm. At the same time, we do have substantial literatures on congressional parties and procedures to draw upon, as we address the implications of high levels of partisanship in a body whose rules have traditionally favored delay, obstruction, and the rights of minorities. (among others, Binder and Smith, 1997; Wawro and Schickler, 2006; and Koger, 2010 on filibusters; on parties, Rohde, 1991; Cox and McCubbins, 1993; and Poole and Rosenthal, 2007). In addition, Keith Krehbiel's "pivotal politics" work (1998), along with various responses to it, has provided a fertile context for analysis of a Senate that so frequently requires supermajorities to function.

Although the legislative politics of the Bill Clinton and George W. Bush eras offered a growing body of evidence that the Senate had entered a new phase of operation in coupling strong partisanship with extensive obstructionism, it has been the experiences of the Obama Administration and the 111th Congress that have moved often obscure Senate politicking even more into the public eye. The Senate of 2010 has come under increasing popular scrutiny, with many calls for its reform – largely surrounding the related issues of filibusters and holds imposed by individual senators. Indeed, perhaps the most influential popular article in this array of criticism, by George Packer (2010) in *The New Yorker*, does not ask *if* the Senate is broken, but rather, *how broken* it is. To be sure, as Barbara Sinclair and others note in this volume, the growth of procedural obstructionism over the past 20-30 years has been substantial, yet defenders of current rules argue that the Senate did pass sweeping health care and financial services reforms, despite the steadfast opposition of the Republican minority. Moreover, filibuster supporters observe (with support from several articles in this volume) that ideology is at least as important as procedure:

> After all, the legislative process has not become "broken." It is largely the same process as it was decades ago. The real change has occurred within the two Senate parties. They are using the filibuster more aggressively in their quest for political success (Cost, 2010).

In the wake of the 2004-5 discussion of changing Senate filibuster rules by a simple majority voter – the so-called "Nuclear Option" – there has been considerable speculation by journalists, politicians, law professors, and political scientists about the how the Senate can or should change its rules on debate. (for example, Gold and Gupta, 2004; Beth, 2005; various articles by Ezra Klein, 2010) With Obama's pursuit of health care legislation in 2009-10, the incidence of obstructionism increased to the point that 70 percent of major legislation was subject to delaying tactics, and even more consideration of possible reforms has occurred. To an extent, this is encouraging; the Senate's anti-majoritarian structure, fashioned by a combination of constitutional, formal, and informal rules, deserves serious analysis that might well lead to procedural change. Indeed, several of the contributors to this volume have testified on Capitol Hill in hearings addressing the possibility and nature of procedural reforms.

Although the essays in this volume do address issues of delay, obstruction, and polarization in a host of ways, they ultimately are not designed to adumbrate a reform agenda. Rather, taken together these twelve original pieces provide a broad picture of the contemporary Senate and how it came to be. If the Senate is to be "reformed," would-be reformers must address the findings and observations found here, many of which place the alleged dysfunction of the chamber in historical and political contexts that demonstrate how difficult it is to change a non-majoritarian, highly individualistic institution with its unique combination of tradition, precedent, and constitutional mandate.

## From Deliberation to Dysfunction: 1960-2010

The Senate of 1960 seems a familiar place for most politically aware Americans, to say nothing of congressional scholars. Thanks to work done by political scientists, Matthews, Ralph Huitt (1961), Randall Ripley (1969), among others, historian Julian Zelizer (2004) and LBJ biographer Robert Caro (2002), we have a well-developed collective view of the Senate of the so-called "Inner Club" era (White, 1957). There is also an understandable tendency, not necessarily by scholars, to romanticize that era, with its greater civility and bipartisanship. In the essay that sets the stage for the remainder of this volume, Eric Schickler provides a detailed version of the Senate at mid-Century, which reinforces much of the "Textbook Congress" landscape while simultaneously emphasizing how party leaders Johnson and Taft rose rapidly in the seniority-oriented institution. Moreover, although the "Inner Club" may well have been powerful, it was scarcely all-powerful, as numerous senators used outsider tactics to affect legislative agendas and inside politics. In various ways, the trends that developed in the 1970s and 1980s had more clear precedents in the Congress of the 1950s than previous analyses have concluded. (Foley, 1980, for example). Schickler argues that the collegial portrait of the 1950s Senate, while generally accurate, needs to be viewed as something of an exception to a Senate that frequently has experienced partisan tensions and successful individualists.

In his exploration of the growing polarization of the U.S. Senate over the past half-century, Alan Abramowitz details the electorate's impact in creating a highly partisan chamber, and he identifies various forces that have played a role. For example, geographical differentiation in the growth of Southern Republicans and the demise of their Northeastern colleagues overlaps with increased racial and ethnic voting trends along party lines. Ambramowitz's article provides an essential background for the rest of the book, in that Senate partisanship is deeply rooted within the electorate especially among those who pay the most attention. His findings must be addressed by anyone who makes the argument that the Senate should simply return to its allegedly golden era of the 1950s and early 1960s, when, in fact, there were many conservative Democrats and a fair number of *liberal* Republicans, such as New York's Jacob Javits and Maryland's Charles Mathias.

The companion piece to Ambramowitz's electoral analysis is Ross Baker's cataloguing of House-Senate relations since 1960. Baker's descriptive chapter tracks the chambers' leadership changes and the evolution of their relations over the course of this period. This is important in that, as he notes, generalizing about bicameral relations is difficult at best; among other elements, personal linkages among leaders are central to their understanding. Likewise, chamber rules and practices have changed substantially over the course of the past five decades, including some that affect both bodies, while others deal with only one, and still others (e.g., the impact of Senate reconciliation procedure on conference reports) that directly impinge on inter-chamber relations. Moreover, partisan developments in one house often have an impact on the other, likewise with rules and practices, especially in the Senate. Baker notes:

> The requirements for unanimous consent to proceed in the Senate, the filibuster, the hold, and the "blue slip" system on presidential nominations vest in individual senators, majority and minority alike, a degree of influence that is enjoyed only by the most senior members of the majority party in the House.

Indeed, he emphasizes the core point that many House members can be ignored, most of the time, whereas no senator who desires to have an impact can be denied. It is no wonder that more and more Senators come from the ranks of the House, and especially the backbenches.

Such a trend is one element in the changing nature of how senators shape their careers. To be sure, as Burdett Loomis points out, senators remain highly interested and eligible potential candidates for president, although only John Kennedy and Barack Obama, at the beginning and end of the 1960-2010 period achieved their goal as senators. Increasingly, senators have come from the House, which has grown more contentious and majority-driven since the 1970s. Senate leaders, often with House experience in the 1990s, have not countered the trends produced by partisan electorates and increasing pressures for party-line votes. This environment may have changed the nature of the Senate career, as senators look toward the private sector for rewarding – both financially and personally – opportunities such as those embraced by Bob Dole, Tom Daschle, George Mitchell, and others. One need not romanticize the old Senate to see that the modern body, with its fund-raising obligations, polarization, delays, and lack of collegiality, imposes increasing costs without commensurate benefits.

Still, there is no shortage of incumbents running for reelection, nor challengers eager to take on the challenge of governing. To do this, they address the central elements of Senate life, circa 2010: partisanship, ideology, and procedure. In what is perhaps the core of this volume, Barbara Sinclair, Frances Lee, and Steven Smith examine these elements of the Senate as they have evolved over the past fifty years and how, in particular, they shape the contemporary institution. Over the past 20 years, Sinclair has chronicled the "new Senate,' and her observations here summarize much of her work. Obstructionism in the Senate, cemented by strong, in not absolute, partisanship has created a body in which trying to reach agreement is at best difficult, and too often impossible. She writes:

> The combination of highly polarized parties and chamber rules requiring supermajorities for most significant decisions makes legislating difficult and majority party leadership a thankless task.

To be sure, others have described the difficulties of leading the Senate in colorful language, as with former Majority Leader Trent Lott's (2005) notion of "herding cats" or political scientist Roger Davidson's (1985) description as "Janitors for an Untidy Chamber." But given the expanded and aggressive use of extended debate, cloture, filibuster threats, and holds, along with the individual agendas of Senators like Jim Bunning, Jim DeMint, Joe Lieberman, and Russ Feingold, the majority and minority floor leaders must struggle to keep the chamber operating, to say nothing of being productive. And given the successful ideologically-based challenges to such mainstream as Republicans Robert Bennett (Col.) and Lisa Murkowski (Alaska), and Democrat Arlen Specter (Pa.), party leaders may well face even more difficulty in moving even ordinary legislative business through the Senate.

It is simple to focus just on growing partisanship in the Senate, but, as usual with this complex institution, simplicity can be misleading. Frances Lee provides some nuances to our understanding, noting how greater polarization has acted to restrict a substantial amount of the individualistic behavior and initiatives that have long characterized the Senate. To be sure, there are many instances of holds and threatened filibusters, but within the legislative process, senators are less likely to offer amendments, especially within the majority. And minority members, who offer the lion's share of amendments, do so within a felt need to establish a party narrative, rather than seeking to improve the ultimate legislative product. We may yearn for an earlier Senate, in which individual legislators such as Daniel Patrick Moynihan, Ted Kennedy, and even Jesse Helms sought to address issue through amendments and debate. Lee sees these relatively recent senators as truly representing a bygone era, even if current senators could match the skills of such former luminaries; she concludes, "For many senators in the contemporary Congress, floor activism may be less a function of their personal stylistic choice than of their majority or minority party status."

If party has tempered individualism within the conventional legislative process, these two characteristics have reinforced each other when it comes to obstruction, delay, and the use of procedure to affect the Senate's ability to conduct business. Drawing upon his considerable expertise on Senate procedure, Steven Smith argues that the body's traditional respect for delay and debate evolved into something more pernicious by 2005 or so, and had grown even more problematic circa 2010. He writes:

> In today's Senate, each party assumes that the other party will fully exploit its procedural options—the majority party assumes that the minority party will obstruct legislation and the minority assumes that the majority will restrict its opportunities. Leaders are expected to fully exploit the rules in the interests of their parties. The minority is quick to obstruct and the majority is quick to restrict. Senators of both parties are frustrated by what has become of their institution.

He labels these practices as the "obstruct and restrict syndrome," which defines actions for all major, and many minor, issues. Though rooted in Senate tradition, the routine use of filibusters, anticipatory cloture motions, and holds, among other tactics, creates a dysfunctional legislative environment. When linked to Abramowitz's and Sinclair's presentation of trends in voting and partisanship, Smith's procedural accounting demonstrates a set of powerful trends that place the Senate at the center of national policy-making, and almost always in ways that diminish the Congress's ability to address major problems, as Oppenheimer develops more fully in a later chapter.

Adding detail to Smith's analysis is Greg Koger's comparison of the filibuster, circa 1960, as opposed to its manifestation in 2010. Koger finds that filibusters, while significant in the 1960s, especially on civil rights, did not grind the legislative process to a halt, as the considerable mythology of filibustering might suggest. Rather, the regular appropriations process moved bills through the process in a timely and regular way, in stark contrast to the contemporary Senate, where filibusters in their modern form are commonplace, and the ability to obstruct disrupts important routine legislation, such as appropriations bills.

In her analysis of judicial confirmations (Ch. 9), Sarah Binder concludes that the contentious nature of these decisions reflects a qualitatively different kind of Senate politics, compared to the 1960s and 1970s. Binder introduces substantial over-time data to develop her argument, and also address the "So what?" question as to the impact of a polarized and obstructionist Senate confirmation process. Binder quotes a federal appeals court judge who states: "Judicial independence is undermined . . . by the high degree of political partisanship and ideology that currently characterizes the process by which the President nominates and the Senate confirms federal judges . . . [and this polarization] may be undermining the very act of judging, as judges on the right or the left may produce opinions not "true to the rule of law." The changing nature of Senate process may well be affecting the judicial branch, and arguably the executive branch as well, given its obstructionist approach to many administration appointments, regardless of party.

If the Senate's impact on the judiciary is speculative, its contribution to short-term policy thinking is not. The Senate was constructed in part to encourage reflection and well-considered judgment, but its current manifestation cuts firmly against this grain. Among the chapters in this volume, none takes more advantage of looking at the entire 1960-2010 period than Bruce Oppenheimer's sober assessment of energy policy in this era. Given his own long-term interest in legislative energy politics, Oppenheimer demonstrates how the Congress as a whole and the Senate in particular has systematically proved incapable of addressing this critical set of issues with thoughtful, long-range initiatives. Although the House members, with their two-year election cycles, have naturally focused on immediate policy implications, Oppenheimer points out that senators have recently responded even more to short-term forces. In particular, the need for 60 votes to enact cloture requires majority building on a rickety, fragile basis.

Moreover, since 1980, the Senate has proved more electorally volatile than the House, with control changing hands six times through 2010, compared to just twice for the House, although that chamber's control also has been in play in virtually every election since 1994. Oppenheimer focuses largely on energy policy, where our long-term vulnerability has been clear for decades, but his analysis applies to many other domestic issues, from health care to social security to infrastructure. Discouragingly, he concludes:

> The Senate of the past half-century has grown increasingly divorced from its traditional role. Its unique ability within the institutional framework of American democracy to pursue the country's longer-term policy interests rather than being responsive to the whims of the electorate has eroded.

In assessing the parallel subject of foreign policy, James Lindsay sees the Senate as changing substantially in how it addresses such policy, but he remains more sanguine in his conclusions; most notably, he finds the Senate as continuing to fulfill its constitutional role of "advice and consent" as laid out by the framers. Lindsay finds the Senate's approach to foreign relations as changing substantially since 1960. He labels the late1950s and 1960s as a period of "consent without advice," in that despite the prestige of the Senate Foreign Relations Committee, it did not offer strong independent advice to an increasingly powerful executive branch. Subsequently, through the 1970s and 1980s, the Senate "reclaimed advice" as it became more assertive in its dealings with the President in the post-Nixon era. More recently, in the 1990s and through the second Bush and Obama administrations, the Senate has entered an "advice, but not necessarily consent" phase, in which foreign policy politics and appointments have become more contentious.

In the end, Lindsay observes an erosion of the long-held "internationalist consensus" in the Senate, as foreign policy has become increasingly framed by partisan politics. Even as he sees real changes in the Senate's handling of foreign policy and the impact of partisanship, Lindsay finds the chamber as meeting its constitutional obligation to take part in, but not dominate, the making of U.S. foreign policy, which lies primarily in the hands of the executive branch, as the framers intended.

Most social scientists are loath to look too far into the future, and David Rohde is no exception, but he does venture forth a bit in his treatment of how the Senate might or might not evolve in upcoming years. To consider the future, Rohde, with the able assistance from the other contributors to this volume, looks back at the arc of Senate development over the past fifty years. He finds little reason to think that the partisan and ideological trends that have dominated the past twenty-plus years will not continue to prevail. Nor does he see much chance of voluntary restraint on the use of delaying procedures that have come to dominate the Senate; minority members see themselves as having too much at stake. Institutional reform remains an option, but even if it only takes 51 votes at the beginning of a session to change the rules, he remains skeptical that members, most of whom have served in the minority in the past (and all of whom can see that possibility in the future), would likely choose to weaken the rules that encourage obstructionism.

All in all, the Senate of 2010 differs greatly from its 1960 predecessor; the last remaining senator among those serving in 1960 was Robert Byrd, who died in 2010. But Byrd's long, remarkable career also illustrates that the Senate is a continuing body, which changes incrementally over the years, while maintaining its constitutional position within the Congress and the national government. The Senate does not face reapportionment, and thus changes in its membership reflect changes within the respective states' electorates. And the voters have become more partisan, often sorting themselves among the states, as in migrations South and West.

The short-term thinking of many senators, and the opportunities beyond the chamber may have lessened the luster of Senate service, at least a bit. Still, the Senate may well remain the "world's most exclusive club," even as it struggles to address the issues of the day. It is the slow institution, to be sure, but new members reshape it every two years, sometimes substantially so. With continuing polarization and partisanship in place, the Senate will proceed, always with the real chance that frequent delay will become institutional dysfunction. But nothing is permanent in such a resilient body. As Don Matthews reminded us, fifty years ago, "the Senate goes on."

# References

Beth, Richard. 2005. "Entrenchment" of Senate Procedure and the "Nuclear Option" for Change: Possible Proceedings and Their Implications, Congressional Research Service Issue Brief, March 28.

Binder, Sarah, and Steven S. Smith, *Politics or Principle? Filibustering in the U.S. Senate*, Brookings 1997.

Caro, Robert A. 2002. *The Years of Lyndon Johnson: Master of the Senate*. New York: Knopf.

Cost, Jay. 2009. "Why the Filibuster Is More Essential Now than Ever," *RealClearPolitics*, January 28. Accessed at *www.realclearpolitics.com*, September 24, 2010

Cox, Gary W. and Mathew D. McCubbins. 1993. *Legislative Leviathan: Party Government in the House*. Berkley and Los Angeles: University of California Press

Davidson, Roger H. 1985. "Senate Leaders: Janitors for an Untidy Chamber?" *Congress Reconsidered*. 3 rd ed., eds. Lawrence C. Dodd and Bruce I. Oppenheimer. Washington, DC: CQ Press.

Foley, Michael. 1980. *The New Senate*. New Haven: Yale.

Gold, M. Gold & D. Gupta. 2004. "The Constitutional Option to Change Senate Rules and Procedures: a Majoritarian Means to Overcome the Filibuster," 28 *Harvard Journal of Law & Pub. Policy* 205, 236–39

Huitt, Ralph K. 1961. "Democratic Party Leadership in the Senate." *American Political Science Review*, 55:333-44

Klein, Ezra. 2010. "How to End the Filibuster with 51 Votes," *Washington Post*, July 27, accessed at www.washingtonppost.com, September 14, 2010.

Koger, Greg. 2010. *Filibustering: A Political History of Obstruction in the House and Senate*. Chicago: University of Chicago Press

Krehbiel, Keith. 1998. *Pivotal Politics*

Lee, Frances. 2009. *Beyond Ideology: Politics, Principles, and Partisanship in the U.S. Senate*. Chicago: University of Chicago Press

Lott, Trent. 2005. *Herding Cats: A Life in Politics*. New York: William Morrow.

Packer, George. 2010. "The Empty Chamber: Just How Broken Is the Senate?" *The New Yorker*, August 9, 2010.

Poole, Keith and Howard Rosenthal. 2007. *Ideology and Congress*. Transaction Publishers

Rohde, David. 1991. *Parties and Leaders in the Post-Reform House*. Chicago: University of Chicago Press

Shepsle, Kenneth. 1989. "The Changing 'Textbook Congress," in *Can the Government Govern?* John E. Chubb and Paul E. Peterson, ed. Washington: Brookings.

Sinclair, Barbara. 1989. *The Transformation of the U.S. Senate*, Baltimore: Johns Hopkins University Press.

Sinclair, Barbara. 2001. "The New World of U.S. Senators," in Lawrence C. Dodd and Bruce I. Oppenheimer, eds., *Congress Reconsidered*, 7th ed. Washington: CQ Press.

Sinclair, Barbara. *Party Wars*. 2006. Norman, Oklahoma: University of Oklahoma Press.

Smith, Steven S. 1989. *Call to Order: Floor Politics in the House and Senate*. Washington: Brookings Institution Press.

Wawro, Gregory, and Eric Schickler. *Filibuster: Obstruction and Lawmaking in the United States Senate*. Princeton University Press, 2006.

White, William S. 1957. *Citadel: The Story of the U.S. Senate*. New York: Harper and Brothers.

# 1

# The U.S. Senate in the Mid-Twentieth Century

Eric Schickler

The Senate at mid-twentieth century forms the backdrop for much of what people see as wrong with today's Senate. The rampant individualism, incessant obstruction, and intense partisan warfare that mark the contemporary Senate are largely missing from our collective understanding of how the Senate worked at mid-century. To be sure, scholars have paid attention to the shortcomings of the Senate of the 1940s and 1950s. These include the ability of southern Democrats to block civil rights initiatives that were beginning to gain the support of a majority of voters and the generalized hostility of the institution to innovation. Regardless of how one weighs the strengths and weaknesses of the mid-century Senate, key features of today's institution stand in stark relief, making the earlier Senate a useful point of contrast for important studies of the modern Senate (see, e.g., Sinclair 1989, 2001; Rohde, Ornstein, and Peabody 1985; Smith 1989).

One reason that the mid-century Senate continues to serve as a starting point for contemporary studies is that we have a rich information base for understanding it. The direct observations and systematic analyses of eminent political scientists such as Donald Matthews, Ralph Huitt, and Nelson Polsby produced a textured account of how the Senate operated as both a social system and as a policymaking body. Influential popular books depicting the Senate of the 1940s and 1950s supplemented this account. Leading examples include William S. White's *Citadel: The Story of the U.S. Senate* (1957) and Rowland Evans and Robert Novak's *Lyndon B. Johnson: The Exercise of Power* (1966). More recent scholarly studies—for example, those undertaken by Barbara Sinclair and Steven Smith—have provided time series data on specific features of Senate politics that provide systematic evidence of how Senate operations have changed since the 1950s. As a result of all this work, one might well assert that there are few periods in Senate

Paper prepared for the Robert J. Dole Institute of Politics Symposium, "Changing the 'Slow' Institution: The U.S. Senate, 1960–2010," University of Kansas, Lawrence, Kan., March 25–26, 2010. The helpful comments of David Mayhew, Burdett Loomis, and the participants in the Dole Institute Symposium are greatly appreciated.

history for which we have as coherent a portrait of how the institution operated as in its mid-century form.

This chapter will focus first on that portrait, providing a sense of what
we have learned about how the Senate operated at mid-century. Much of
the collective portrait of that Senate stands the test of time. However, the
second part of this chapter will revisit some of the common assumptions
about the coherence and stability of the mid-century Senate. In particular,
I will argue that some features often associated with that institution were
not consolidated until the early to mid-1950s—only to fade away soon
thereafter—while other features were subject to significant exceptions and
complications. Although the conventional portrait of the Senate as a social
and political system continues to offer important insights into the Senate
of the 1950s, the fragility and contradictions inherent in that system may
warrant greater attention than they have received.[1]

## I. Prevailing Themes in the Study of the Mid-Century Senate

Several interconnected themes emerge when one considers the nature
of the mid-century Senate. First, scholars have long highlighted the role of
norms and folkways in creating expectations that shaped the behavior of
individual senators. These norms gave rise to an environment of restraint in
which senators—mindful of the need to maintain good relationships with
their colleagues—did not push individual prerogatives to the limit. This
restraint was especially evident in a second key feature of the mid-century
Senate that contrasts sharply with today's Senate: the limited use of the
filibuster. A third key theme is the central role of an "Inner Club" of senior,
institutionally oriented senators in enforcing norms and running the Senate.
This club was largely composed of southern Democrats and Republicans,
and thus is linked to a fourth key feature of the mid-century Senate: the
power of the conservative coalition. Finally, Democratic leader Lyndon
Johnson came to symbolize the core features of the mid-century Senate, so
that it has often been referred to as "the Johnson Senate."

### Norms and Folkways at Mid-Century

The single most influential scholarly portrait of the mid-century Senate was
that of Donald Matthews in his book *U.S. Senators and Their World* (1960).

---

1. It is important to emphasize that contemporary scholarship on the Senate does not
accept the conventional portrait uncritically and has greatly advanced our understanding of
the incentives underlying the patterns of behavior identified in earlier work. It is also worth
noting that several of my specific "revisions" to the conventional portrait of the Senate can
be traced to Ralph Huitt's studies of the Senate (see, e.g., Huitt 1961a, 1961b).

Matthews observes that "the Senate of the United States, just as any other group of human beings, has its unwritten rules of the game, its norms of conduct, its approved manner of behavior. Some things are just not done; others are met with widespread approval" (92). Matthews depicts the Senate as an inward-looking, relatively closed institution in which a set of norms—referred to as folkways—regulated behavior. These norms instructed senators on how they should view their job: new senators should wait a substantial amount of time before participating actively in policy debates (*apprenticeship*); each senator should specialize, focusing on a handful of matters that are under the jurisdiction of his committees or that have a direct impact on his state (*specialization*); and a good senator will focus on legislative tasks rather than seeking publicity (*legislative work*). These norms also governed how senators treat one another and the institution as a whole. Personal attacks on other senators should be avoided (*courtesy*); senators should show restraint in their use of individual prerogatives and should be willing to help their colleagues out when they are in need, with the expectation that they will be repaid in kind (*reciprocity*); and senators should protect the prestige of the Senate (*institutional patriotism*).[2] Matthews readily acknowledges that not all senators abided by these norms, but he argues that those who conformed tended to be the most influential, effective members (see also White 1957).

Empirically documenting the strength of norms is notoriously difficult, but considerable evidence supports the idea that apprenticeship and specialization were meaningful norms.[3] Smith (1989: 136) shows that in the 1950s senators in their first term were considerably less likely than senior members to sponsor floor amendments. For example, the average first-term senator sponsored fewer than four amendments in the 84th Congress, while the average senator with more than six years of seniority sponsored more than twice as many. Smith argues that the apprenticeship norm started to fade after the 1958 election, with the influx of a number of ambitious but electorally vulnerable programmatic liberals. Indeed, by the time Matthews' book was published in 1960, apprenticeship was "under severe, and apparently successful, challenge" (Smith 1989: 133). Smith shows that the senior-junior gap in amending activity had completely disappeared by the end of the 1960s.

With respect to specialization, Sinclair (1989) documents the extent to which senators focused their activity on a limited number of issues in the

---

2. See Rohde, Ornstein, and Peabody (1985) for an excellent summary and analysis of these norms.

3. Richard Fenno's *The Power of the Purse* (1966) offers arguably the best demonstration of the importance of norms of specialization and reciprocity in shaping congressional behavior in this era.

mid-century Senate, at least in comparison to the contemporary Senate. For example, she shows that only thirty-three senators in the 84th Congress (1955–56) offered and pushed to a roll call at least one amendment that concerned bills from committees on which the member did not sit. A mere six senators did so more than once. By contrast, non-committee amendments are now routine. More generally, Smith (1989) finds that committees faced far fewer floor challenges to their products in the 1950s than in subsequent decades, reinforcing the contention that norms of specialization and committee deference held sway in the 1950s. Again, both Smith and Sinclair attribute the shift away from these norms largely to the influx of programmatic northern liberals in the late 1950s and 1960s. These members believed that they had to move quickly and decisively to achieve liberal policy innovations—and to make a name for themselves with their constituents—in order to be reelected and to redress what they saw as the major policy problems facing the country (see also Rohde, Ornstein, and Peabody 1985). Norms such as apprenticeship and specialization stood in the way of achieving these goals and thus were increasingly ignored.

Sinclair (1989) adds that the transformation of the Washington policy community in the 1960s undermined mid-century norms of restraint. As the role of the national government expanded with the Great Society, the number and diversity of groups active in Washington exploded. With new, controversial issues on the agenda—and an attendant proliferation of groups eager to recruit senators as advocates for their causes—senators saw the opportunity to play a more active policy leadership role. Norms of deference and specialization were jettisoned as senators took advantage of these opportunities to take on a leading role in setting Washington's political agenda and responding to the entreaties of issue advocates.[4]

## The Filibuster at Mid-Century

The characterization of the mid-century Senate as an institution in which individual restraint was prized fits nicely with the limited use of the filibuster in that era. In their pioneering study of the filibuster, Sarah Binder and Steven Smith (1997) point out that the late 1930s through the early 1960s constitutes a "quiet period" in the use of minority obstruction. The frequency of filibusters in the 1940s and 1950s was well below that in the early twentieth century and in later periods. Drawing primarily upon data

---

4. See Frances Lee (this volume) for an analysis of changing patterns of minority and majority party amendments from the 1950s to the present. Lee's finding that the minority party makes much greater use of amendments to embarrass the majority party in today's Senate is consistent with the idea that norms of reciprocity and restraint have faded amid larger changes in the political context.

compiled by the Congressional Research Service's Richard Beth, Sinclair (2001) notes that there was an average of just one filibuster per Congress in the period 1951–1960 and just two cloture votes in that period. By contrast, there were roughly twenty-seven filibusters and nearly forty cloture votes per Congress by the late 1980s (see Beth 1994). In short, the frequency of filibusters in the 1950s was far below the levels reached in the 1970s and 1980s, let alone the contemporary era in which little gets done in the upper chamber absent supermajority support.

Many scholars have attributed this dearth of obstruction to norms of reciprocity and specialization that discouraged floor activism (see, e.g., Sinclair 1989). Binder and Smith (1997) argue that these norms in large part reflected the underlying power distribution in the Senate: starting in the late 1930s the Senate typically had a relatively conservative floor majority, which meant that there was little need for opponents of liberal policy initiatives to make use of obstruction. Since conservatives had a relatively modest policy agenda of their own, liberals too had little incentive to obstruct business.[5]

Of course, the few filibusters that did take place in the 1940s and 1950s often focused on one of the central policy battlegrounds of the era: civil rights.[6] Southern Democrats notoriously wielded unlimited debate to defeat several major civil rights bills in this era. In the public mind—and among political observers—the filibuster thus became fused with southern opposition to civil rights. Liberals led repeated efforts to use rules changes or parliamentary rulings to roll back the filibuster in this era. These efforts fell short, however, resulting in only modest compromise reforms in 1949 and 1959 (see Wawro and Schickler 2006). In this context, the only civil rights bills that could garner the necessary two-thirds super-majority to invoke cloture put forward weak policies with little or no teeth.

## The Inner Club

The centrality of southern civil rights filibusters contributed to still another aspect of the Senate's image at mid-century: that of an inward-looking, conservative institution dominated by senior members of an "Inner Club"

---

5. Gregory Koger (2010: 161) attributes the paucity of filibusters in this period in part to a reaction against Huey Long's excessive—and at times clownish—use of obstruction during his brief Senate career in 1932–1935. Senators believed Long's obstruction undermined the Senate's reputation and thus were more willing to use social sanctions against "inappropriate filibustering" (161).

6. This is not to say that liberal initiatives in other areas might not have also faced filibuster problems had they gained majority support. For example, had Democrats found a formula to win a majority for Taft-Hartley repeal in the 81st Congress (1949–50), Republicans and southern Democrats may well have attempted a filibuster. But they did not need to resort to this tactic given the lack of a supportive floor majority.

(see Ripley 1969; White 1957; Davidson, Kovenock, and O'Leary 1966; Evans and Novak 1966). White famously argued in *Citadel: The Story of the U.S. Senate* that an informal group made up primarily of southern Democrats and Midwestern Republicans dominated the inner life of the Senate. To White, the Inner Club included those members who had a primary allegiance to the Senate as an institution and did not seek excessive personal publicity. Politics was an insider game, in which longtime senators such as Richard Russell (D-Ga.), Lyndon Johnson, and William Knowland (R-Calif.) worked the levers of power through bargaining with their fellow "Club" members. The "outsiders" who refused to go along with the Club and instead sought personal publicity did not amount to much within the Senate. Johnson himself cultivated the image of an Inner Club running the Senate, going so far as to provide copies of *Citadel*—autographed by both White and Johnson!—to new senators (see Polsby 1969). Presumably Johnson believed that senators would be more likely to defer to his leadership if they believed that doing so was necessary in order to gain influence in the chamber.

The theme of an Inner Club found its way into both popular and academic accounts of the mid-century Senate. Robert Caro (2002) traces how Hubert Humphrey (D-Minn.) initially found himself ostracized by Senate Club members due to his outspoken advocacy of civil rights in the 1948 campaign. Humphrey arrived in the Senate determined to transform the institution, and his maiden speech criticized the Senate for being too cozy and conservative. The new senator brought an African American staff member to eat in the Senate dining room, insisting that the staffer be accommodated after being told that they could not eat together. Humphrey's assertiveness was rewarded by poor committee assignments and overt snubs by his colleagues, both on and off the floor. Interestingly, the consummate insider, Lyndon Johnson, eventually reached out to Humphrey, viewing him as a bridge to the Senate's growing liberal contingent (Caro 2002). White goes so far as to argue that Humphrey had become part of the Club by the mid-1950s, distinguishing him from other liberals who remained outsiders, such as Democrat Paul Douglas of Illinois and Republican-turned-Democrat Wayne Morse of Oregon (see also Clark 1963 on the idea of a "Senate Establishment").

Indeed, the flip side of the Senate Inner Club was the idea that there were a handful of "mavericks" who did not abide by the Club's norms and thus found themselves with little influence in the Senate. These mavericks—Douglas, Morse, Estes Kefauver (D-Tenn.), and William Proxmire (D-Wis.) are often cited as examples—sought to make a name for themselves through appealing to "outside" groups. They did not defer to their more senior colleagues and instead spoke out on a range of issues early in their careers. White and Matthews both suggest that such individuals were aberrations and did not amount to much within the Senate.

While some critics challenged the idea that there ever was a Senate Inner Club (Polsby 1969; Huitt 1961b; see discussion below), the more common view emerging from the literature on the mid-century Senate is that the Club had been real in the 1940s and 1950s but then dissipated in the 1960s. For example, Randall Ripley (1969) argues that the Inner Club's influence had only recently faded away as more liberals and ambitious junior members entered the Senate. Thus, the prevailing account of the Inner Club's role in the Senate fits in with the more general view of the Senate as a relatively insular, conservative institution in which norms of reciprocity and restraint played a crucial role. It was only the influx of a generation of ambitious, programmatic liberals in the 1958 and 1964 elections that ultimately spelled the doom for not only the Club, but also other core features of the mid-century Senate.

## The Conservative Coalition

While most accounts suggest that the Inner Club was not limited to conservatives, the senators typically identified as important Club members were either southern Democrats or conservative Republicans. Thus, the idea of a Club was closely linked to still another feature of the mid-century Senate: the centrality of the cross-party conservative coalition in Congress.

As David Rohde, Norman Ornstein, and Robert Peabody (1985) show, the 1950s Senate was in many ways dominated by conservative Democrats and Republicans. Committee leadership positions and the best committee assignments were concentrated in the hands of the Senate's most conservative members (see also Sinclair 1989). Key committees, such as Appropriations and Finance, were generally more conservative than the Senate chamber as a whole (Rohde, Ornstein, and Peabody 1985; Sinclair 1989). Thus, in the 85th Congress (1957–58), 53 percent of the members of prestige committees had conservative coalition scores of 81–100, as compared to 42 percent of the Senate as a whole. Liberals—those with conservative coalition scores below 20—constituted just 8.3 percent of the membership of prestige committees, while constituting 17.5 percent of the Senate. Ripley (1969) shows that southern Democrats in particular were overrepresented on key committees and as committee chairs for much of the 1940s and 1950s.

Beyond dominating key committees, the conservative coalition possessed considerable floor strength in this period. The coalition appeared on only approximately 20 percent of Senate roll calls in the 1950s, but emerged victorious in a substantial majority of these cases. Conservative strength was particularly evident on labor-related issues, a central front in battles over New Deal liberalism. Liberal Democrats failed dismally in their efforts to repeal the Taft-Hartley Act of 1947. Instead, the most noteworthy labor legislation of the 1950s—the Landrum-Griffin Act of 1959—was a Democratic setback that tightened regulation of unions.

Although conservatives succeeded in actively rewriting labor law in 1947 and 1959, a more common theme in analyses of the conservative coalition is the defeat of liberal legislation that sought to extend the New Deal. Broad full employment legislation, federal aid to education, national health insurance, and civil rights measures with genuine enforcement authority each failed enactment in the 1940s and 1950s (see Sundquist 1968). While the filibuster received much of the blame for the failure of civil rights, conservative strength was considerable in both chambers. Indeed, for a time there was even a literature that asked why the Senate was more liberal than the House, though the balance of evidence suggests that the two chambers were, on the whole, roughly equally conservative (see Mayhew 2011; Kernell 1973). Again, this theme of Senate (and congressional) conservatism began to give way following the big liberal gains in the 1958 and 1964 elections, which allowed notable liberal policy successes, particularly with the adoption of the Civil Rights Act of 1964, the Voting Rights Act of 1965, and Medicare (1965).

## The Johnson Senate

A final key feature of the conventional portrait of the mid-century Senate is the central role played by Lyndon Johnson as Democratic leader and as a broker who worked effectively with all three major ideological groupings in the Senate: southern Democrats, Republicans, and northern Democrats. When Johnson entered the Senate in January 1949, his sights were already set on climbing within the Senate's internal leadership and on one day winning the presidency. From the start, he courted senior southern leaders, such as Russell, gaining a seat on the Armed Services Committee and winning key support to create a defense preparedness subcommittee, which the freshman senator chaired (Evans and Novak 1966). At the same time, Johnson sought to distance himself publicly from the Russell-led "Southern Caucus"; several accounts noted that Johnson, along with fellow presidential aspirant Kefauver, chose not to attend the Caucus meeting called by Russell at the start of the 81st Congress in 1949 (Evans and Novak 1966). Caro (2002) suggests that Johnson was engaged in a double-game of sorts: refusing to be identified publicly with the Southern Caucus but also attending at least some of its meetings and maintaining close contacts with key members.

Johnson's ascent within the Senate was remarkably quick, aided in part by the electoral defeats of Democratic leaders Scott Lucas (D-Ill.; defeated in 1950) and Ernest McFarland (D-Ariz.; defeated in 1952). Johnson served as Democratic whip after just two years in the Senate and became minority leader in January 1953, following McFarland's defeat. The Texan spent two years as minority leader and then became majority leader following Democratic gains in the 1954 midterms.

Johnson's tenure as leader has become something of a legend among political observers; indeed, it is often the point of comparison when critics lament the lack of genuine leadership in today's Senate. While scholars have cast considerable doubt on the view that Johnson dominated the Senate (see discussion below), it is important to trace the conventional account of the Johnson years since it has helped define the way in which professional political observers view the mid-century Senate.

The Johnson "Treatment" is often viewed as the hallmark of Johnson's leadership. As Rowland Evans and Robert Novak (1966) described it in their biography of Johnson:

> Its tone could be supplication, accusation, cajolery, exuberance, scorn, tears, complaint and the hint of threat. It was all of these together. It ran the gamut of human emotions. Its velocity was breathtaking, and it was all in one direction. Interjections from the target were rare. Johnson anticipated them before they could be spoken. He moved in close, his face a scant millimeter from his target, his eyes widening and narrowing, his eyebrows rising and falling. From his pockets poured clippings, memos, statistics. Mimicry, humor, and the genius of analogy made The Treatment an almost hypnotic experience and rendered the target stunned and helpless. (104)

Political scientists have also credited Johnson's dominating personality as a significant resource in his wielding of floor leadership, while moving away from the view that he bullied members into backing his positions (see, e.g., Ripley 1969; Davidson 1989). In a classic—and nuanced—essay on the Johnson years, Huitt (1961a) highlights the main sources of Johnson's success as leader. First, Johnson was at the center of his party's communication networks; no other senator had contacts with as wide a range of senators as Johnson. This gave him a crucial informational advantage over his rivals in building coalitions. Second, Johnson nurtured close ties to many Republicans, making it easier for him to build cross-party coalitions and to use GOP votes to offset defections from within his own party. Third, Huitt notes Johnson's skills in bargaining and in structuring parliamentary situations so that members could more easily side with him: Johnson saw that senators play multiple, conflicting roles and "that one task of leadership is to structure a situation so that a member can select a role which will allow him to stand with the party" (Huitt 1961a: 339; see also Ripley 1969). Finally, Johnson fostered an image of invincibility by steadfastly avoiding fights that he could not win. Huitt highlights the importance of divided party government in facilitating this aspect of Johnson's leadership: with a Democrat in the White House, Johnson might have found himself pressured to push for liberal programs with little chance of success. The dismal record of Johnson's predecessors, Scott Lucas and Ernest McFarland, were likely in part attributable to the difficulty of trying to pass a presidential agenda that deeply divided party members (Huitt 1961a). With the moderate Republican Eisenhower in office, Johnson was not expected to win passage of a major domestic agenda and instead could select his battles based on what he could sell to his membership.[7]

Several scholars have emphasized that Johnson's strong personal leadership in the 1950s ultimately contributed to the decline of the Inner Club and gradually ushered in a more individualistic, open Senate environment. Most importantly, Johnson built support for himself among junior members by instituting the so-called Johnson Rule in 1953. Prior to 1953, the Democratic Steering Committee doled out committee assignments based entirely on seniority. The Johnson Rule entitled each Democratic senator to one major committee assignment before any senator would receive a second major slot. This meant that liberal freshman senators would receive good committee positions far earlier in their careers than in the past. Rohde, Ornstein, and Peabody (1985) quote a conservative southern ally of Johnson on the impact of this change: "When Johnson started putting a freshman guy on a major committee, he immediately broke down the strength of the inner club" (159; see also Polsby 1969).

Still, Johnson in many ways personified the conventional portrait of the mid-century Senate. He was the consummate insider—a southern Democrat articulating the view that one has to work with the Inner Club and abide by norms of restraint in order to succeed in the tradition-bound chamber.

## II. Revisiting the Mid-Century Senate

The conventional portrait of the mid-century Senate summarized above captures important facets of the institution that stand in particularly sharp contrast to today's Senate, with its intense partisan warfare, unrestrained use of the filibuster, and near-universal individual activism. Yet this stylized portrait of the Senate leaves out several important facets of the institution, which may lead to an exaggerated sense of the mid-century Senate as a long-lasting "system" in a coherent and stable equilibrium.

Perhaps most importantly, the idea of a Senate governed by an Inner Club of senior "Senate types" who are focused on the internal life of the institution rather than on reaching for higher office is in tension with the

---

7. Johnson also played a role in turning unanimous consent agreements into a leadership tool, though as Steven Smith (1993) points out, the agreements were still relatively simple in the Johnson years.

rapid rise of the two most important leaders of the Senate in the 1940s and 1950s: Robert Taft (R-Ohio) and Lyndon Johnson. Observers have long noted that Johnson's rise to power was swift, yet the implicit assumption has been that this constituted a rare exception, rather than speaking to a more general permeability of Senate leadership. Taft's rise was every bit as remarkable as Johnson's speedy ascent, despite the supposed power of seniority and apprenticeship norms.[8] Taft entered the Senate in January 1939 and quickly established himself as one of the most important Republican critics of President Franklin Roosevelt and the New Deal. James Patterson (1972: 187) notes that Taft gave forty-four floor speeches in his first year in office, evidently in blatant disregard of the idea that freshmen senators are supposed to keep quiet on the floor. Taft launched his first presidential campaign in August 1939, again hardly a sign of respect for the notion that a member ought to toil in the Senate for several years before actively pursuing the presidency. Journalistic accounts label Taft as the leading Republican—and perhaps the most significant senator—by the early 1940s (Patterson 1972; see also Drury 1963). Taft had the opportunity to become floor leader in 1944, but instead pressed for creation of a new Steering Committee that he would chair and that would become a tool to develop Republican policies (Schickler 2001; Drury 1963). Taft used the Steering Committee to frame policy initiatives in 1945–46; it was then renamed the Policy Committee as part of the Legislative Reorganization Act of 1946. Taft continued to lead the Policy Committee until 1953, when he somewhat reluctantly took on the role of floor leader.

In many ways, Taft's approach to leadership was the direct opposite of Johnson's: where Johnson thrived on personal relationships and on understanding each member's particular political needs, Taft focused far more on promoting an ideological vision and on policy details and design.[9] Yet both were regarded as extremely successful Senate leaders in the mid-century period, which suggests that there were multiple avenues for gaining influence. Patience and deference to more senior members were not necessary to their rise to power.[10]

Beyond such formal party leaders as Johnson and Taft, Huitt (1961b) argues that ambitious senators in the 1940s and 1950s had a well-established, successful model to follow if they did not want to abide by the informal rules of the Inner Club. Specifically, Huitt observes that the role of outsider or

---

8. Huitt's (1961b) classic essay highlights precisely this point and helped shape much of the argument made below.

9. William White (1954, 62) even comments on Taft's rudeness to his fellow senators, arguing that Republicans forgave this trait, perhaps due to their respect for hierarchy.

10. William Knowland (R-Calif.), a less well-known figure than Taft and Johnson, became majority leader in 1953 after having served fewer than eight years in the Senate.

maverick has a rich history in the Senate. Rather than viewing such senators as Proxmire, Kefauver, Morse, and Douglas as deviants, Huitt argues that they were playing an accepted role in the Senate, with such models as Robert La Follette Sr. and George Norris to draw upon for inspiration. Interestingly, the general public has often shown considerable support for so-called mavericks, and several have served in the Senate for many years. Huitt notes that when political scientists who studied Congress were asked to rank the best senators in 1950, they put Douglas, Kefauver, Morse, and Herbert Lehman (D-N.Y.) at the top. Granted, political scientists' ideological and partisan preferences likely played a role in generating these rankings, but they at least suggest that being a maverick was not necessarily associated with the perception of ineffectiveness. Huitt adds that when senators selected five outstanding late members to honor in 1955, they put the outsider La Follette on the list. And La Follette's main competitor for the slot was George Norris, again suggesting that senators view the outsider as a distinct and legitimate type. The bottom line, according to Huitt, is that the image of a cohesive Senate establishment consistently invoking a set of widely shared norms against maverick behavior is overdrawn, to say the least.[11]

A further underemphasized feature of the mid-century Senate's conventional portrait is the heated ideological conflict that permeated the chamber prior to the mid-1950s. The so-called textbook Congress, in which a rough ideological consensus allowed for a politics based on reciprocity and restraint, appears to be a far cry from the Senate of the 1940s and early 1950s. In the 1940s, northern Democrats were engaged in a pitched battle against Republicans and many southern Democrats over the scope of New Deal liberalism. Where the northern liberals were seeking something resembling a social democratic system featuring strong national unions and "cradle-to-grave" social insurance (including national health care), conservatives viewed this agenda as a threat to core American values. The result was a series of intensely ideological fights in the House and Senate concerning such issues as full employment policy, labor regulation (culminating in Taft-Hartley but echoing later in unsuccessful bids for repeal), price controls, aid to education, and national health insurance.[12] Liberals were on the losing side of most of these battles, but they were fought out in public

---

11. The Senate mavericks of the 1950s did not enjoy access to some of the resources that *all* of today's senators take for granted, such as extensive personal staff and press offices. At the same time, they competed in a Washington environment that was less densely populated with interest groups and in which parties made far weaker claims on their members. These factors no doubt made life as a maverick different —though not necessarily more difficult or frustrating—in the 1950s than today.

12. Civil rights could be added to this list, though the battle lines on the issue were more complicated, as Republicans were split on the issue rather than united with the southern Democrats (see Schickler, Pearson, and Feinstein 2010).

campaigns that involved high-profile investigations (e.g., of labor union wrongdoing) and vigorous appeals for popular support. Senate politics in the 1940s were thus infused by broad ideological and policy disagreements that were at the core of battles over the role of government. The "clubby," internally focused Senate described by Matthews and others may well have been a short-lived aberration, dependent on the political stalemate induced by the combination of a moderate Republican president and a divided Democratic majority.

The most famous example of ideological warfare is, of course, the rise of Joseph McCarthy in 1950 and his investigative activism prior to his 1954 censure. But it is crucial not to view McCarthy as an isolated exception. Long before McCarthy rose to prominence, Republicans and many southern Democrats were pursuing accusations of disloyalty in government as part of an effort to link the New Deal to communism (Goldman 1960). McCarthy was hardly the only loyalty investigator in the Senate. For example, Pat McCarran (D-Nev.) and William Jenner (R-Ind.) led the Internal Security Subcommittee of the Judiciary Committee, which aggressively investigated charges of subversion in the early 1950s. More generally, David Mayhew's (2000: 112–113) analysis of significant member actions in the public sphere identifies a cluster of more than two dozen such actions in the 1947–1954 period; these focused on anti-communism, blended with an "Asia First" critique of Democratic foreign policy mistakes (i.e., "Who Lost China").

Republican leader Taft's relationship with the loyalty investigators was complicated, but by no means unfriendly. Taft himself undertook a series of speeches in 1946 linking Democrats to communism (Patterson 1972). With McCarthy's initial rise to prominence, Taft found himself dealing "with an individual who ignored the folkways and civilities of the Senate" (Patterson 1972: 445). When the GOP Policy Committee met to respond to McCarthy's initial salvo, Taft told reporters that it would not treat the charges as a policy matter but that he personally thought that the Wisconsin senator should keep it up (Patterson 1972: 446). Other leading Republicans, such as Kenneth Wherry (R-Neb.) and Styles Bridges (R-N.H.), were also personally wary of McCarthy but decided to cooperate with him (Goldman 1960). It was only when McCarthy directed his investigators to the Eisenhower administration—in particular, the army—that leading Republicans turned against him. This example again suggests the wide berth given to ambitious members to make a name for themselves through aggressive public campaigns, even as they risked embarrassing the Senate as an institution.[13]

---

13. The ideological warfare surrounding foreign policy receives less attention in the political science literature on Congress from this period than in works by historians. Robert Dahl's *Congress and Foreign Policy* (1950) is one of the few works by political scientists of the era focusing on America's growing international role. By contrast, standard historical accounts give heavy play to foreign policy (see, e.g., Goldman 1960).

# III. Conclusions

Studies of the mid-century Senate have provided a textured portrait of the upper chamber. There is no question that core features of the Senate at mid-century are sharply different from the contemporary Senate. Indeed, one might argue that if Richard Russell, Lyndon Johnson, or Robert Taft were transported to today's Senate, they would find themselves deeply puzzled by the combination of extreme individualism, intense party polarization, and routine use of obstruction to stall the majority's program.

But depictions of the mid-century Senate have tended to focus on the mid to late 1950s, while making at least an implicit assumption of considerable continuity from the 1940s. That is, the notion of a "mid-century" Senate brings to mind an equilibrium institution that had existed for a few decades, but that was later upset by major external shocks, such as the election of 1958 and the political upheavals of the 1960s. Yet if one looks back to the 1940s and early 1950s in attempting to understand the mid-century Senate, a more complicated, open, and changing institution emerges. Johnson's speedy rise to power becomes less of an aberration when coupled with Taft's equally impressive ascent; together the two cases suggest a Senate that was open to ambitious and talented members making a quick mark. It is especially striking that Taft's policy-oriented leadership approach was so different from Johnson's intensely personal strategy. Similarly, taking in a broader time frame makes it clear that the relative political quiet and insulation of the mid-1950s was really—at most—just a brief respite in an otherwise turbulent era. Finally, when one thinks of the Senate of the 1940s and early 1950s, several apparent "outsiders" used a combination of high-profile investigations, major speeches, and cooperation with national interest groups to create broad constituencies that forced their opponents to take notice and respond. These outsiders included both conservative loyalty investigators, such as McCarthy, McCarran, and Jenner, and liberals, such as Kefauver, who used his Crime Committee investigation to build a national following. They also included liberals like Humphrey, Douglas, Morse, and (after 1957) Proxmire, who worked with liberal interest groups, such as Americans for Democratic Action, to build momentum for their causes.

The initial wave of behavioral studies of Congress depicted an institution in which committees dominated, norms of reciprocity and restraint were strong, and ideological battles were largely submerged (see, e.g., Shepsle 1989 for a useful review). A close look at the mid-century Senate suggests that the time may be ripe for a more general effort to revisit what we think we know about the textbook Congress, including the mid-century Senate.

# References

Beth, Richard S. 1994. "Filibusters in the Senate, 1789–1993." Memorandum, Congressional Research Service, February 18.

Binder, Sarah A., and Steven S. Smith. 1997. *Politics or Principle? Filibustering in the United States Senate*. Washington, D.C.: Brookings Institution.

Caro, Robert A. 2002. *The Years of Lyndon Johnson: Master of the Senate*. New York: Knopf.

Clark, Joseph S. 1963. *The Senate Establishment*. New York: Hill and Wang.

Dahl, Robert A. 1950. *Congress and Foreign Policy*. New York: Harcourt Brace.

Davidson, Roger H. 1989. "The Senate: If Everybody Leads, Who Follows?" In Lawrence C. Dodd and Bruce Oppenheimer, eds., *Congress Reconsidered*, 4th ed. Washington, D.C.: CQ Press.

Davidson, Roger H., David M. Kovenock, and Michael K. O'Leary. 1966. *Congress in Crisis: Politics and Congressional Reform*. Belmont, Calif.: Wadsworth Publishing.

Drury, Allen. 1963. *A Senate Journal, 1943–1945*. New York: McGraw-Hill.

Evans, Rowland, and Robert Novak. 1966. *Lyndon B. Johnson: The Exercise of Power*. New York: New American Library.

Fenno, Richard F. 1966. *The Power of the Purse: Appropriations Politics in Congress*. Boston: Little, Brown.

Goldman, Eric. 1960. *The Crucial Decade and After: America, 1945–1960*. New York: Vintage Books.

Huitt, Ralph K. 1961a. "Democratic Party Leadership in the Senate." *American Political Science Review* 55: 331–344.

———. 1961b. "The Outsider in the Senate: An Alternative Role." *American Political Science Review* 55: 566–575.

Kernell, Samuel. 1973. "Is the Senate More Liberal than the House?" *Journal of Politics* 35: 332–366.

Koger, Gregory. 2010. *Filibustering: A Political History of Obstruction in the House and Senate*. Chicago: University of Chicago Press.

Matthews, Donald R. 1960. *U.S. Senators and Their World*. New York: Vintage Books.

Mayhew, David R. 2000. *America's Congress: Actions in the Public Sphere, James Madison through Newt Gingrich*. New Haven, Conn.: Yale University Press.

——— 2011. *Partisan Balance: Why Political Parties Do Not Kill the U.S. Constitutional System*. Princeton, N.J.: Princeton University Press.

Patterson, James T. 1972. *Mr. Republican: A Biography of Robert A. Taft*. Boston: Houghton Mifflin.

Polsby, Nelson W. 1969. "Goodbye to the Inner Club." *Washington Monthly*, August, 30–34.

Ripley, Randall B. 1969. *Power in the Senate*. New York: St. Martin's Press.

Rohde, David W., Norman J. Ornstein, and Robert L. Peabody. 1985. "Political Change and Legislative Norms in the U.S. Senate, 1957–1974." In Glenn R. Parker, ed., *Studies of Congress*. Washington, D.C.: Congressional Quarterly.

Schickler, Eric. 2001. *Disjointed Pluralism: Institutional Innovation and the Development of the U.S. Congress*. Princeton, N.J.: Princeton University Press.

Schickler, Eric, Kathryn Pearson, and Brian Feinstein. 2010. "Shifting Partisan Coalitions: Support for Civil Rights in Congress from 1933–1972." *Journal of Politics* 72: 672–689.

Shepsle, Kenneth A. 1989. "The Changing Textbook Congress." In John E. Chubb and Paul E. Peterson, eds., *Can the Government Govern?* Washington, D.C.: Brookings Institution.

Sinclair, Barbara. 1989. *The Transformation of the U.S. Senate.* Baltimore and London: Johns Hopkins University Press.

———. 2001. "The New World of U.S. Senators." In Lawrence C. Dodd and Bruce Oppenheimer, eds., *Congress Reconsidered*, 7th ed. Washington, D.C.: CQ Press.

Smith, Steven S. 1989. *Call to Order.* Washington, D.C.: Brookings Institution.

———. 1993. "Forces of Change in Senate Party Leadership and Organization." In Lawrence C. Dodd and Bruce Oppenheimer, eds., *Congress Reconsidered*, 5th ed. Washington, D.C.: CQ Press.

Sundquist, James L. 1968. *Politics and Policy: The Eisenhower, Kennedy, and Johnson Years.* Washington, D.C.: Brookings Institution.

Wawro, Gregory, and Eric Schickler. 2006. *Filibuster: Obstruction and Lawmaking in the United States Senate.* Princeton, N.J.: Princeton University Press, 2006.

White, William S. 1954. *The Taft Story.* New York: Harper and Brothers.

———. 1957. *Citadel: The Story of the U.S. Senate.* New York: Harper and Brothers.

# 2

# U.S. Senate Elections in a Polarized Era

### Alan I. Abramowitz

The rise of ideological polarization in the U.S. Congress over the past half century has been well documented by scholars (Rohde 1991; Poole and Rosenthal 1991, 2007; Bond and Fleisher 2000; Fleisher and Bond 2004; Poole 2005; Smith and Gamm 2005; Sinclair 2006). In both the Senate and the House of Representatives, the ideological divide between the parties has widened dramatically: the Democratic Party has moved steadily to the left since the 1960s while the Republican Party has moved steadily to the right. Conservative Democrats and liberal Republicans, who exercised considerable influence in Congress from the end of World War II through the 1960s, have almost completely disappeared. And the rise of polarization cannot be attributed to partisan gerrymandering as some scholars and journalists have claimed (Ornstein and McMillion 2005; Eilperin 2006) since the increase in polarization has been almost as great in the Senate as in the House of Representatives (Ono 2005; Poole 2005).

In recent years, moderates have become relatively rare even in the Senate, as the evidence in Figure 2.1 demonstrates. This figure displays the locations of senators in the 111th Congress on a liberal-conservative scale based on votes during 2009. Figure 2.1 shows very clearly the ideological chasm separating the parties in the contemporary Senate. In marked contrast to the situation that existed forty or fifty years ago, there is no overlap at all between the two parties. The most conservative Democrat, Ben Nelson of Nebraska, is located to the left of the most liberal Republican, Olympia Snowe of Maine.

The ideological polarization that characterized the 111th Senate represents a dramatic change from the situation that existed forty years ago. The data displayed in Table 2.1 show that there has been a dramatic increase in ideological polarization over the past forty years. In the 91st Senate (1969–71), moderates made up 41 percent of the membership while strong liberals and conservatives made up only 22 percent. In contrast, in the 111th Senate, moderates made up only 8 percent of the membership while strong liberals and strong conservatives made up 45 percent.

Both parties have contributed to growing ideological polarization, although the movement away from the center has been somewhat greater

**Figure 2.1**   Ideologies of Democrats and Republicans in the 111th Senate

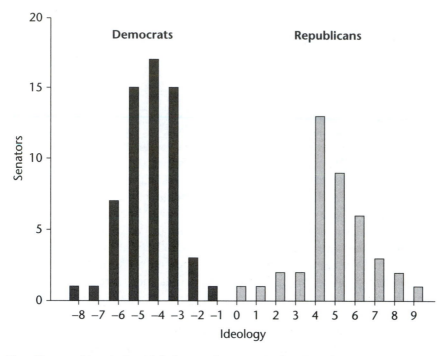

Note: To create this scale, I multiplied senators' scores on the first dimension of the DW-Nominate scale by 10 and rounded them off to the nearest whole integer.

Source: http://voteview.com/dwnomin.htm.

on the Republican side than on the Democratic side. Between the 91st Senate (1969–70) and the 111th Senate (2009–10), the proportion of Democratic senators classified as moderate fell from 36 percent to 7 percent while the proportion classified as strong liberal rose from 22 percent to 40 percent. Over the same time period, the proportion of Republican senators classified as moderate fell from 48 percent to 10 percent while the proportion classified as strong conservative rose from 21 percent to 52 percent.

The rise of ideological polarization has had important consequences for the legislative process in both chambers of Congress, making bipartisan cooperation increasingly difficult and strengthening the hand of party leaders (Aldrich and Rohde 2000; Smith and Gamm 2005).

But the consequences of polarization have been greater in some ways for the Senate than for the House because the House has traditionally operated in a much more partisan fashion than the Senate. In the House of Representatives, the rules governing debate and floor voting have long

**Table 2.1**    Ideology in the 91st and 111th Senates

| Ideology | 91st Senate | 111th Senate |
|---|---|---|
| Moderates | 41 | 8 |
| Liberals and conservatives | 37 | 47 |
| Strong liberals and conservatives | 22 | 45 |

Note: In order to compare ideological polarization in the Senate over time, I collapsed DW-Nominate scores into five categories: senators with DW-Nominate scores below –.5 were classified as strong conservatives, those with scores between –.5 and –.2 were classified as conservatives, those with scores between –.2 and +.2 were classified as moderates, those with scores between .2 and .5 were classified as liberals, and those with scores of .5 or higher were classified as strong liberals.

Source: http://voteview.com/dwnomin.htm.

given crucial advantages to the leaders of the majority party. And increasing polarization may make it easier for leaders of the majority party to keep their own members unified on the floor since there are now fewer ideological outliers to persuade (Schickler and Pearson 2005).

In the Senate, however, reliance on unanimous consent agreements (see Chapter 7 in this volume) and the filibuster rule have provided the minority party with much greater influence (Evans and Lipinski 2005). For most purposes it takes sixty votes to pass legislation, and this usually requires both near unanimity within the majority party and at least a few votes from members of the minority party. As we have seen in the 111th Congress, this has become very difficult to achieve, requiring delicate negotiations between the majority party leadership and a handful of moderates in both parties who hold the balance of power.

## Polarization in the Electorate

While scholars generally agree on the importance of increasing partisan polarization in Congress, there has been much less agreement on the extent and significance of polarization in the American electorate. The central argument of this chapter is that polarization is not just an elite phenomenon. I will present evidence that over the past several decades there has been a substantial increase in polarization in the electorate and that this has had important consequences for Senate elections and for the relationship between senators and their constituents.

Four major trends have contributed to the growth of polarization in Senate elections over the past half century. First, the parties' electoral coalitions have become increasingly distinct both racially and ideologically. The nonwhite share of the U.S. electorate has increased dramatically since the

1960s, reaching a record 26 percent in 2008, and this trend is almost certain to continue based on the racial make-up of the youngest and oldest age groups in the population. Because of the overwhelming preference of non-white voters for the Democratic Party, the growth of the nonwhite elector-ate has led to an increasing racial divide between the Democratic and Republican electoral coalitions. At the same time, the parties' electoral coalitions have become increasingly distinct ideologically as a result of a gradual realignment within the electorate (Abramowitz and Saunders 1998). Democratic voters have grown more liberal while Republican voters have become increasingly conservative.

Second, as a result of the growing racial and ideological differences between the Democratic and Republican electoral coalitions, party loyalty and straight-ticket voting have increased in Senate elections. This increase in party loyalty at the individual level means that state partisanship is now a stronger determinant of the outcomes of Senate elections than in the past and that winning candidates' electoral coalitions have become more party based.

Third, the changing racial composition of the electorate and ideo-logical realignment have increased geographic polarization. States with relatively liberal electorates have been trending Democratic while states with relatively conservative electorates have been trending Republican. As a result, the South has become the most Republican region in the nation while the Northeast has become the most Democratic region. Although the overall balance of power between the parties in the nation has been rela-tively close in recent years, the number of states dominated by one party has increased while the number of evenly balanced states has decreased. In the color-coded language of media commentators, there are more dark blue and dark red states and fewer purple states.

The combination of increased geographic polarization and increased party loyalty in voting means that it is now much more difficult for a candi-date from the minority party to win a Senate election. Fewer senators represent so-called swing states, or those states that remain competitive for both parties, while more senators represent states that are relatively safe for their own party. As a result, fewer senators need to worry about appealing to voters who identify with the opposing party.

Finally, Senate elections have become more nationalized. As ideo-logical differences between the two parties have grown, voters have increas-ingly come to see a Senate election as a choice about not just who will represent their state but which party will control the chamber. Therefore, in choosing a Senate candidate, voters are increasingly influenced by their opinions on national political issues and especially their assessment of the president's performance. This has resulted in greater consistency in the party direction of seat turnover, larger seat swings, and more frequent changes in party control of the Senate.

There is a mutually reinforcing relationship between polarization in the Senate and polarization in the electorate. Polarization in the Senate has contributed to both increased party loyalty and the increased influence of national issues in Senate elections. With the near-disappearance of conservative Democrats and liberal Republicans, most Senate contests now involve a clear choice between a liberal Democrat and a conservative Republican. As a result, there is less incentive for voters to cross party lines. At the same time, increasing polarization within the electorate has served to reinforce the divisions between Democrats and Republicans in the Senate. One of the main reasons why Democratic and Republican senators are deeply divided on major issues such as health care is that Democratic and Republican voters are deeply divided on these issues. Rather than indicating that there is a "disconnect" between politicians and voters (see Fiorina, Abrams, and Pope 2006; Fiorina and Levendusky 2006; Fiorina 2010), polarization in Congress actually indicates that Democratic and Republican members are accurately reflecting the views of the voters who elected them.

## Diverging Party Coalitions

The growth of the nonwhite electorate, beginning with African Americans in the 1960s and 1970s and continuing with Hispanics and Asian Americans since the 1980s, has had profound consequences for the party system and the electoral process in the United States. African American and Hispanic voters now comprise a large proportion of the electoral base of the Democratic Party. This trend played a major role in the election of the nation's first African American president, Barack Obama. According to the 2008 national exit poll, African Americans made up 24 percent of Obama voters while Hispanics and other nonwhites made up 16 percent of Obama voters. In contrast, despite the rapid growth in the proportion of nonwhite voters over the past two decades, the Republican Party's electoral base has changed very little and remains overwhelmingly white. According to the 2008 national exit poll, African Americans made up less than 1 percent of all McCain voters while Hispanics and other nonwhites made up only 9 percent.

The same demographic trends that contributed to Barack Obama's victory have had a powerful impact on U.S. Senate elections. Figure 2.2 displays the trends in the nonwhite proportions of Democratic and Republican senate voters between the 1950s and the first decade of the twenty-first century. During this time period, even as the nonwhite share of the electorate has increased, the Republican Party's strategy has continued to emphasize appealing to conservative white voters. This strategy has been successful: Republican identification among conservative white voters has increased dramatically. However, the gap in nonwhite support for the two

**Figure 2.2**    Nonwhite Share of Democratic and Republican Senate
Voters, by Decade

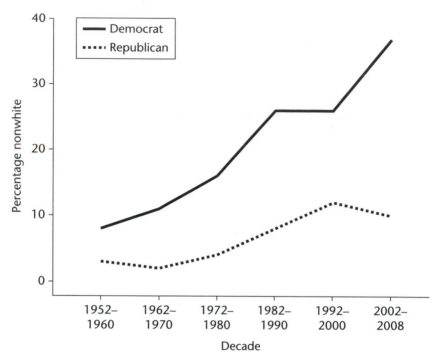

Source: American National Election Studies. Available at www.electionstudies.org.

parties has also increased dramatically. During the 1950s, nonwhites made
up about 8 percent of Democratic Senate voters and about 4 percent of
Republican Senate voters. By the 2000s, nonwhites made up almost 40 percent of Democratic Senate voters but less than 10 percent of Republican
Senate voters.

If the Republican Party does not improve its performance among nonwhite voters, it is likely to face an increasingly challenging electoral environment in the coming decades. Conservative whites have been shrinking as a
share of the overall electorate for some time, and at close to 90 percent
identification the GOP may have already maxed out its support among this
group. At the same time, the nonwhite share of the U.S. electorate is certain
to continue growing well into the twenty-first century. This can be seen by
examining exit poll data on the racial composition of the 2008 electorate as
well as Census Bureau data on the racial composition of the U.S. population
by age. According to the 2008 national exit poll, non-Hispanic whites made
up 81 percent of voters over the age of 45 but only 66 percent of voters

under the age of 45; African Americans made up 15 percent of voters under the age of 45 compared with only 9 percent of those 45 and older while Hispanics and other nonwhites made up 19 percent of voters under the age of 45 compared with only 10 percent of those 45 and older.

A 2007 Census Bureau study shows that there is a dramatic difference between the racial composition of the oldest and youngest age groups in the U.S. population. According to the Census Bureau, non-Hispanic whites make up over 80 percent of Americans over the age of 65 but less than 60 percent of those under the age of 18. In contrast, African Americans make up more than 15 percent of the population under the age of 18 compared with only 8 percent of the population over the age of 65, and Hispanics make up more than 20 percent of the population under the age of 18 and almost 24 percent of the population under the age of 5, compared with less than 7 percent of the population over the age of 65. While the nonwhite share of the electorate will probably continue to lag behind the nonwhite share of the population due to lower citizenship and turnout rates, these data indicate that we can expect the nonwhite share of the U.S. electorate to continue to grow for many years.

Along with the racial divide, the ideological divide between supporters of the two major parties has widened considerably since the 1960s. The gradual disappearance of conservative Democrats and moderate-to-liberal Republicans has had a clear impact on the electoral coalitions of Democratic and Republican Senate candidates. Figure 2.3 displays the trends in the average scores of Democratic and Republican Senate voters over the past four decades on the American National Election Study (ANES) 7-point liberal-conservative scale. Over this time period, the gap between the average location of Democratic and Republican voters has more than doubled, from .8 units to 1.7 units. In 1972 conservative identifiers made up 30 percent of Democratic Senate voters and 43 percent of Republican Senate voters. In 2008 conservative identifiers made up 19 percent of Democratic Senate voters and 72 percent of Republican Senate voters.

The growing ideological identification gap between Democratic and Republican voters is especially significant because there has also been a substantial increase in the relationship between ideological identification and a wide range of policy preferences. For example, according to ANES data, between 1984 and 2008 the correlation between ideological identification and abortion preference increased from .28 to .47, the correlation between ideological identification and health insurance policy preference increased from .24 to .49, and the correlation between ideological identification and government spending/services preference increased from .32 to .52. As a result, as Democratic and Republican voters have moved apart on the ideological identification scale, they have also moved apart on a wide range of policy issues.

**Figure 2.3**    Mean Liberal-Conservative Score of Democratic and Republican Senate Voters, by Decade

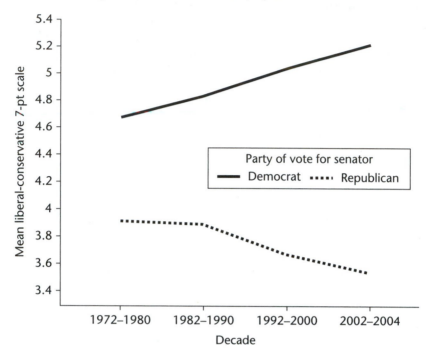

Source: American National Election Studies. Available at www.electionstudies.org.

It is also important to note that partisan polarization is greatest among the most politically engaged members of the public—those who care about politics, pay attention to what their elected representatives are doing, vote regularly, and engage in political activities beyond voting. According to data from the 2008 ANES, the correlation between ideological identification and Senate vote was .30 for those whose political involvement was limited to voting, .58 for those who engage in one activity beyond voting, and .73 for those who engaged in at least two activities beyond voting.

Among Republican Senate voters, the average score on the 7-point liberal-conservative scale was 4.7 for those whose involvement was limited to voting, 5.2 for those who engaged in one activity beyond voting, and 5.6 for those who engaged in at least two activities beyond voting; among Democratic Senate voters, the average score was 3.8 for those whose involvement was limited to voting, 3.4 for those who engaged in one activity beyond voting, and 2.9 for those who engaged in at least two activities beyond voting.

The most politically engaged Republican voters were much more conservative than those who were less politically engaged while the most politically engaged Democratic voters were much more liberal than those who were less politically engaged. And it is the engaged partisans whose preferences are of greatest concern to candidates and elected officials, including U.S. senators.

## The Decline and Resurgence of Partisanship

Since the 1970s, the growing racial and ideological divisions between supporters of the two parties have contributed to a marked increase in partisan voting in Senate elections. Far fewer voters feel cross-pressured by their ideological orientation and their party identification. Therefore, far fewer are tempted to defect to the opposing party. This can be seen in Figure 2.4, which displays the trends in two measures of partisan voting, party loyalty and straight-ticket voting, between the 1950s and the first decade of the twenty-first century.

**Figure 2.4**   Party Loyalty and Ticket Splitting in U.S. Senate Election, by Decade

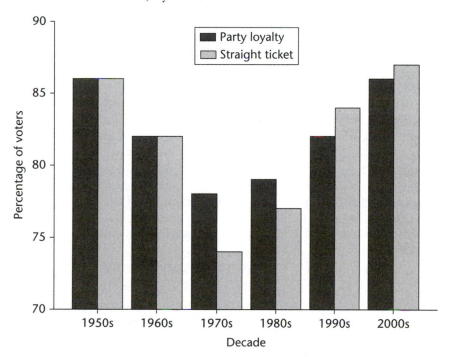

Source: American National Election Studies. Available at www.electionstudies.org.

Between the 1950s and the 1970s there were substantial declines in both party loyalty and straight-ticket voting in Senate elections. Based on this trend, political scientists concluded that the United States was experiencing a period of partisan "dealignment" during the 1970s. In 1972 partisanship reached its nadir when only 76 percent of Democratic and Republican identifiers (including leaning independents) voted for their own party's Senate candidate and just 72 percent of voters chose a presidential and Senate candidate from the same party. Since then, however, both of these measures have rebounded to levels not seen since the 1950s. In 2008, 87 percent of Democratic and Republican identifiers voted for their own party's Senate candidate, and 88 percent of voters chose a presidential and Senate candidate from the same party.

## The Rise of Geographic Polarization

As the racial and ideological divisions between the parties have deepened, one of the most important consequences for Senate and presidential elections has been growing geographic polarization. Conservative states and regions have trended toward the Republican Party while more liberal states and regions have become more Democratic. The results of these trends were clearly apparent in 2008. Although there were more blue states and fewer red states, the divide between the two was even deeper than in 2004. Across all fifty states the average statewide margin of victory for the winning presidential candidate increased from 13.9 points in 2004 to 16.2 points in 2008: the average margin of victory for Barack Obama was 16.8 points while the average margin of victory for John McCain was 15.4 points. There were more landslide and near-landslide states and fewer closely contested states. The number of states in which the winning candidate's margin of victory was greater than 15 points increased from 21 to 26, while the number in which the winning candidate's margin of victory was less than 5 points decreased from 11 to 6. Of the seven most populous states, only Florida and Ohio were decided by less than 5 points while New York, California, and Illinois were decided by more than 20 points.

There was wide divergence in support for the presidential candidates across states and regions of the country. Although Barack Obama made inroads into the Republican Party's southern base by carrying Virginia, North Carolina, and Florida, John McCain carried the other eight states of the old Confederacy along with the border states of Kentucky and Oklahoma, winning most of them by double-digit margins. Altogether, McCain won 54 percent of the popular vote in the South while Obama won 57 percent of the popular vote in the rest of the country. The 2008 election was a landslide for Barack Obama outside of the South and a near-landslide for John McCain in the South.

The regional voting patterns in the 2008 presidential election reflected a long-term ideological realignment within the American electorate. This has had a dramatic impact on the regional composition of the Democratic and Republican parties in the Senate. The conservative South has been transformed from a Democratic stronghold into a Republican one. In the 86th Congress (1959–61), Democrats held all twenty-two Senate seats from the eleven states of the old Confederacy. In the 111th Congress, even after suffering some losses in the 2006 and 2008 elections, Republicans held fifteen of the twenty-two Senate seats from these states. At the same time that the South was moving toward the GOP, however, the liberal Northeast was moving in the opposite direction. In the 86th Congress, Republicans held fourteen of the twenty-two Senate seats from eleven states in the Northeast: New York, New Jersey, Pennsylvania, Maryland, Delaware, Maine, Vermont, New Hampshire, Massachusetts, Connecticut, and Rhode Island. In the 111th Congress, Republicans held only three of these twenty-two seats.

This regional realignment has altered the distribution of power within the two parties in the Senate. Fifty years ago, southern conservatives chaired many key committees and exercised considerable influence within the Democratic Party in the Senate while northeastern liberals made up a large and influential bloc within the Senate Republican Party. Today the strength of the Democratic and Republican parties in the major regions of the country is much more consistent with the ideological orientations of the voters in those regions. As a result, northeastern liberals make up the largest bloc in the Senate Democratic caucus while southern conservatives constitute by far the largest bloc in the Senate Republican caucus (Black and Black 2007).

The high degree of geographic polarization in 2008 is consistent with the pattern evident in other recent presidential elections, including 2004, but it represents a dramatic change from the voting patterns of the 1960s and 1970s, as the evidence in Table 2.2 demonstrates. In the competitive 1960 and 1976 elections, for example, there were many more closely contested states and far fewer landslide states than in recent presidential elections. In 1960 twenty states were decided by fewer than 5 points and only nine by more than 15 points; in 1976 twenty states were decided by fewer than 5 points and only ten by more than 15 points.

The trends shown in Table 2.2 along with increasing party loyalty among voters have important, direct implications for Senate elections. As the number of states that strongly favor one party has increased and party loyalty has increased, we would expect to find an increase in the number of senators holding relatively safe seats and a corresponding decline in the

**Table 2.2**  Geographic Polarization in Four Competitive
Presidential Elections

| State margin (percent) | 1960 | 1976 | 2004 | 2008 |
|---|---|---|---|---|
| 0–4.99 | 20 | 20 | 11 | 6 |
| 5–9.99 | 14 | 11 | 10 | 9 |
| 10–14.99 | 7 | 9 | 8 | 9 |
| 15 + | 9 | 10 | 21 | 26 |
| Total | 50 | 50 | 50 | 50 |

Source: unselectionatlas.org.

number holding marginal or high-risk seats. And this is exactly what has
happened according to the data displayed in Table 2.3.

Table 2.3 compares the partisan orientations of states represented by
Democratic and Republican senators in two congresses separated by just
over three decades: the 95th Congress (1977–79) and the 111th Congress
(2009–11). States were classified based on the vote for the presidential
candidate of the senator's party in the state compared with the national
vote for that candidate. States classified as safe were at least 10 points more
supportive of the senator's party than the nation, those classified as solid
were between 5 and 10 points more supportive of the senator's party than
the nation, those classified as competitive were within 5 points of the vote
for the senator's party in the nation, and those classified as high risk were
at least 5 points less supportive of the senator's party than the nation. The
data in Table 2.3 show that there was a dramatic change in the competitive-
ness of states represented by Democratic and Republican senators during
this time period: the number of senators representing states classified as
safe or strongly supportive of their party increased from twenty-five to fifty-
nine while the number representing states classified as competitive fell
from sixty to twenty-eight.

**Table 2.3**  Changing Partisan Composition of States Represented
by Democratic and Republican Senators

| Partisan composition | 95th Senate, 1977–79 | 111th Senate, 2009–11 |
|---|---|---|
| Safe solid | 25 | 59 |
| Competitive | 60 | 28 |
| High risk | 15 | 13 |

Source: Data compiled by author.

## Competition in Senate Elections

Given the growing number of senators representing states in which their party is strongly advantaged, it is not surprising that there has been a marked decline in competition in Senate elections in recent years. Table 2.4 displays the trends in the proportions of competitive and one-sided Senate contests by decade since the 1960s. The data in this table show that since 2002, only 22 percent of Senate contests have been decided by a margin of fewer than 10 percentage points while 55 percent have been decided by a margin of at least 20 percentage points. These elections had the smallest proportion of competitive contests and the largest proportion of one-sided contests in the past five decades. During the 1960s, for example, 40 percent of Senate contests were decided by a margin of less than 10 percentage points and only 38 percent were decided by a margin of at least 20 percentage points.

Despite the decline in competition for individual Senate seats, however, competition for control of the Senate has actually increased in recent years. The data in Table 2.5 show that the average number of Senate seats switching parties has remained fairly stable since the 1960s, except for a temporary bump during the 1970s. Meanwhile, the frequency of switches in party control of the Senate has actually increased over time. There were no switches in party control between 1962 and 1970, only one between 1972 and 1980 and between 1982 and 1990, but two between 1992 and 2000 and two more between 2002 and 2008.

Part of the explanation for the increasing frequency of switches in party control of the Senate in recent years is a shift in the balance of power between the parties. Between 1962 and 1980, Democrats controlled the large majority of Senate seats. Since 1980, however, the two parties have

**Table 2.4**   The Decline of Competition in U.S. Senate Election, by Decade

| Decade | Margin of victory (percent) | | | |
| | Less than 10 | 10–20 | More than 20 | Number of contests |
| --- | --- | --- | --- | --- |
| 1962–1970 | 40 | 22 | 38 | 180 |
| 1972–1980 | 39 | 23 | 38 | 170 |
| 1982–1990 | 30 | 17 | 53 | 168 |
| 1992–2000 | 32 | 24 | 44 | 174 |
| 2002–2008 | 22 | 23 | 55 | 136 |

Source: *CQ Guide to U.S. Elections*, CNN election data.

**Table 2.5**    Seat Changes, Seat Swing, and Majority Control
Changes in U.S. Senate Elections, by Decade

| Decade | Average seat changes | Same direction | Average swing | Average majority | Control changes |
|---|---|---|---|---|---|
| 1962–1970 | 6.0 | 77% | 3.2 | 61.4 | 0 |
| 1972–1980 | 10.8 | 69% | 4.0 | 57.8 | 1 |
| 1982–1990 | 5.2 | 73% | 2.4 | 54.6 | 1 |
| 1992–2000 | 6.0 | 73% | 2.8 | 53.6 | 2 |
| 2002–2008 | 6.5 | 88% | 5.0 | 54.0 | 2 |

Source: *CQ Guide to U.S. Elections,* CNN election data.

alternated in power and the balance of power has generally been much closer. The size of the average Senate majority fell from over sixty-one seats during the 1960s to around fifty-four seats during the 1990s and 2000s. As a result, it took a much smaller inter-party seat swing to produce a switch in party control.

But the narrower majorities of the past two decades are not the entire explanation for the greater frequency of switches in party control. Another factor contributing to increased competition for control of the Senate has been an increase in the average inter-party seat swing in elections. The data in Table 2.5 show that the average inter-party swing of five seats between 2002 and 2008 was higher than the average for any of the previous four decades. Even though the average number of seats switching party control has not been increasing, and was actually considerably larger during the 1970s, the data in Table 2.5 demonstrate that the average inter-party seat swing increased because the direction of these seat switches became more consistent. Between 2002 and 2008, an average of 88 percent of seat switches in each election favored the same party. This meant that the net seat swing produced by a given number of seat switches was considerably larger than in previous decades. In fact, in both 2006 and 2008 all of the seat switches were in one direction, with Democrats picking up six Republican seats in 2006 and eight Republican seats in 2008 for a net gain of fourteen seats in two elections. This trend continued in 2010 with six seats switching from Democratic to Republican control and none switching from Republican to Democratic control.

The close balance of power in the Senate in recent years, combined with relatively large inter-party seat swings and frequent switches in party control, may themselves be exacerbating tensions between Democrats and Republicans in the chamber. Since 1994 control of the chamber has been in question in almost every election, and, given the large ideological differences between the parties, this means that the stakes in these elections are enormous. Despite the chamber's tendency toward obstructionism (e.g., the filibuster rule), a Democratic Senate and a Republican Senate are going to produce very different legislative outcomes.

## The Nationalization of Senate Elections: The Presidential Referendum Effect

Increased uniformity in the direction of seat switches in recent years appears to reflect the growing influence of national issues on voting in Senate elections. As ideological differences between the two major parties have increased, voters appear to increasingly view individual House and Senate contests as referenda on the performance of the national parties. As a result, in choosing a candidate to represent their district or state they are more and more influenced by their evaluation of the president's performance. This can be seen in Table 2.6, which displays the correlations between voters' evaluation of the president's job performance and their House and Senate votes over the past four decades, since the ANES began asking a presidential job performance question.

The data in Table 2.6 show that there has been a fairly dramatic increase in the influence of evaluations of the president's performance on voting for both House and Senate candidates over this time period. The size of the correlations has increased in every decade for both House and Senate elections. In the 1970s, presidential evaluations explained less than a tenth of the variance in House and Senate candidate choice. By the 2000s, however, presidential evaluations explained over a quarter of the variance in House candidate choice and almost a third of the variance in Senate candidate choice.

The influence of presidential evaluations on candidate choice appears to have been even stronger in some of the key Senate contests of 2006, the election in which Democrats gained six seats to take back control of the

**Table 2.6**   Average Correlations of House and Senate Votes with Presidential Job Evaluations, by Decade

| Decade | House vote | Senate vote |
| --- | --- | --- |
| 1972–1980 | .31 | .28 |
| 1982–1990 | .39 | .42 |
| 1992–2000 | .43 | .50 |
| 2002–2008 | .51 | .57 |

Source: American National Election Studies. Available at www.electionstudies.org.

**Table 2.7**    Percentage Voting Democratic by Bush Job Evaluation in Eight Competitive 2006 Senate Contests

| State | Approve | Disapprove | Correlation |
|---|---|---|---|
| Virginia | 7 | 87 | .80 |
| Montana | 15 | 85 | .70 |
| Missouri | 10 | 86 | .75 |
| Pennsylvania | 15 | 88 | .73 |
| Ohio | 17 | 85 | .67 |
| Minnesota | 18 | 90 | .72 |
| Tennessee | 9 | 85 | .76 |
| Rhode Island | 12 | 67 | .48 |

Note: Correlation coefficient is Spearman's rho.

Source: 2006 Exit Polls.

Senate. Table 2.7 displays the relationship between evaluations of incumbent president George W. Bush's performance and Senate voting decisions in eight of these competitive Senate races, including all six contests in which Democrats picked up previously Republican seats: Virginia, Montana, Missouri, Pennsylvania, Ohio, and Rhode Island.

In seven of these eight contests, voters were presented with a choice between a moderately or very liberal Democrat and a moderately or very conservative Republican. The only exception was Rhode Island, where the Republican incumbent, Lincoln Chafee, generally regarded as the most moderate Republican in the Senate, faced a liberal Democrat, former state attorney general Sheldon Whitehouse. In all seven contests involving a choice between a liberal Democrat and a conservative Republican, there was a very strong relationship between evaluations of the president's performance and the Senate vote. The overwhelming majority of those approving of President Bush's performance voted for the Republican candidate, and the overwhelming majority of those disapproving of President Bush's performance voted for the Democratic candidate. The correlations for these seven states ranged from .67 to .80. In the case of Rhode Island, however, the correlation was a much weaker .48. That was because Chafee, a Republican who had broken with the Bush administration on the war in Iraq and other major issues, won a third of the vote among those who disapproved of the president's performance. This was more than twice the vote share of any other Republican candidate among voters disapproving of the president's performance. Nevertheless, Chafee could not overcome the president's unpopularity in heavily Democratic Rhode Island and lost his general election race to Whitehouse.

Moderates like Lincoln Chafee are an endangered species in the Senate. That is because Senate primaries now almost always result in the nomination of a relatively liberal Democrat and a relatively conservative Republican. In the Republican Party, especially, moderate incumbents have frequently had to contend with primary challenges from their right. Chafee survived a difficult primary challenge from a strong conservative in 2006 before losing in the general election. More recently, one of the few remaining GOP moderates, Arlen Specter of Pennsylvania, switched parties in order to avoid a primary challenge in 2010 from the same hard-line conservative who almost defeated him in a 2004 primary. Ironically, he lost the Democratic primary to a more liberal opponent.

The evidence from the 2006 election suggests that the rise of polarization in the Senate over the past several decades has contributed to changes in the behavior of voters. Thirty or forty years ago, there were many moderate-to-liberal Republicans like Lincoln Chafee in the Senate along with a large number of moderate-to-conservative Democrats. They won elections by building coalitions that cut across party lines. As a result many of them were able to win in politically hostile territory and survive downturns in their party's fortunes. The disappearance of these centrists means that the vast majority of Senate contests now involve a clear-cut choice between a relatively liberal Democrat and a relatively conservative Republican, thereby reinforcing the influence of national issues such as presidential performance on voter decision-making.

## Partisan Polarization and Representation: The Case of Health Care Reform

The rise of polarization in the Senate and in the public has had important consequences for the relationship between senators and their constituents. Since Barack Obama's inauguration a number of political commentators have expressed disappointment at the continued bickering and lack of cooperation between Democratic and Republican leaders in Washington. But calls for bipartisanship ignore the deep ideological divide between the two parties in Washington and in the electorate. Nowhere has this been more evident than on the most important and contentious policy issue of Obama's first two years in office—health care reform.

Despite attempts to make health care legislation more palatable to Republicans by dropping provisions such as a public insurance option, and despite weeks of negotiations among a bipartisan group of senators known as the "gang of six," Democratic efforts to win Republican support for health care reform were completely unsuccessful. Not a single Republican representative or senator voted for the final version of the bill, and Democrats ultimately had to resort to use of the controversial reconciliation procedure in the Senate to avoid a Republican filibuster.

Democrats and Republicans in Congress remain deeply divided over health care policy. In fact, the first action taken by the new Republican majority in the House of Representatives in 2011 was to repeal the Afford-able Care Act passed by the Democratic 111th Congress.But the partisan divide on this issue is not confined to Washington. Based on the opinions expressed by Democratic and Republican voters in 2008, the divisions between Democratic and Republican leaders appear to mirror the divisions between Democratic and Republican voters. Figure 2.5 displays the opin-ions of Democratic and Republican voters on a health care policy scale included in the 2008 American National Election Study. The ANES ques-tion asked respondents to place themselves on a 7-point scale indicating support or opposition to a plan to have the federal government pay for all of the cost of medical care for Americans.

The evidence in Figure 2.5 demonstrates that even before the debate over health care reform began in earnest in Washington, the American

**Figure 2.5**    Preferences of Democratic and Republican Senate
Voters on Universal Health Care, 2008

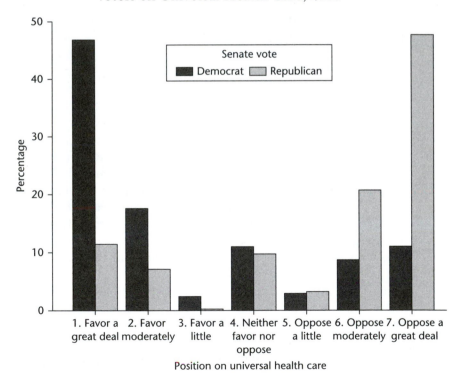

Source: 2008 American National Election Study. Available at www.electionstudies.org.

public was deeply divided on this issue, with Democratic identifiers and leaners overwhelmingly supporting a universal health care plan and Republican identifiers and leaners overwhelmingly opposing such a plan: almost three-fourths of Democrats placed themselves at 1 or 2 on the scale while almost two-thirds of Republicans placed themselves at 6 or 7. Contrary to the argument of Morris Fiorina and his colleagues that there is a disconnect between a polarized political elite and a moderate electorate (Fiorina and Levendusky 2006; Fiorina 2010), this evidence shows that on the issue of health care, the deep divide in Washington reflects a similar division within the American electorate.

## Polarization and the Future of the Senate

Since 1980 Senate majorities have generally been relatively narrow and shifts in party control of the Senate have occurred fairly frequently. Even with the loss of the late Ted Kennedy's seat in Massachusetts, the 111th Congress's fifty-nine-seat Democratic majority was unusually large. In fact, one has to go back to 1977–79 to find a larger majority. The question this raises is whether this expanded Democratic majority signals a long-term shift in party strength or whether it will turn out to be a temporary phenomenon caused by dissatisfaction with the performance of the Bush administration. The results of the next few elections will answer this question. In 2010 Republicans gained six Senate seats, narrowing the Democratic majority from fifty-nine seats to fifty-three seats, and in 2012 Republicans are likely to pick up additional seats because Democrats will have to defend twenty-three of the thirty-three seats that will be up for election.

In the long run, Democrats will probably find it very difficult to maintain anything approaching a sixty-seat majority in the Senate. Since the end of World War II, Senate majorities of sixty or larger have been unusual, and the large majority Democrats enjoyed in the 111th Congress represented a sharp break with the recent pattern of relatively small majorities. While Democrats have enjoyed an edge in party identification in recent years, their advantage among voters is much smaller than it was thirty or forty years ago. Moreover, the evidence in Table 2.8 shows that even after losing six seats in the 2010 midterm elections, Democrats continue to hold a large number of seats that would appear to be vulnerable in the event of an incumbent retirement or a national Republican tide. According to these data, Democrats currently hold eleven seats in states that were carried by the Republican Party in all three presidential elections since 2000 as well as eight seats in states that were carried by the Republicans in two of these three elections. In contrast, Republicans only hold six seats in states that were carried by the Democratic Party in all three presidential elections and only two additional seats in states that were carried by the Democrats in two of these elections.

**Table 2.8**  Number of Times Senator's Sate Carried by Party's Presidential Candidate, 2000–2008

| Number of times carried | Democrats | Republicans |
| --- | --- | --- |
| 0 | 11 | 6 |
| 1 | 8 | 2 |
| 2 | 4 | 6 |
| 3 | 30 | 33 |

Source: uselectionatlas.org.

One of the main reasons for the greater vulnerability of Senate Democrats is the upper chamber's small state bias that gives Republicans a significant advantage. Republicans have carried twelve of the twenty least populous states in all three presidential elections since 2000 while Democrats have only carried five of these states in all three elections. Taken together, the twenty least populous states have about six million fewer residents than the state of California. However, these states elect 40 percent of the Senate. Republicans only hold two of the ten seats from the five small Democratic states. But Democrats currently hold nine of the twenty-four seats from the twelve small Republican states, including both seats from Montana and West Virginia. Incumbent retirements or a national Republican tide could put many of these Democratic seats in jeopardy.

Regardless of which party controls the Senate or the size of its majority, the ideological divide separating the parties is almost certain to remain very large, making bipartisanship an elusive goal for the foreseeable future. That is because the divisions between Democrats and Republicans in the Senate reflect divisions between partisans in the electorate, and those divisions are greatest among those who pay attention to what their elected representatives are doing and vote in primary elections.

Based on the evidence presented in this chapter, polarization is not going away any time soon, and this has potentially important implications for the legislative process in the Senate. Polarization is producing growing frustration among members of the majority party in the Senate, where rules are in place that allow the minority party to block or delay legislation. We have seen clear signs of this frustration in threats by Republican leaders to invoke the "nuclear option" to prevent filibusters over judicial nominations during President Bush's second term and in the recent, successful effort by Democrats to use the reconciliation process to overcome a Republican filibuster of health care reform legislation in 2010.

Given the deep ideological divide that separates the two parties today, a return to relatively narrow majorities in the future is likely to increase the level of frustration of members of the majority party as cloture becomes even more difficult to invoke. At some point, this may well lead to renewed efforts to change the Senate's rules to reduce the ability of the minority party to block legislation by making it easier to invoke cloture or to use floor procedures that prevent filibusters— efforts that are likely to reinforce the deep partisan divide in the upper chamber.

# References

Abramowitz, Alan I., and Kyle L. Saunders. 1998. "Ideological Realignment in the U.S. Electorate." *Journal of Politics* 60: 634–652.

Aldrich, John, and David Rohde. 2000. "The Consequences of Party Organization in the House: The Role of the Majority and Minority Parties in Conditional Party Government." In Jon R. Bond and Richard Fleisher, eds., *Polarized Politics: Congress and the President in a Partisan Era*. Washington, D.C.: CQ Press.

Black, Earl, and Merle Black. 2007. *Divided America*. New York: Simon and Schuster.

Bond, Jon R., and Richard Fleisher. 2000. "Congress and the President in a Partisan Era." In Jon R. Bond and Richard Fleisher, eds., *Polarized Politics: Congress and the President in a Partisan Era*. Washington, D.C.: CQ Press.

Eilperin, Juliet. 2006. *Fight Club Politics*. New York: Rowman and Littlefield.

Evans, C. Lawrence, and Daniel Lipinski. 2005. "Obstruction and Leadership in the U.S. Senate." In Lawrence C. Dodd and Bruce I. Oppenheimer, eds., *Congress Reconsidered*, 8th ed. Washington, D.C.: CQ Press.

Fiorina, Morris P. 2010. *Disconnect: The Breakdown of Representation in American Politics*. Norman: University of Oklahoma Press.

Fiorina, Morris P., and Matthew Levendusky. 2006. "Disconnected: The Political Class versus the People." In Pietro S. Nivola and David W. Brady, eds., *Red and Blue Nation?* Vol. I. Washington, D.C.: Brookings Institution.

Fiorina, Morris P., Samuel J. Abrams, and Jeremy C. Pope. 2006. *Culture War? The Myth of a Polarized America*, 2nd ed. New York: Pearson Longman.

Fleisher, Richard, and Jon R. Bond. 2004. "The Shrinking Middle in the U.S. Congress." *British Journal of Political Science* 34: 429–451.

Ono, Keiko. 2005. "Electoral Origins of Partisan Polarization in Congress: Debunking the Myth." *Extensions* (Fall): 15–19, 25.

Ornstein, Norman, and Barry McMillion. 2005. "One Nation, Divisible." *New York Times*, June 24, A-23.

Poole, Keith T. 2005. "The Decline and Rise of Party Polarization in Congress during the Twentieth Century." *Extensions* (Fall): 6–9.

Poole, Keith T., and Howard Rosenthal. 1991. "Patterns of Congressional Voting." *American Journal of Political Science* 35: 228–278.

———. 2007. *Ideology and Congress*. New York: Transaction Books.

Rohde, David W. 1991. *Parties and Leaders in the Postreform House*. Chicago: University of Chicago Press.

Schickler, Eric, and Kathryn Pearson. 2005. "The House Leadership in an Era of Partisan Warfare." In Lawrence C. Dodd and Bruce I. Oppenheimer, eds., *Congress Reconsidered*, 8th ed. Washington, D.C.: CQ Press.

Sinclair, Barbara. 2006. *Party Wars: Polarization and the Politics of National Policy-Making.* Norman: University of Oklahoma Press.

Smith, Steven S., and Gerald Gamm. 2005. "The Dynamics of Party Government in Congress." In Lawrence C. Dodd and Bruce I. Oppenheimer, eds., *Congress Reconsidered*, 8th ed. Washington, D.C.: CQ Press.

# 3

# A Half-Century of Bicameralism

Ross K. Baker

Since 1960 many things in Congress have changed. But a surprising number have remained the same, although in somewhat different form. The House has undergone the largest number of alterations, some of which have been reversed by one party and restored by the other. These changes have principally involved the distribution or redistribution of power between party leaders and chairs of committees. Changes in the Senate have largely affected the procedures by which the Senate operates. And, in a manner characteristic of the Senate, many of those changes have come about informally or have been changes in application rather than the result either of formal modifications of party or chamber rules.

A person who went into a deep sleep in 1960 and was revived fifty years later would see two recognizable chambers with the same two parties. Some committees would have been renamed, some eliminated, and others would have had their jurisdictions realigned. Minor committees would have been eliminated or had their jurisdictions assumed by other panels. But beneath these reassuringly familiar sights for the reawakened visitor from 1960 would be a political system dramatically altered, a spirit of partisanship (in both chambers) significantly intensified, a supporting cast of lobbyists vastly expanded, and hard-copy journalism community supplanted by cable news, bloggers, tweeters, and citizen journalists. One thing would not have changed: the low levels of approval for Congress as an institution. The degree of disapproval has only deepened over the years.

## The Challenges of Generalization

Because of the span of time and developments both on and off Capitol Hill, drawing general conclusions about fifty years of House-Senate relations confronts us with a daunting tangle of variables, beginning, for example, with the matter of party control of each chamber at any given time. Starting in 1955, Democratic control of both houses of Congress persisted until the election of 1980 when majority control passed to the Republicans in the Senate. That pattern prevailed until the 1986 election that returned Senate Democrats to the majority. Unified Democratic control continued until the election of 1994 when both houses came under Republican majorities. Those majorities endured until the election of 2000 when the Senate deadlocked at 50–50 and the tie-breaking vote was given first to the outgoing vice president and defeated presidential candidate, Al Gore, and then, upon the swearing-in of George W. Bush as president, to Vice President Dick Cheney. The wafer-thin GOP control of the Senate was maintained only until May 2001 when Vermont Republican James Jeffords announced that he would henceforth caucus with the Democrats, making them the majority party.

Democratic control of the Senate agenda lasted only until the 2002 election when the Republicans reclaimed the majority, which they held until the 2006 election when both chambers were recaptured by the Democrats. Democrats' margins of control in both houses were augmented in the 2008 election, with the Senate Democrats reaching sixty members in mid-2009, only to have their majority cut to fifty-nine after a Massachusetts special election to fill Edward Kennedy's seat. All else being equal, a unified Congress will probably act differently than one in which the majorities in each chamber differ. Over this entire period the margin of majority control tended to be closer in the Senate than in the House. The narrowness of majority party control in the Senate is exaggerated by the requirement of a sixty-vote majority to secure cloture (see Chapters 5, 6, and 7 in this volume).

The alignment of the party of the president and the majorities in Congress adds another obstacle to general statements that hold true over a fifty-year span. During the early years of the 1960s through 1980, whatever the party of the president, both houses of Congress were almost certain to be controlled by the Democrats. That expectation was upended with the 1980 election that brought Ronald Reagan to the White House and the GOP to the majority in the Senate. But the pre-1980 pattern was reestablished in 1986 with the reassumption of majority control by the Democrats, which lasted through the entire administration of George H.W. Bush only to end with the 1994 election that confronted Democrat Bill Clinton with bicameral Republican majorities.

The evenly divided Senate and the razor-thin Republican majority, and the brief reversion to Democratic control in the spring of 2001, posed problems for George W. Bush, but with the 2002 election the strength of congressional Republicans combined with an aggressive GOP president to produce an unusually high degree of White House dominance over Congress, most notably the House. The George W. Bush years also saw periodic strains between Senate and House Republicans on a number of important issues. House GOP leaders applied the principle that no legislation would issue forth unless it enjoyed the support of "a majority of the majority." This produced a deeply dyed Republican and conservative coloration to House legislation in anticipation of the fact it would almost certainly be diluted by a Senate with its empowered minority.

If these changes are not sufficiently daunting, those seeking to generalize about bicameral relations over half a century would also need to confront the fact that, although the names of the two parties have not changed, the internal composition and relative homogeneity of the two have in fact changed dramatically over the years. The Democrats of 1961 were still tied strongly to their historical roots in the American South, where their party's dominance not only made general elections a formality but created a privileged caste of long-tenured southern members in both House and Senate whose accumulation of seniority led to the domination of chairs by members from Dixie, most of whom worshiped the household god of racial segregation. Northern Democrats were often treated as dangerous stepchildren who needed to be penned up in marginal committees and denied advancement. Within the electorate, the voting rights legislation of the 1960s sent Dixie voters in two different directions: newly enfranchised African American voters embraced the Democrats while many white voters turned Republican.

The congressional Republican caucuses in both houses in 1961 contained many of the same elements of the party caucuses of the twenty-first century, such as farm-state members from the Great Plains. But in most other ways, the congressional Republicans of fifty years ago exhibited considerably more diversity. A notable presence was a substantial number of eastern seaboard Republicans who were generally more liberal than their midwestern colleagues. The more conservative northern Republicans had, since the late 1930s, voted frequently with conservative southern Democrats against the proposals of Democratic presidents. Efforts by Democratic presidents and party liberals in Congress to attack racial segregation ran into the implacable barriers of a House Rules Committee dominated by conservative southern Democrats and the Senate filibuster (or the threat to employ it) wielded by southern Democrats. In both chambers, Republicans, other than the party liberals, were inclined to stand aside and relish the family quarrel within the opposing party.

By the mid-1970s primordial House-Senate differences became even more complicated by national demographic changes and political reactions that erupted in 1977 over President Jimmy Carter's legislative program and his signature energy proposals. "The [oil and gas] producing states of the South and West were increasingly more Republican and conservative; they had proportionately more power in the Senate than in the House. . . . [T]he House, on the other hand, was controlled by a liberal Democratic leadership that embraced the energy-consuming states of the Northeast and Midwest and environmentalists from around the nation" (Farrell 2001: 465).

Another factor that needs to be considered in relation to this time span is the differential impact of institutional change on the two chambers. Beginning with the 1970s, Democratic House reformers who had struggled against the tide of entrenched seniority and the unchecked power of standing committee chairs used their increased numbers in the party caucus to engineer significant changes in the distribution of power in the House. This included deposing senior chairs, broadening leadership opportunities, and strengthening the hand of Democratic leaders vis-à-vis the chairs of the standing committees. The second wave of reform came after the election of 1994, when GOP reformers led by Speaker Newt Gingrich introduced many innovations, including further reductions in the importance of seniority, a vastly increased leadership influence in the selection of committee chairs, and the institution of term limits on these chairs. In contrast to the sweeping House changes, Senate changes were more circumspect. The most notable institutional reforms in the Senate were procedural. The most important came in 1975 with the reduction from sixty-seven to sixty votes required for cloture. And the upsurge in the frequency of filibusters, threatened filibusters, holds (both secret and open), and, accordingly, the filing of cloture petitions has marked the most recent period in the Senate (see Chapters 3 and 4 in this volume).

Procedures in both houses were changed substantially by the enactment of the 1974 Budget Act, which, in effect, added a third dimension to the legislative process and occasioned a number of procedural novelties such as the annual budget resolution, the budget reconciliation that protects much of the budget from the filibuster, and the Byrd Rule in the Senate that limits the introduction of extraneous amendments to budget legislation. In the Senate, the protection accorded the budget resolution from the filibuster produces an annual "vote-a-rama" of amendments that would otherwise be vulnerable to filibusters. But the rule also became a source of friction between the two chambers, and "House members bitterly complain that a Senate rule dictates what can and cannot be included in reconciliation bill conference reports" (Sinclair 2007: 102).

The virtual abandonment of formal conference committees in the late twentieth and early twenty-first centuries can probably be laid at the door of the heightened levels of political polarization in Congress. Conferees from both chambers were traditionally selected for their disposition to compromise and to uphold the position of their chamber, but it became increasingly the case that conferees were picked for their partisan combativeness. The nadir of the process was the exclusion or marginalization of members of the minority party by the majority. House-Senate differences on legislation passed by both houses came to involve "ping-ponging" of bills back and forth between the two chambers. A conspicuous reversal of this trend away from volleying bills was the televised House-Senate conference on legislation to reform financial services that took place in the spring of 2010.

If the partisan complexion of the chambers, the fit between the president's party and that of Congress, and the distinct and differential procedural innovations were not sufficient to complicate the task of generalizing about a half-century of bicameralism, the personalities of the leaders of Congress over the past fifty years also contribute to the elusiveness of facile generalizations.

## Fifty Years, Many Leaders

The period 1960–2010 began in the House with the twilight of the speakership of Sam Rayburn, who had presided over the House since before the United States entered World War II and, in partnership with fellow Texan Lyndon B. Johnson, guided the congressional Democrats in the 1950s. Despite Rayburn's legendary reputation, he was frequently at the mercy of House conservatives such as Howard Smith (D-Va.), chair of the Rules Committee, who Rayburn reluctantly challenged by "packing" his committee in 1961 with members more amenable to the Kennedy program.

Transition occurred in congressional leadership in 1961 with the death of the tough but companionable Rayburn and ascension of the starchy and pedantic John McCormack (D-Mass.). On the Senate side, Lyndon Johnson found himself kicked upstairs to the vice presidency. His replacement by the taciturn, hands-off Mike Mansfield (D-Mont.) provided the Senate with a welcome respite from Johnson's high-powered style. Johnson's departure as majority leader marked the end of a unique period in Senate history in which an institution unaccustomed to muscular leadership acquiesced to a leader's style.

One episode in 1962 dramatized the relative power of committee chairs in both the House and Senate vis-à-vis party leaders. The chairs of House and Senate Appropriations Committees battled over whether the House would enjoy the exclusive power to initiate spending bills. The chair of the Senate committee, Carl Hayden (D-Ariz.), acknowledged the constitutional primacy of the House in initiating revenue bills but claimed that the Senate had as much right to begin the appropriations process as the House. This assertion was vigorously disputed by the chair of the House Appropriations Committee, Clarence Cannon (D-Mo.), who argued that custom decreed the House go first on spending bills. The clash eventually degenerated into a squabble over which side of the Capitol the appropriations conference committees would meet. So acrimonious did the dispute become that the federal government faced a shutdown over the feud between these two elderly chairs. The appropriations crisis of 1962 is mentioned here only because it illustrates the superordinate influence of committee chairs at the time. Both Majority Leader Mansfield and Speaker McCormack stood by, almost helplessly, as these two committee titans battled out an issue that had widespread support in both chambers.

Still, it was Lyndon Johnson as president and Mansfield and McCormack as his congressional allies who brought about the enactment of a cascade of liberal legislation in the mid-1960s: the Civil Rights Act of 1964, the Voting Rights Act of 1965, Medicare, and the Open Housing Act of 1968. The success of those initiatives is as much a tribute to the Mansfield-McCormack partnership as to the energy and determination of LBJ. Mansfield's relationship with McCormack dated to the time that Mansfield was a House member and McCormack was majority leader. Mansfield sought the post of majority whip in the belief that the incumbent whip, Percy Priest (D-Tenn.), was planning to relinquish it. When Priest decided to remain whip, McCormack gave Mansfield the consolation prize of chief deputy whip (Oberdorfer 2003: 89–90). While McCormack was a Bostonian and Mansfield a Montanan, both were Irish Catholics. McCormack was the more devout of the two, although Mansfield was observant. Johnson, in a conversation with Vice President Hubert Humphrey, referred to the two disparagingly as "the Catholics" and believed that John F. Kennedy had advised the two to ignore Johnson when LBJ was vice president (Oberdorfer 2003: 224). Nonetheless, the Johnson-Mansfield-McCormack team compiled an unprecedented record of social legislation.

Carl Albert of Oklahoma, who succeeded McCormack in 1971, was in many ways a transitional figure. Burdened by a troubled marriage and a drinking problem, the Speaker was relatively ineffective in managing a restive membership that was divided on critical issues such as Vietnam. Majority Leader Hale Boggs (D-La.), also faced with periodic bouts of excessive drinking, was not always able to support Albert effectively. It was during Albert's tenure as Speaker that the Watergate scandal and President Gerald Ford's pardoning of Richard Nixon unleashed the fury of the electorate on the Republicans in the election of 1974. What followed was the surge of reforms from the majority Democrats that reshaped the House and provided the opportunity for the party leadership at long last to reduce the power of the committee chairs. But, as Nelson Polsby (2004) observed, "Albert was more aware of [the changes] than some of his colleagues, but he was as Speaker little inclined to use in an aggressive way the new levers of power that the caucus pressed upon him" (111).

The House Democrats, in addition to their sweeping reforms, also took up the campaign to extricate the United States from Vietnam, but the debate divided their caucus, which still had its share of "hawks." One of the most energetic opponents of the war was the man who was to succeed Carl Albert, Majority Leader Thomas P. "Tip" O'Neill (D-Mass.), whose liberalism was far more in harmony with the Democratic rebels than was Albert's tentativeness. In the Senate, Mike Mansfield, an old Asia hand, harbored serious reservations about President Johnson's escalation but resisted breaking openly with Johnson. Neither, however, could restrain such colleagues as Idaho's Frank Church, New Jersey Republican Clifford P. Case, and the formidable chairman of the Foreign Relations Committee, J. William Fulbright. It was characteristic of Mansfield's laissez faire approach to leadership that he did not obstruct the antiwar Democrats. Accordingly, in 1970 the Senate was able to pass a bipartisan amendment sponsored by Church, a Democrat, and Republican John Sherman Cooper to the Foreign Military Sales Act to cut off funds for combat operations in Cambodia that had spilled into that country from Vietnam. As evidence of the continuing split among House Democrats on the war, the Cooper-Church amendment, which had passed the Senate easily, was tied up for six months in conference with the House.

While the mid-1970s represented the flood tide of liberal reform in the House, in the Senate Republican conservatives shook off the trauma of Watergate to organize the Senate Steering Committee to build cohesion within the Republican caucus in opposition to the Democrats. The advent of the Carter administration in 1977 saw a change of majority leadership in both houses of Congress with the emergence of the O'Neill speakership in the House and Mike Mansfield yielding to Robert C. Byrd (D-W.V.) in the Senate; on the minority side, Howard Baker replaced Hugh Scott in the Senate while John J. Rhodes, the House Republican floor leader who had held the post since 1973, provided some continuity. The solidifying liberal hold on the majority House Democrats and their new, highly partisan Speaker was recognized by Baker, who wrote, "[O'Neill] was the most fiercely partisan man I ever dealt with. Personally, he was a sweetheart but in a political mode he was the devil. No statement by a Republican was taken at face value. No promise by a Republican was accepted. After a while, it's terrible to say, I never expended much energy trying to figure him out or reason with him" (Farrell 2001: 17).

O'Neill's speakership represented an assertively liberal caucus's culmination of the takeover of House standing committees, which occurred "not because the reformers wanted to undermine the committee system, nor because they wanted to so disperse power that the system was incapable of action. Rather, they wanted to remove the chair's capability to frustrate the wishes of the majority of the party" (Rohde 1991: 26).

If liberals were dominant in the House Democratic caucus of the 1980s, House Republicans were in transition. As William Connelly and John Pitney (1994) put it, "In previous decades, the Northeast and Midwest had supplied the House GOP Conference with a significant number of liberal members [but a]s the 1990s began . . . the more-conservative South and west were defining House Republicanism." They add that, "By 1993, only one-sixth of the House Republicans belonged to the GI generation, while more than a third were 'baby boomers' born after 1945" (22). The Republican generation warp could be summed up in the lives and careers of Robert

H. Michel (R-Ill.), who became the Republican floor leader in 1981, and Newt Gingrich (R- Ga.), who became GOP whip in 1989 and Speaker in 1995. Michel served as a combat infantryman in World War II and was awarded two Bronze Stars and a Purple Heart; he received his college degree after military service. In 1948 he began his political career as a congressional staff member and served as a House member from 1957 until 1995. Michel sought the type of bipartisan harmony that had prevailed between Rayburn and Republican leader Joe Martin in the 1950s.

Gingrich's only connection with World War II was a father who had been a career soldier in uniform during that conflict; Gingrich spent much of his youth on army bases. Gingrich was basically an academic who turned to politics. This lack of generational connection was to have important implications for bicameral relations when, after 1994, Gingrich as House Speaker was teamed with Senate majority leader Bob Dole (R-Kans.). Dole's age and World War II military service had much more in common with Michel than with Gingrich.

If one were to sum up the view of the younger Republican House members toward their leadership during the 1980s, when the Republicans were still frozen out of power in the House, it would be that of a collaborationist government in a country under foreign occupation. The chamber's seemingly eternal dominance by Democrats combined with the essentially majoritarian nature of the House inevitably resulted in the Democrats enjoying a sense of entitlement coupled with a disdain for the minority. Long-term Republican members seemed to their younger party colleagues supplicants grateful for whatever crumbs fell from the majority banquet table. The perplexing picture in the minds of the party insurgents who formed Newt Gingrich's Conservative Opportunity Society group was of a party leader, Bob Michel, taking the afternoon off to go golfing with Tip O'Neill—a vivid expression of their own irrelevance in an arena where Republicans seemed to have accepted the role of permanent minority.

In the Senate, the election of Ronald Reagan brought Howard Baker to the leadership of the new Republican majority. Baker, who had opposed Reagan in the 1980 GOP primaries and criticized Reagan's economic policy as "a river boat gamble," was now placed in the position of enacting the very policy he had so vocally questioned. As his fellow-Republican Warren Rudman recalled, "Howard's great challenge in the early months of 1981 was to pass Reagan's economic program. . . . Both Howard and I had serious doubts about this theory, but we swallowed hard and supported the Reagan plan, to our eventual regret" (Rudman 1996: 36).

Baker was viewed with wariness by the growing number of conservative senators, who held against him his prominent role on the Senate Watergate committee and his question, "What did the president know and when did he know it?" and his partnership with Sen. Edward Kennedy in the 1967 effort to accelerate congressional redistricting to comply with the Supreme Court's one-man–one-vote rulings.

In 1980 eighteen new senators were elected, sixteen of whom were Republican; this represented the largest infusion for the GOP since 1946. Of these sixteen, six were former House members. Some observers contend that this period of infusion brought significant change to the Senate. Historian Louis Gould (2005) suggests that "[a]n influx of Republicans who had previously served in the House brought the highly polarized tactics of that body across the Capitol" (293). This argument may help explain what some regard as the coarsening of the Senate and the decline in its vaunted civility.

In fact, the actual number of former House members actually declined between 1976 and 1980, from thirty-six to thirty-two (though it subsequently rose; see Chapter 4 in this volume), but there was certainly a more conservative tinge to the 1980 Senate freshmen. One notable piece of House-Senate asymmetry was rectified through the efforts of Baker, who sought television coverage of floor debate. In 1979 the House began broadcasting its floor proceedings on C-SPAN. Baker had pushed strongly for television coverage of the floor, but it was only after Baker left, in 1986, that the Senate accepted the cameras.

When Baker departed, the leadership of the Republican majority devolved upon Bob Dole, former Republican National Committee chair during the Watergate scandal and the 1976 vice-presidential candidate. Both of these positions had conferred on Dole a reputation as a hard-edged partisan, but he proved to be the ideal leader in his dealings with the Democratic House and its leaders, Speaker O'Neill and Majority Leader Jim Wright. One Democratic colleague praised him as the most effective majority leader since Lyndon Johnson (Talmadge 1987: 228).

Ironically, the House Democratic leadership during this period got along less well with the Democratic floor leader, Sen. Robert C. Byrd; most of the communication passing between them was carried on at the staff level (Barry 1989: 62). Symptomatic of the tensions of the period was the common complaint heard in the House—a lament heard much more frequently in recent years—that the House acts with dispatch on politically risky legislation and then waits, often in vain, for the Senate, which acts slowly or sometimes not at all.

In 1987, shortly after Jim Wright succeeded Tip O'Neill as Speaker and the Democrats were restored to the majority in the Senate under the leadership of Byrd, the matter of a congressional pay raise surfaced, largely because for eight years Congress had exempted itself from the raises given to other parts of the federal government. Suffering from the erosion of inflation but fearful of taking an up-or-down vote on the raise, the leaders of Congress created a bipartisan commission to make recommendations on a substantial pay raise. For political cover and to avoid a vote, the recommendations of the commission were to become effective in thirty days unless cancelled by a vote of both houses of Congress. "Wright, Michel, Byrd and Senate GOP Leader Bob Dole had agreed to let the thirty-day clock expire, putting the pay raise into effect . . . [b]ut. . . the Senate voted 88-6 for a resolution killing the pay raise. It was pure hypocrisy; senators knew that Wright would prevent a House vote" ( Barry 1989: 112).

Still, on some important issues the chambers could work together. That same year the Iran-Contra scandal erupted, and what might have been a constitutional crisis or an opportunity for partisan advantage became instead an outstanding example of bicameral and bipartisan cooperation when House and Senate leaders agreed that a single select committee composed of members of both houses and both parties would investigate the arms-for-hostages deal.

By the late 1980s, however, partisan animosity was beginning to intensify. George H.W. Bush's nomination of Sen. John Tower to the post of Secretary of Defense was rejected by the Senate on an almost straight party-line vote. Speaker Jim Wright pointed to the rejection of Tower in the Senate as the occasion for an attack upon him in the House. Shortly after the Senate vote, a Republican colleague of Wright's approached him, claiming, "[W]e're under heavy pressure to make an example of you. The Gingrich crowd is putting Bob Michel and the moderates through a virtual inquisition. They want to make your personal downfall a litmus test of party loyalty" (Wright 1996: 484–485).

President Bush sent the Senate the name of House minority whip Dick Cheney as a replacement for Tower. Cheney's imminent resignation from the party leadership caused Newt Gingrich to make a bold bid for his post. The heir apparent to Michel was fellow-Illinoisan Edward Madigan, a Republican very much in the mellow midwestern mold. Significantly, in a show of dissatisfaction with the accommodationist leadership, Gingrich was elected whip by a two-vote margin. He used his new position to level ethics violations charges against Speaker Wright and eventually also against Majority Whip Tony Coelho. Even though Gingrich himself came under suspicion for ethical lapses, the Democratic majority leadership took the fall. In May 1989, Wright resigned the speakership, and Majority Leader Thomas Foley (D-Wash.) was chosen to replace him. Where Wright was a tough, even overbearing partisan leader, who took on the Reagan administration on both domestic and foreign policy issues, Foley "reverted to the traditional role of a speaker almost above party" (Kuttner 1991).

The term of Foley's speakership coincided with the six years that George Mitchell of Maine served as Senate majority leader. "Where Byrd seemed an old-fashioned inside player evocative of another era, Mitchell, although reliably liberal, was modern, articulate, and telegenic. A former federal judge and a genuinely nice man, he seemed anything but a wheeler-dealer. Mitchell also had a substantive interest in policy, having offered a full programmatic blueprint in 1988 that was largely ignored by the press" (Kuttner 1991). Moreover, while Mitchell could be highly partisan, he generally worked well with his Senate counterpart, Bob Dole, another pragmatic partisan.

In 1994 Newt Gingrich devised a strategy to nationalize the congressional contests to a degree rarely seen in a midterm election. This was the "Contract with America," a manifesto that promised to bring ten important issues to the floor of the House. It capitalized on the scandals that had erupted in Congress, most notably those surrounding the so-called House bank scandal, in which representatives were given unlimited overdraft privileges. The contract embraced reforms both inside and outside Congress. It called for term limits on members, limits on the terms of committee chairs, a ban on proxy voting in committees, and a reduction in the number of congressional committees. The internal reforms, Gingrich hoped, would be embraced by Republicans in both chambers when, as he anticipated, the GOP would take majorities in both chambers in November 1994. Gingrich proved prescient and highly effective as a campaign leader; one significant casualty was Speaker Foley, who was defeated in his eastern Washington district.

Gingrich did spark some enthusiasm among Senate Republicans, notably from two senators who had previously served in the House, Trent Lott (R-Miss.) and Phil Gramm (R-Texas). Gingrich organized a demonstration on the front steps of the Capitol to kick off the campaign. As Lott recalled, Gingrich approached him and said, "'The media are prepared to cover that assembly intensely. Trent, why don't you and your fellow Republicans in the Senate join us out there?' Phil Gramm and I both thought it was a terrific idea, and we both separately approached Bob Dole." Then, in a response that foretold a great deal about the future of House-Senate relations under the Republicans, Dole replied, "Nah, we don't want to do that" (Lott 2005: 127). Later, however, despite their differences, Gingrich would credit Dole for getting "an amazing amount of the Contract With America through the Senate" (Gingrich 1998: 10).

Gingrich, in a moment of levity, had once referred to Dole as "the tax collector for the welfare state" for his instrumental role in the 1983 Tax Equity and Fiscal Responsibility Act that reversed many of Ronald Reagan's 1981 tax cuts in the interest of lowering the deficit. The relationship between the two was never close. Gingrich looked upon Dole as a kind of dinosaur; Dole regarded Gingrich as an ideologue. But the 1994 election yoked them uneasily together.

In pursuit of the presidency, Dole resigned the majority leader post in 1996. Gingrich's departure from the speakership in 1998 was less felicitous. He had withstood both a palace coup mounted in 1997 by members of the Class of 1994 unhappy with his leadership and a series of ethics charges. But the fatal blow came with the Republicans' poor showing in the 1998 mid-term elections. The Republicans had believed they could strengthen their numbers in the House, but in fact they lost five seats. Their optimism was based on the scandal surrounding President Bill Clinton and his relationship with White House intern Monica Lewinsky. The affair and its fallout resulted in Clinton's impeachment by the House on a straight party-line vote, after it rejected the lesser penalty of censure. In a remarkable display of Senate bipartisanship, the Senate agreed to proceed with a trial in the full knowledge that there were insufficient votes for conviction. The Republicans got their trial and the Democrats their acquittal, but in institutional terms the reputation of the House as a strongly partisan institution was reinforced. The Senate, in contrast, emerged as a paragon of statesmanship, at least for the time being.

In the immediate aftermath of the 1998 election, a leadership crisis developed for House Republicans when Gingrich resigned and his most likely successor, Appropriations chair Robert L. Livingston, withdrew from the race upon admitting that he had engaged in an extramarital affair. Leadership devolved on Dennis Hastert, a low-key member from Illinois. The gray eminence behind him was Majority Leader Tom DeLay of Texas who ratcheted up the partisanship of an institution that, by its nature, is already a more partisan institution than the Senate (a reality not necessarily reflected in recent roll call voting data; see Chapter 00). But even in the Senate, the dawn of the twenty-first century saw an institution whose characteristic stately pace was slowed even further by heightened partisanship. Significantly, what did not change was the frustration experienced by House members, even Republicans, with a Senate that was either slow to act or disposed to dilute legislation emerging from the south side of the Capitol.

The period of George W. Bush's presidency from 2001 until the loss of Republican majorities in the election of 2006 saw the House GOP marching in virtual lockstep with the legislative program of the president, a remarkable display of party discipline overseen by Majority Leader DeLay. In the Senate, the majority was typically more constrained by the Democrats' use of the filibuster, especially on judicial nominations. This led to a threat by Republicans to resort to a "nuclear option"—the use of parliamentary rulings from the vice president and possible rules changes to blunt the effect of the filibusters. The crisis was eased when a bipartisan group of moderates, "The Gang of Fourteen," proposed curbing the filibuster except on judicial nominees deemed too extreme.

The increased alienation between House and Senate Republicans during the Bush years was exacerbated by a leadership crisis in 2002 when Trent Lott, who had been majority leader since 1996, was forced to step down after making an impolitic remark at a celebration marking Sen. Strom Thurmond's 100th birthday that seemed to praise Thurmond's segregationist past. Lott was succeeded by Bill Frist of Tennessee, a physician who had been elected in 1994 and who never seemed completely comfortable in his floor leader role.

From the start, Frist struggled under the burden of having been seen by his Republican colleagues as the choice of the Bush White House who was foisted on the Senate. Unlike Lott, a creature of both the House and Senate, Frist was innocent of any prior political experience and soon proved himself unequal to the task of managing the Senate floor. The contrast between the well-disciplined Hastert-DeLay vote whipping operation in the House and Frist's inability to follow suit became a source of House-Senate friction. "Tensions ran so deep between the House and Senate after Bush's re-election in 2004 that the House approved a rules change . . . allowing members to criticize the Senate or individual senators during speeches on the House floor. . . . Democrats [when they became the majority party in 2006] kept the rule, in a sign that tensions between the chambers run deeper with the majority" (O'Connor 2007: 1).

The ambitious agenda of the Obama administration placed similar strains on House-Senate relations when House Democrats went on record in support of controversial and politically risky legislation such as "cap-and-trade" to curb global warming. After only thirteen months of the Obama administration frustrated House Democrats had compiled a list of 290 bills passed by the House that had not been acted on by the Senate. In January 2010, House majority whip James Clyburn (D-S.C.) suggested that the Senate was out of touch with Americans, and did not differentiate between the two parties: "Senators tend to see themselves as a House of Lords and they don't seem to understand that those of us that go out there every two years stay in touch with the American people. . . . We tend to respond to them a little better" (Rushing 2010).

Rarely, if ever, is there return fire from the Senate. Whether this silence reflects embarrassment or a senatorial hauteur that dictates silence in the face of criticism from fellow partisans, senators rarely rise to the chamber's defense, and in particular they make no comment on the excessive resort to the filibuster.

In the prolonged negotiations over the Obama stimulus package, health insurance reform, and the restructuring of financial regulations, one aspect of House-Senate relations should be noted: the remarkably good rapport between House Speaker Nancy Pelosi and Senate Majority Leader Harry Reid. By temperament and political philosophy these legislative leaders were not natural allies. Although both have demonstrated a disposition to blurt out impolitic statements on occasion, and the political terrain on which each operates could hardly be more different, they proved adept at working together. Reid is usually elected by slender margins; Pelosi represents one of the most comfortable Democratic districts. In the

110th Congress (2007–09), Pelosi's margin of partisan control (around forty seats) was generally enough for her to push through legislation, even with the defection of some conservative "Blue Dog" Democrats. Reid, on the other hand, only briefly achieved the super-majority of sixty essential to cloture and the shut down of filibusters.

What made them a successful team in enacting the Obama administration's legislative priorities was the fact that each is a tough and resourceful operator with a skilled staff. There was also a high degree of personal mutual regard, as reflected in the frequency of their meetings, often over dinner.

More than most Speakers, Pelosi seems to have had genuine sympathy for the plight of the Senate floor leader. Early in the Obama administration, when the economic stimulus bill was being debated, House Majority Leader Steny Hoyer, a one-time Pelosi rival, urged the Speaker to get tough with Reid. He expressed frustration that Reid had not forced Republicans to mount old-fashioned filibusters and thus unmask them as obstructionists. Pelosi understood, perhaps more acutely than Hoyer, the reality that modern filibusters are no more than repeated requests for roll calls, and she defended Reid, saying in an interview on MSNBC, "This is the legislative process. We act. They act. We reconcile. And in order to get their votes, they [the Senate Democratic leadership] had to make certain changes in the legislation" (O'Connor and Bresnahan 2009).

The relative harmony between these two very different Democrats produced the greatest volume of important legislation since the 89th Congress (1965–66) which enacted the Great Society programs before suffering substantial Democratic losses in the subsequent midterm election.

## Persistence and Change in House-Senate Relations

The Clinton administration's 1993–2000 efforts to reduce the federal deficit, stimulate the economy, and pursue a policy of liberalizing trade with the nations of Latin America illustrated some of the enduring characteristic differences between the contemporary House and Senate. In the first instance, Clinton proposed an economic plan designed to stimulate the economy and reduce the deficit in the spring of 1993. The stimulus portion was passed by the House but defeated in the Senate by a Republican filibuster. Using the budget process with its limitation on filibusters as the vehicle, a reconciliation package that embodied most of Clinton's economic program passed the House by two votes. The Senate passed the budget bill on a 50–50 tie broken in the bill's favor by Vice President Al Gore. But in a pattern that would be repeated in the Clinton administration and later in the Obama presidency, House Democrats "walked the plank" by supporting a politically risky energy tax that was scuttled in the Senate with Democratic votes. Resentment among House Democrats directed to their fellow partisans in the Senate became a familiar theme on Capitol Hill.

The underlying reason for the inability of Senate Democrats to follow suit on Clinton's legislative program was the increasing use of the filibuster. "To an extent unprecedented in modern American history, the filibuster became a partisan tool during the 103rd Congress. Republicans wielded the weapon throughout the Congress but especially at the end, when time pressure makes obstructionism especially effective" (Sinclair 2000: 81; see also Chapters 5, 6, and 8 in this volume).

Characteristic House-Senate differences also expressed themselves in the 1993 debate over the North American Free Trade Agreement (NAFTA). In this instance, the House-Senate differences were based less on partisanship than on other factors, including the distinctive nature of House and Senate constituencies. Senators, representing entire states, tend to embrace more diverse constituencies than do House members, who might be influenced by how a particular bill would affect a single major economic interest in their district. Many House Democrats, for example, depended heavily on labor union support, and organized labor was virtually unanimous in its opposition to NAFTA.

While many Democratic senators also enjoyed labor support, few were uniquely dependent on the votes of union members. As journalist Chris Matthews succinctly put it: "Senators represent the big picture. Congressmen can be affected if one factory in their district stands to get hurt. It's the sheer scale of the state and all that's going on in it that makes the difference for the Senate guy. In a congressional district, if you have one factory that might get hurt you've got to vote against NAFTA, whereas a senator says, 'Wait a minute. I've got other things going on here. I've got agriculture. I've got shipping.' So senators look at things in terms of sectors, not so much in terms of individual industries or individual factories" (quoted in Baker 1995: 228–229).

The contention that Senate constituencies are, in general, larger and arguably more diverse than House constituencies and that these differences yield distinctive policy differences has come under attack from several quarters. One revisionist argument maintains that "[s]tates and congressional districts are not as different as a superficial view would have us believe. States are not exceptionally heterogeneous, nor are congressional districts unusually homogeneous" (Gronke 2000: 59). A subsequent study that examined trade policies specifically concluded that, although there were significant House-Senate differences on trade policy throughout history, "[t]he case is overwhelming that constituency size does not account for notable differences in preferences . . . on trade issues evident in recent decades" (Karol 2007: 491).

The House-Senate differences in constituency size and diversity, however, do appear to have an effect in terms of distributive politics. Frances

Lee (2004: 185, 204) found that in the case of transportation grants House members tend to favor the use of earmarks and narrow categorical programs to bring resources to their constituencies while senators resort to large formula grants. These more narrowly targeted projects favored by House members promote "credit-claiming" "in order to make their contribution more visible." Lee also found that the Senate has had a greater impact on the overall distribution of federal funds to the states than has the House and, less surprisingly, that Senate formulas disproportionately benefitted smaller-population states.

One feature of House-Senate differences over time has been party unity on roll call votes with party line voting commonly as low as in the 70 to 75 percent range in both chambers in the 1970s. In the Senate this lower level of partisanship persisted, particularly among Senate Democrats, into the mid-1980s. Beginning in the 1990s, the party unity scores in both houses and for both parties began to converge so that by the decade after 2000, 90 percent party unity scores were common in both houses, for Republicans and Democrats alike (Stanley and Niemi 2008: 224–225). While greater partisanship in both houses is undeniable—roll call vote tallies testify to this eloquently—it would be a mistake to conclude that the interaction of the two parties in both chambers is indistinguishable one from the other. The requirements for unanimous consent to proceed in the Senate, the filibuster, the hold, and the "blue slip" system on presidential nominations vest in individual senators, majority and minority alike, a degree of influence that is enjoyed only by the most senior members of the majority party in the House.

House members, particularly those both junior and in the minority, can be routinely disregarded; one disregards an individual senator at one's own peril. What this leads to, and what roll call voting data do not reveal, is a degree of inter-party consultation and personal interaction that continues in the Senate. What it has not produced during the first years of the Obama administration is important legislation with anything more than token bipartisan support. And while scholars can continue to debate the extent of House-Senate convergence, one thing that cannot be denied is that the pathogen of hyper-partisanship has invaded both bodies.

# References

Baker, Ross. 1995. *House and Senate*, 2nd ed. New York: W. W. Norton.
Barry, John M. 1989. *The Ambition and the Power*. New York: Penguin.
Connelly, William F., Jr., and John J. Pitney Jr. 1994. *Congress' Permanent Minority?* Lanham, Md.: Littlefield Adams Quality Paperbacks.
Farrell, John A. 2001. *Tip O'Neill*. New York: Little, Brown.
Gingrich, Newt. 1998. *Lessons Learned the Hard Way*. New York: Harper Collins.
Gould, Louis. 2005. *The Most Expensive Club*. New York: Basic Books.

Gronke, Paul. 2000. *The Electorate, the Campaign, and the Office.* Ann Arbor: University of Michigan Press.

Karol, David. 2007. "Does Constituency Size Affect Elected Officials' Trade Policy Preferences?" *The Journal of Politics* 69: 483–494.

Kuttner, Robert. 1991. "Congress without Cohabitation: the Democrats' Morning-After." *The American Prospect.* http://www.prospect.org/cs/articales?article=congress_without_cohabitation_the_democrats_morningafter. Accessed September 24, 2010.

Lee, Frances E. 2004. "Bicameralism and Geographic Politics: Allocating Funds in the House and Senate." *Legislative Studies Quarterly* 29: 185–213.

Lott, Trent. 2005. *Herding Cats.* New York: Harper Collins.

Oberdorfer, Xxxxx. 2003. *Senator Mansfield.* Washington, D.C.: Smithsonian Books.

O'Connor, Patrick. 2007. "House Republicans Learn to Appreciate Their Senate Peers." *Politico.* http://dyn.politico/printstory.cfm?uuid=70E05366-3048-5C12-0083BB8BE9BB610F. Accessed March 21, 2007.

O'Connor, Patrick, and John Bresnahan. 2009. "Hoyer to Pelosi: Stand up to Senate." *Politico.* http://dyn.politico.com/printstory.cfm?uuid=818FA9E9-18FE-702B2-A8828A58699D8384. Accessed February 17, 2009.

Polsby, Nelson W. 2004. *How Congress Evolves.* New York: Oxford University Press.

Rohde, David W. 1991. *Parties and Leaders in the Postreform House.* Chicago: University of Chicago Press.

Rudman, Warren B. 1996. *Combat, Twelve Years in the Senate.* New York: Random House.

Rushing, J. Taylor. 2010. "Senate Sitting on 290 Bills Already Passed by House; Tension Mounts." *The Hill.* http://thehill.com/homenews/house/83059-senate-sitting-on-290-house-bills. Accessed February 2, 2010.

Sinclair, Barbara. 2000. "The President as Legislative Leader." In Colin Campbell and Bert A. Rockman, eds., *The Clinton Legacy.* New York: Chatham House Publishers.

———. 2007. *Unorthodox Lawmaking: New Legislative Processes in the U.S. Congress.* Washington, D.C.: CQ Press.

Stanley, Harold W., and Richard G. Niemi. 2008. *Vital Statistics on American Politics 2007–2008.* Washington, D.C.: CQ Press.

Talmadge, Herman E. 1987. *Talmadge, A Memoir.* Atlanta: Peachtree Publishers.

Wright, Jim. 1996. *Balance of Power.* Atlanta: Turner Publishing.

# 4

## The Changing Careers of Senators, 1960–2010: Coming, Going, Choosing

### Burdett Loomis

I've given most of my life to serving the people of West Virginia, and it began here 59 years ago.

Sen. Robert Byrd, 2008

Easy, boy.

Former Senator Robert Dole,
speaking to his dog at the end of a
Britney Spears Pepsi commercial, 2001[1]

The U.S. Senate has traditionally valued the individual legislator, such as a Robert C. Byrd (D-W.Va.), who could chart his or (increasingly) her course through the chutes and ladders of a legislative career. Although political eras may change the nature and value of Senate service, understanding how individual careers develop is integral to assessing both senators and the Senate. For example, in 1958 William Proxmire (D-Wis.), after about six months in the chamber, concluded that he could not abide by the restricting norms of a highly collegial chamber and decided that "he would 'be a senator like Wayne [Morse] and Paul [Douglas]'; he would talk when he pleased on whatever he chose and would not worry about his influence in the Senate. He had found his role" (Huitt 1969). Within the so-called textbook Congress of the late 1950s, the norms of reciprocity and apprenticeship remained fully operational (Matthews 1960). Senator Proxmire could choose to flout them and suffer the consequences. He did, even as he carved out a long and satisfactory Senate career that never placed him near the core of the institution's power.

In 2004 former representative Tom Coburn (R-Okla.) won a Senate seat and proceeded in his first term to speak his mind, to frequently tie the Senate in knots, and to express little concern over the consequences. Coburn has embraced his "Dr. NO" nickname, bestowed in recognition of

---

1. See http://www.youtube.com/watch?v=Jt8uNG02ixA.

his willingness to obstruct large numbers of spending bills, which often irritated the Republican leadership, to say nothing of the majority Democrats. "When it comes to obstructing bills, he is part of a very tiny pantheon in the history of the Senate," observed political scientist Ross Baker (Leibovich 2009). Although Coburn has received his full complement of criticism for his obstructionist tactics, the "maverick" label has infrequently been applied to him, even as he defined his own singular role within the institution. In fact, the maverick role embraced by Proxmire has largely ceased to exist in a contemporary Senate that has become simultaneously highly partisan and thoroughly individualistic at the expense of much of the norm-based collegiality that existed in earlier times (Sinclair 2006).

Careers—whether Proxmire's or Coburn's or Byrd's—develop within a context of opportunities, resources, expectations, and formal rules that change over time. This chapter examines some of the ways in which Senate careers have changed since 1960 and what the implications have been for the body and for American politics more broadly, as increasing numbers of former senators continue to make their mark for many years after leaving the chamber. The focus here is on careers *and* the Senate, rather than just careers *in* the Senate. Indeed, leaving the Senate may well be an important part of a public-service career, if we are to take two-term senator Evan Bayh (D-Ind.), age 54 when he retired, at his word: "At this time [February 2010], I simply believe I can best contribute to society in another way: creating jobs by helping grow a business, helping guide an institution of higher learning, or helping run a worthy charitable endeavor" (Bayh 2010).

Although skepticism should accompany any pronouncement like Bayh's—especially given his March 2011 announcement that he was joining a major D.C. law firm—the fact remains that many former senators have constructed post-Senate careers whose contributions to society may well match their impact within the institution. These include David Boren's long run as the president of the University of Oklahoma, Alan Simpson's service on various national commissions, and George Mitchell's host of negotiating missions—from Northern Ireland to the Middle East to Major League Baseball's steroids controversy. With increasing longevity and an ever-growing range of opportunities, especially in Washington, it makes sense to examine post-Senate careers and rethink the nature of the costs (including opportunity costs) and benefits of serving in the country's presumptive "Most Exclusive Club" (Gould 2005).

If there were any doubt of the relevance of post-Senate careers, it should have been laid to rest by the exodus of senior (but not old) legislators in 1996. These included Bill Bradley, William Cohen, Bennett Johnson, David Pryor, Paul Simon, and Alan Simpson, among others (see Ornstein

1997).[2] Whether in the private sector, public service, education, or some combination, these legislators and others from that group demonstrated how one might prosper, literally and figuratively, after leaving the Senate.

In mid-1996, Senate Majority Leader Bob Dole took the unprecedented step of resigning his Senate seat, after twenty-seven years of service, to devote his full energies to running for president. Given the abysmal success rate of senators running for the White House, it was probably not a bad idea for him to leave the Senate, even though his ultimate performance was poor (less that 41 percent of the popular vote) (Burden 2002). Still, Dole could not have envisioned the post-Senate career that lay before him. He could well have foreseen that his services as a lawyer/lobbyist/"rainmaker" would be in demand, but the Dole enterprise, including staff and associates, moved far beyond the traditional role of post-Senate power brokering. With a host of commercials (Viagra, Pepsi, among others), books on political humor and his World War II service, and board memberships, Dole made far more money than he ever had before—or had ever anticipated. But financial rewards represent only one aspect of his career in the wake of his resignation.

Equally important, as a major political personality he was in a position to address a host of causes in which he had maintained a long-standing interest (for example, raising $100 million for the World War II memorial) or function in an official capacity (for example, serving as chair of the International Commission on Missing Persons in the former Yugoslavia). He worked with former president Bill Clinton to raise more than $120 million for families of victims of the September 11, 2001, terrorist attacks. And he helped found and fund an Institute of Politics at the University of Kansas, which supports a bipartisan approach to politics and emphasizes, among other things, civil discourse on politics and major issues. In these ways, Dole has remained active in political life. Most recently, he worked in 2009 with former Senate majority leader Tom Daschle and others to craft and actively advocate for a bipartisan set of health care proposals (Seelye 2010). Indeed, beyond "doing well" in financial terms and "doing good" on behalf of various causes, Dole continues—as a highly engaged politico—to have fun as part of the game that was his vocation and avocation for over a half century.

Although Dole is not typical (e.g., Viagra ads), he is no complete outlier, either. Former senators increasingly live long, lucrative, relevant lives after their legislative careers have ended. The growing number of these individuals offers continuing, visible examples to sitting senators, whose levels of frustrations in a contentious, unpopular, and often unproductive body may lead them to consider leaving the chamber to pursue alternative endeavors.

---

2. I have added Bob Dole, who retired midway through the 104th Congress, to this group.

What follows will largely focus on the members of the 86th Congress (1959–60) and the 101st Congress (1989–90). The 86th Congress is important given the large, disproportionately Democratic "class" of 1958, which helped define many elements of the Senate; the 101st Congress is not so distinctive, but looking at senators from a twenty-year vantage point, as of 2010, means that enough time has passed to assess the post-Senate careers of the seventy-five or so who departed Capitol Hill, at least as elected officials.

## Why Study Senators' Careers?

In *U.S. Senators and Their World*, Donald Matthews examined the pre-Senate backgrounds of those who served in the 1947–1957 period and provided some descriptively useful, if unsurprising data. Senators were scarcely typical of the population, as if there was any expectation that they would be. They were largely lawyers, almost all male, and all white. They didn't vary much by party, and could be divided into categories, based on prior political experience, although this characteristic didn't seem to predict much in terms of their congressional behavior (Matthews 1960). The Senate of the 1950s had become more careerist, senators stayed longer, and for most this office was simultaneously the pinnacle and end point of their political careers (see Chubb 1994; Hibbing 1994).

Still, these kinds of observations tell us relatively little about the institution. What was important, as Matthews lays it out, were the Senate's norms, which did shape the behavior of almost all its members while allowing others (Douglas, Proxmire) to understand that they could not play the collegial, deferential inside game. Importantly, Matthews ended his data gathering in 1957, one year before the 1958 elections blew in a large number of new, disproportionately liberal Democratic senators who would prove instrumental in transforming the Senate over the next twenty-plus years (Sinclair 1989; Foley 1980).

This group of insurgents won good committee seats and collectively made their mark quickly, even though for individual members the traditional norms of apprenticeship and seniority slowed their progress. Again, the question is raised as to the importance of individual career patterns and choices. Joseph Schlesinger offers the first systematic analysis. In *Ambition and Politics* (1966) he lays out a rough rational choice model of career advancement, which Gordon Black and David Rohde, among others, articulated with more precision in the 1970s (Black 1972; Rohde 1979). Indeed, most subsequent examination of Senate careers specifically and congressional careers generally has been anchored in examining ambition for higher office, either getting to the Senate or moving from it (Hibbing 1994). Internal careers have been given short shrift, even though they are arguably as important, or more so, than moving into or out of the chamber. For example, within the House of Representatives, Newt Gingrich won the GOP whip position in 1987 by two votes, over Illinois moderate Ed Madigan. Had that turned out differently, the Republican takeover of the House in 1994 arguably might not have happened.

Overall, the simple, career-based formulation first proposed by Black, $u(O) = (PB) - C$, or the value of the prospective office equals the benefits times the probability of success minus the costs, remains powerful, largely because it addresses not just the decision to seek higher office, but also the paths taken within a legislative body and the decision to resign or retire from that body, as well as seeking higher office (Black 1972). Moreover, it addresses not just the benefits and probability of success (PxB), but also the costs (C) of seeking office, which can be large and varied. While difficult to measure, the costs of office holding can be high, whether personal, campaign related, or policy based. If a senator has five children to put through college, must raise $20 million to wage an uncertain reelection campaign, and has little hope of pushing a policy agenda through the chamber, he or she might think twice (or more) about running again, especially if attractive career options exist outside the Congress. Indeed, one major category of costs for an ambitious politician, or even one who does not seek to advance, is that of opportunity costs.

As with other, lower offices within the structure of American politics, a senator's range of options roughly parallels those laid out by Albert Hirschman: exit, voice, or loyalty (Hirschman 1970).[3] Exit can mean choosing to leave the institution by seeking to move up (the presidency or vice presidency)[4] or retiring, while voice and loyalty relate more to a senator's internal career. Given that the opportunity structure narrows considerably for those in the Senate and that most career analysis focuses on ambition for higher office, it is scarcely surprising that the lion's share of attention on Senate careers has emphasized seeking the presidency (see Burden 2002; Peabody, Ornstein, and Rhode 1976; Hess 1986). The post–World War II era has seen a considerable rise in the number of Senate candidacies for president, but few successes—although 1960 and 2010, the bookend years for this study, do reflect the exceptions that prove the rule. Indeed, many

---

3. Hirschman's formulation has been applied in dozens of contexts, but only infrequently in legislative analyses, and then in comparative contexts.

4. Many senators (e.g., Barack Obama, Joseph Biden, Hillary Clinton) do run for the presidency (or hope to be chosen vice president) without exiting the Senate, and some exit (Bill Bradley) in preparation for a presidential run. Lyndon Johnson famously guided a bill through the Texas legislature so he could run simultaneously for president and reelection to the Senate.

senators hear the call of the presidency and thus structure their chamber in ways that may help their ambitions. Citing Nelson Polsby, political scientists Robert Peabody, Norman Ornstein, and David Rohde (1996) note changes in Senate activities by the mid-1970s: "The need to cultivate national constituencies, to formulate and discuss the important issues of the day, to come up with new policy proposals which may later be the basis for legislation—these broader objectives are not unrelated to a Senate in which presidential hopefuls are increasingly at home."

The important thing for Senate careers is *not* whether large numbers of senators win the presidency; rather, it is that large numbers think they have a chance to do so, whether realistic (Joe Biden in 2008?) or not. To paraphrase Richard Fenno, we get the kind of Senate the members give us, and the modern institution allows most senators the chance to think about seeking the White House, even if their odds are slim.

Winning the presidency (or being named to a successful ticket as vice president) reflects one kind of exit. Defeat is another, although usually beyond one's control (see Fenno 1992). But retirement is a choice, and one, we shall see, made increasingly by senators when leaving office. Jeffrey Bernstein and Jennifer Wolak find that age and majority party status (not formal position) are most strongly linked to retirement, but they also note that institutional structures frame retirement decisions. In the individualistic but partisan Senate, the "retirement choices of Senators reflect more personal choices . . . [and] how legislators respond to changes in institutional environments." In particular, as the Senate grows more partisan, "career decisions reflect this, as minority party status [actual or projected] becomes a more influential determinant in the decision to seek reelection or retire" (Bernstein and Wolak 2002).

Still, most senators do decide to stay at any given time, and most do not actively seek the presidency. So, within Hirschman's framework, they must satisfy themselves with some combination of loyalty and voice. For example, Senator Coburn has opted for voice within the GOP ranks, while Indiana's senator, Richard Lugar, has chosen loyalty as a core value. To be sure, Coburn is generally loyal and Lugar has an important voice on key issues, especially on foreign policy. Increasingly, in a strong-party era, scholars have depicted legislative parties as teams that seek to build an effective brand. Senators must not only decide whether they want to remain within the institution, but whether they want to maintain their partisan brand association; these choices fit neatly with Hirschman's notions of exit and voice for dissatisfied members of an organization (Hirschman 1970). One implication of both Black's and Hirschman's basic formulations is that politicians in general, and senators here, may continually reassess their career prospects, much as Fenno has demonstrated in many of his studies of legislators.[5] Fenno argues, "it will be useful to think of each representative in terms of his or her career and in terms of his or her continuous negotiations with constituents" (Fenno 2000: 7). We choose to see career decisions made continually—that is, in a series of discrete decisions rather than in a continuing, uninterrupted manner. Still, in recent years the abrupt resignations of Robert Dole, Trent Lott, and Mel Martinez, among others, do indicate that rethinking one's career trajectory can occur at any time.

In addition, and of great importance, Black and Hirschman remind us of the problematic side of political careers—the costs that elected officials, and especially career politicians, must bear. Legislators must consciously decide whether to run for reelection every two or six years. For many, in most circumstances, these decisions appear routine; the papers are filed, the campaign committees reorganized, and constituency work segues into reelection politics. But it remains a formal choice that must be made, and remade (see Theriault 1998). Political circumstances can and do tip the scales, as with Connecticut senator Chris Dodd's decision not to seek reelection in 2010, but often the generalized *costs* of continuing simply outweigh the *benefits* of remaining, even if the probability of reelection is very high (as with many of the 1996 retirees).

As life expectancy increases (current senators average about 64 years of age) and the potential benefits of work outside the Senate grow, senators in their late sixties and seventies may well assess the cost/benefit ratio increasingly toward exit, even if (maybe especially if) they wish to remain active. Senators like Dole, Daschle, Mitchell, and Simpson, among others, demonstrate convincingly that an ex-senator can "do well" and "do good" at a fraction of the costs of remaining in the chamber (see Loomis 2003). At the same time, running for reelection remains the default option, even for fairly senior senators. The costs of serving may have risen, but the perceived benefits of serving, including prestige, endure (see Zeleny 2010).

## Outlines of the Senate Career, 1960 and 2010

The picture of the U.S. Senate circa 1960 is rich, if often impressionistic, although Barbara Sinclair and Donald Matthews do shore up the journalistic and case-study approaches provided by William White and Ralph Huitt (Sinclair 1989; Huitt 1969; White 1957; Matthews 1960). Sinclair provides a lucid assessment of the changing Senate membership in the early 1960s,

---

5. Most obviously in *Home Style* (Fenno 1978) and its assessment of "expansionist" and "protectionist" styles, but also in his work on the career building of Sen. Arlen Specter (then-R, Penn.) and the comparative analyses of representatives Jack Flynt (D-Ga.) and Mac Collins (R-Ga.) in their largely similar Georgia district, twenty years apart (Fenno 2000).

as the locus of power within the Democratic caucus begins to shift (Sinclair 1989; Foley 1980). But there are no systematic analyses of Senate careers in the modern era, in large part because at any given time there are 100 over-lapping careers, unfolding both individually and simultaneously. This analy-sis takes a close look at those individuals who constituted the Senate in the 86th Congress (1959–60) and the 101st Congress (1989–90), with some additional snapshots of other congresses between 1960 and 2010. The rea-soning is straightforward. The 86th Congress aligns with the 1960 starting point of this overall analysis; it also provides a full articulation of the politi-cal careers of all its members. The 101st Congress was chosen because it offers a reasonably complete picture of the modern Senate career, even though twenty-five members of that Congress remained in office in 2010. That leaves seventy-seven members of the 101st Senate who have died, retired, lost elections, or otherwise left the chamber—a number sufficient to draw some tentative conclusions about contemporary careers. In particu-lar, we can examine the post-Senate actions of these legislators.

## The Senate Career: Entrance and Exit

Perhaps the best starting point to examine Senate careers lies in an actu-arial study of the careers of 209 senators who left office between 1945 and 1970 (Treas 1977). Using a life-table approach to Senate exits, demogra-pher Judith Treas finds that defeat (40 percent), retirement (29 percent), and death (almost 25 percent) make up the three leading causes of exit. She observes, "like a general mortality table, the Senate table exhibits an initially high attrition rate which soon falls to very low levels. Mortality changes only gradually thereafter" (Treas 1977). Treas finds that surpris-ingly only about half of the senators served more than one full term, but as we shall see this result derives from (1) high numbers of appointees, who serve temporarily in the wake of an elected senator's death, and (2) the electoral vulnerability of first-term senators. Both these conditions became less common over the succeeding decades. Nevertheless, many senators did enter the chamber as appointees, and a fair number stayed (see Sinclair 1989).[6]

*The Decline of Careerist Senators Entering as Appointees.*    Through the 1960s, more than 10 percent of all senators (excluding "seat-warmers" who do not

---

6. We also know a lot about how *internal* Senate careers developed over the 1950s and 1960s, with the importance of committee-based seniority, even though committees, by and large, were less important to senators' careers than to members of the House of Represen-tatives. This chapter will not examine internal Senate careers at any great length, but the rise of the individualist Senate of the 1970s and beyond did change the nature of senators' careers within the chamber.

**Table 4.1**    Entering the Senate

|  | 86th Congress, 1959–60 (N = 103) | 91st Congress, 1969–70 (N = 102) | 96th Congress, 1979–80 (N = 101) | 101st Congress, 1989–90 (N = 102) | 106th Congress, 1999–2000 (N = 102) | 111th Congress, 2009–10 (N = 103) |
|---|---|---|---|---|---|---|
| Elected | 90 | 88 | 95 | 96 | 98 | 97 |
| Appointed[a] | 13 | 14 | 6 | 6 | 4 | 6 |

Note: Includes all senators who served and sough reelection ("seat-warmers" are excluded); N = 100 + due to death, resignation, and subsequent appointments.

[a] Excludes those appointed after winning a general election, due to resignation of sitting senator, to enhance the newcomer's seniority ranking (such senators are included in "Elected" category).

seek to retain their appointed seats) in the modern era began their careers as appointees; since then the number has averaged about 5 percent (see Table 4.1). One reason for this decline is straightforward: latterly, fewer senators died in office. Of the 103 senators serving in the 86th Congress, twenty-four died in office—more than were defeated in general elections. Although advancement and resignation also opened some seats to appointment, in the twentieth century the death of a predecessor in office was the most common avenue to senatorial appointment and an apparent advantage in an ensuing bid for election, even though, as Treas documents, many appointed senators did not subsequently run for a full term.

The data here mirror Treas's findings for the textbook Congress era— that is, senators' deaths frequently opened up the possibility of a Senate career through appointment; our findings also track with the spadework of Forrest Maltzman, Lee Sigelman, and Sarah Binder on congressional passing (see Maltzman, Sigelman, and Binder 1966). Indeed, it appears that senators, given their greater age and seniority, may well have contributed disproportionately to the funeral business in the 1960s and 1970s, as the members of the 86th Congress went to their reward. Overall, Americans' life expectancy at age 65 in 1960 was 14.4 years, increasing to 17.4 by 1990 (Center for Disease Control 2010). Males, however, could expect fewer years, so the increasing numbers of women entering the Senate in the 1980s and beyond may well increase post-chamber longevity in years to come. Indeed, to date no elected female senator has died in office.

*Positions, Occupations, and Entry: Political Careerism on the Rise.*   Over time, governors have lost power in appointing prospective careerist senators, while some of the usual suspects—House members or prominent state legislators, in particular—have seen their stock rise. Moreover, governors themselves have become less inclined to run for the Senate (and self-appointment is

**Table 4.2**   Immediate Previous Service to Senate

|  | 86th Congress, 1959–60 (N = 104) | 101st Congress, 1989–90 (N = 102) | 111th Congress, 2009–10 (N = 100) |
|---|---|---|---|
| Governor | 19 | 14 | 8 |
| U.S. House | 38 | 37 | 48 |
| State legislature | 7 | 7 | 9 |
| Other statewide office | 11 | 14 | 13 |
| Sub-state office | 7 | 12 | 9 |
| Private sector | 18 | 14 | 11 |
| National appointed office | 4 | 2 | 2 |

Note: "Seat-warmers" omitted.

almost entirely ruled out[7]) (see Codispoti 1987), in part due to the increasing success of running for the White House from the state house (Sabato 1983). Over the course of the past fifty years (and more, given that many of the 86th Congress's senators entered the chamber in the 1930s and 1940s), the penultimate position from which to move to the Senate has changed modestly, but significantly (see Table 4.2).

House members have historically been the most common aspirants for Senate seats, and that tendency has only increased in recent years, with small-state representatives especially holding a distinct advantage (Codispoti 1987). Given representatives' established fund-raising machinery and name recognition, their prominence is scarcely surprising. But the growing number of state legislators who have moved to the Senate is somewhat unexpected, and reflects substantial success in small population states where fund-raising requirements may not be as onerous and the number of prospective competitors may be few. In the 111th Congress, the most heavily populated state that promoted a state legislator to the U.S. Senate was North Carolina (nine million), while Alaska, Wyoming, and Montana (all with one U.S. House member and fewer than a million residents) each elected a sitting state lawmaker.

As noted, governors increasingly appear less willing to run for the Senate, although there remain eight senators who moved from the governor's office to the U.S. Capitol. Indeed, other statewide offices offer solid positions from which to run for the Senate—especially attorney general, but also

---

7. For example, Minnesota governor Wendell Anderson helped destroy a promising political career with his self-appointment to Walter Mondale's seat; he lost his initial try for election in 1978.

auditor, treasurer, and lieutenant governor. There has been no significant movement of senators toward the nation's state houses, with the exceptions of Pete Wilson (R-Calif.), Frank Murkowski (R-Alaska), and, more recently, Sam Brownback (R-Kan.). Given term limits on most governors, the structure of ambition continues to move governors toward Capitol Hill, but the pathway may not be as clear or the incentives as strong in 2011 as they were fifty years ago (Schlesinger 1966). The number of entrants from the private sector has declined steadily over the past half-century, and the nominal figures certainly overestimate the number of actual private-sector advancements. Of the eleven senators who moved to the chamber from the private sector in the 111th Congress, only Orrin Hatch (R-Utah), Herb Kohl (D-Wisc.), Bob Bennett (R-Utah), Al Franken (D-Minn.), and, to a lesser extent, Jim Webb (D-Va.) truly had extensive private careers in their run-up to candidacy. More telling, Arlen Specter (R/D-Penn.), Kay Bailey Hutchinson (R-Texas), Susan Collins (R-Maine), Frank Lautenberg (D-N.J.), and Lamar Alexander (R-Tenn.) did come from the private sector, but all qualify as career politicians, as does Hillary Clinton, although she may be beyond category. For all the emphasis on amateurs in the Senate of the late twentieth century (Canon 1990), today's chamber has very few, as even Bennett (son of a senator, who managed his campaigns) and Webb (former Navy Secretary) were politically experienced when they arrived.

The contemporary Senate is filled with political pros, and increasingly they are arriving via the highly contentious, highly partisan House of Representatives. Combined with state legislators, fifty-seven of 100 sitting senators in the 111th Congress came straight from legislative bodies, in which political perspectives are often partisan and parochial. Of the four top leaders, only Minority Leader Mitch McConnell (R-Ky.) was not a House member; Harry Reid (D-Nev.; majority leader), Richard Durbin (D-Ill.; majority whip), and Jon Kyl (R-Ariz.; minority whip) all served there in the era of intensifying partisanship and declining comity. Moreover, Durbin and Kyl won their respective Senate seats in 1994, a watershed election in terms of partisanship. The advancement of members from the contentious House to the Senate is surely not the only reason for the chamber's growing polarization, but this trend has almost certainly contributed to it.

## Leaving the Senate: A New Career Stage

> If a due participation of office is a matter of right, how are vacancies to be obtained? Those by death are few; by resignations, none.
>
> Thomas Jefferson

Jefferson notwithstanding, voluntary retirements have historically represented the most common way for senators to leave office. Of course, some

**Table 4.3**  Leaving the Senate: Subtotals and Percentage of Those No Longer Serving

|  | 86th Congress, 1959–60 (N = 103) | 91st Congress, 1969–70 (N = 102) | 96th Congress, 1979–80 (N = 101) | 101st Congress, 1989–90 (N = 102) | 106th Congress, 1999–2000 (N = 102) |
|---|---|---|---|---|---|
| Retired | 44 (42%) | 49 (48%) | 54 (57%) | 47 (61%) | 25 (50%) |
| General election defeat | 21 (21%) | 29 (28%) | 24 (26%) | 13 (17%) | 15 (30%) |
| Primary election defeat | 9 (9%) | 5 (5%) | 1 (1%) | 2 (3%) | 1 (2%) |
| Died in office | 24 (23%) | 12 (12%) | 8 (9%) | 6 (8%) | 6 (12%) |
| Higher office | 3 (3%) | 3 (3%) | 3 (3%) | 5 (6%) | 2 (4%) |
| Resigned | 2 (2%) | 3 (3%) | 4 (4%) | 4 (5%) | 1 (2%) |
| Serving 111th Congress | 0[a] | 1 | 7 | 25 | 52 |

Note: Percentage refer to proportion of senators who have left the chamber.

[a] Sen. Robert Byrd died during the 111th Congress; count is at end of a Congress.

of those "voluntary" decisions reflected a realistic reading of the political tea leaves. Still, in the modern Congress (Table 4.3) the trend is clear: most members of the Senate choose to leave, whatever the circumstances. And most continue working after their retirement, another trend that has strengthened over the past fifty years. Comparing the exit data for those who served in the 86th, 91st, 96th, and 101st Congresses (the 106th Congress offers little insight, save that many of the weakest members do lose early in their careers), the rise of voluntary retirements is paired with declines in deaths and primary defeats. By and large, the careers of senators, for all their individualism, have become increasingly predictable.

Among members of the 86th Congress, more than half would leave the chamber involuntarily (death or defeat); so far, just over a quarter of those who served in the 101st Congress have met such a fate, and there were two more retirements (Kit Bond, Christopher Dodd) in 2010, along with Specter's primary defeat. With an average age of 65, the eight 2010 Senate retirees are not unusually young, yet they generally can look forward to years of productive, often lucrative work, if they so desire. In this sense, choosing when to retire has become a part of the Senate career, with a transition to related lines of work (see below), often carried out inside the Beltway. The question is, do such prospects change senators' behavior while in office? There are many facets to this question, and no analysis to date, but one study from

**Table 4.4**    Principal Pose-Senate Occupation

|  | 86th Congress, 1959–60 (N = 76) | 101st Congress, 1989–90 (N = 72) |
|---|---|---|
| Business/finance | 13 (21%) | 16 (22%) |
| Law | 16 (26%) | 8 (11%) |
| Lobbying/consulting | 3 (5%) | 15 (21%) |
| Education | 10 (16%) | 14 (19%) |
| Publicservice | 7 (11%) | 6 (8%) |
| Author/media | 2 (3%) | 2 (3%) |
| Nonprofit | 0 | 3 (4%) |
| Retired | 10 (16%) | 8 (11%) |
| Incarcerated[a] | 1 (2%) | 0 |
| No data | 14 | — |

Note: In the 86th Congress, some "no data" are likely retired; percentages are for N = 62. In the 101st Congress, "no data" excluded; four are undetermined, while many hold multiple positions across categories.

[a] Harrison Williams (D-N.J.).

the U.S. House does provide some clues. Adolfo Santos (2004) examined retirements from the House between 1976 and 1998 and found that "those who left the House to become lobbyists remained significantly more active than those who did not. This is particularly true among those House members who left public life under their own volition."

Such a finding may well track with the actions of contemporary ex-senators, but given the dearth of lobbyists emerging from the 86th Congress, it does not likely reflect the behavior of the earlier era. The data are somewhat sketchy for this previous cohort, but most departees remained active, although they did their work outside Washington (see Table 4.5, below). Many continued to practice law, and some resumed business careers; others taught, largely on a part-time basis. But whatever endeavors they undertook, they often did so in their home states. Even though the occupations pursued are similar across eras (see Table 4.4), today the content of the work is different, largely because of the opportunities made possible by policy communities in Washington and beyond that increasingly value ex-senators' expertise and reputations.

Moving forward thirty years, to the 101st Congress, a modified pattern emerges. More important than any particular distribution of post-chamber activities is the simple preponderance of them. Even as they move into their seventies and eighties, senators work—and often work hard. As with their predecessors in the 86th Congress, more than half of departed senators return to the private sector (law, lobbying/consulting, business/finance). Today's ex-senators, however, enjoy much greater financial rewards. Many go into education, from serving as a university president (Boren) to starting a public policy institute (Simon), among others. And various former senators have moved back and forth between the private and public sectors, as with Indiana's peripatetic Dan Coats, who worked as a lobbyist and served as the U.S. ambassador to Germany before successfully winning a second tour of Senate service in 2010.

Overall, the experiences of this generation of ex-senators has demonstrated the range of opportunities—to do well and to do good—that stretch out before them once leaving elective office. Aside from generating income far exceeding a Senate salary, many departing members have created (or assisted in creating) institutions named for them that address policy and governance issues related to their Senate careers. At least fifteen senators from the 101st Congress have such eponymous centers. And while their degree of involvement varies substantially, these institutions provide the senators a way to remain active and pursue their particular interests. In such cases, not even death will affect the institutionalization of these senators' values, as their legacy lives on through the activities of these organizations.

*Ex-Senators as Lobbyists: Inside and Beyond the Beltway.*    While the data are less than clear for members of the 86th Congress, it is safe to say that not many of them worked extensively as D.C. lobbyists. Still, Russell Long, Clifford Case, and George Smathers did lobby; Long and Smathers, in particular, foreshadowed the career paths of future departing senators. At age 68, in 1987, Long left the Senate after thirty-eight years of service and an extended tenure as chair and ranking member of the Finance Committee. His expertise and connections were highly attractive to prospective clients, and he prospered after forming his own firm, located in Baton Rouge and Washington.[8] Smathers, on the other hand, despite three terms in the Senate (1951–1969), was never a power broker, but his friendship with John F. Kennedy and others helped make him a sought-after lawyer/lobbyist after retiring at age 55, when he began an extended and extremely lucrative post-legislative career.

The departing members of the 101st Congress have worked in the post-lobbying reform era in which registration with the Senate is required of most lobbyists (Senate Office of Public Records 2010).[9] Among seventy

---

8. This pairing of home-state and D.C. offices has become somewhat more common, given communication and transportation options; it sometimes clouds the assessment of whether one remains in the capital or not.

9. Passed in 1995, the registration requirements have been twice modified, most recently in the 110th Congress. Although there are exceptions and interpretations that allow some lobbying without registration, most active lobbyists must register.

living ex-senators from this Congress, exactly half (35) have registered at some time as a lobbyist. The remainder, including Vice President Joe Biden, have not. The registration numbers surely overestimate a bit the number of actual lobbyists. For example, Paul Simon registered as a lobbyist for Southern Illinois University, but probably did not meet the minimum time threshold required. Others, like Howard Metzenbaum (Consumer Federation of America) and Tim Wirth (Better World Foundation), lobbied for a single nonprofit. Still, this class of legislators does contain major lobbying figures, such as John Breaux and Trent Lott, who formed a powerful bipartisan firm upon departing the Senate.

Conversely, former floor leader Tom Daschle has never registered as a lobbyist, despite his affiliations with Alston and Bird and later DLA Piper, two powerhouse lobbying firms, where his title has been "senior policy advisor" (DLA Piper Press Release 2010). It may be that registrations among ex-senators will decline in the future, given a two-year period in which they are restricted from lobbying and a general trend toward avoiding registering if not absolutely required.

In the end, more ex-senators have registered to lobby than have remained in Washington (see below), demonstrating the ability to maintain capital connections while returning home (or to a new location) after leaving the Senate. The financial incentives to lobby are great, the opportunities numerous. It is not the choice for everyone, but increasingly it has become a regular feature of the post-Senate career.

*You Can Go Home Again: But Do You Want to, Need to?*    Given the level of activity of most recently departed senators and the incidence of lobbying registrations, it is somewhat surprising to find that only about four in ten ex-senators make the D.C. area their principal residence (see Table 4.5).[10] Still, that's far more than those in the 86th Congress, who mostly did retire back in their home states or some place other than D.C. (Sun City, Arizona, and New Canaan, Connecticut, for example). The expectation was that you would return to your state and implicitly that Washington had not become "home." Again, Bob Dole offers a striking contemporary example. After living in Washington since the 1960s, first as a congressman, then a senator, his social, economic, and policy worlds all revolved around the capital and—especially—the Capitol. He lived in the Watergate, was married to a former Labor Secretary (soon to be a senator herself), worked for a major D.C. law firm, raised funds for the building of the World War II memorial on the National Mall, and so forth. Rather than moving back to Russell, Kansas, he

---

10. Absent a little more digging, it is difficult to pin down where some ex-legislators spend the bulk of their time; often they have at least two residences, a carryover from their years in the Senate.

**Table 4.5**    Do They Go Back to Pocatello?

|  | 86th Congress, 1959–60 (N = 81[a]) | 101st Congress, 1989–90 (N = 70[a]) |
|---|---|---|
| Reside mainly in D.C. area | 22 (28%) | 27 (39%) |
| Reside mainly outside D.C. area | 59 (72%) | 43 (61%) |

[a] Undetermined are omitted; several have dual residences.

eventually bought the adjoining Watergate apartment (owned by Monica Lewinsky's mother) and greatly enlarged his living space.

These choices, however, did not mean that Dole didn't return to Kansas, raise funds for the Dole Institute of Politics at the University of Kansas, and participate, at a distance, in state politics. Ditto for Tom Daschle, who is married to a major airline lobbyist, and many other former senators. And even when a senator does return home, as with James McClure from Idaho, he or she can retain strong D.C. lobbying connections—in McClure's case, to the mining industry.

Many members of the 86th Congress served in the Senate in the days of July adjournments and long annual stays back home. Those in the 101st had always served with jet aircraft and lengthy sessions; many did return home (or leave D.C. for New York or other cities), but for an increasing number of former senators, Washington has become home to their families and the location for their future economic livelihood. Moreover, for many former senators, living much of the year outside Washington does not preclude them from remaining active in lobbying inside the Beltway.

## Discussion

This study has assessed only some changes (and continuities) in senators' careers. It has not addressed senators' seeking the presidency or the implications of the increasing number of women in the chamber or the nature of careers *within* the Senate as the institution moved from an arena of collegiality to one that is simultaneously individualistic and partisan. Without question, however, contemporary senators, such as South Carolina's Jim DeMint, have become active and influential senators even in the course of their first terms of service.

This chapter has focused on patterns of senatorial entry and, especially, exit, and the possible implications of changes in senators' post-Senate careers. In particular, I have emphasized the need to make fuller, more sophisticated assessments of the prospective costs and opportunities that senators address in deciding to leave the Senate, or stay. John

Hibbing, in his 1994 overview of legislative careers, observed, "A position in the Senate is truly a capstone for most who make it that far." Very few advance to the presidency or vice presidency (Hibbing 1994). In many ways, the Senate probably does remain a "capstone," yet it is one that may have become tenuous, given both the rewards of a post-Senate career and the opportunity costs of continuing to serve. A recent article argued that relatively few incoming senators "enter the institution with plans to spend a lifetime there"—choosing instead "to use the Senate as a launching pad for a higher form of celebrity . . . rather than view[ing] it as a place to master the art of policy making and die with their boots on" (Senior 2010). As noted, few senators leave feet first these days, even if most legislative careers remain fairly long. And there can be an extensive, rewarding life after the Senate. If the personal and political costs of winning elections and of taking part in the continuing scrum of lengthy, filibuster-laden, often uncivil Senate sessions continue to increase, the benefits of private life may look all the better.

The contemporary Senate may well attract certain kinds of legislators (e.g., from the House, well accustomed to partisanship, such as DeMint or New York Democrat Charles Schumer), while discouraging others, such as those who enter from the private sector. And it may disproportionately retain some kinds of senators, while alienating others. We do not know much about how these politicians decide, nor do we know if sitting senators act differently once they have decided to retire (Chris Dodd on becoming a more aggressive banking reformer after announcing his retirement?). What is clear is that post-Senate careers in recent years can be productive and high in remuneration. Whether retired by their own choice (George Mitchell) or by the voters' decision (Tom Daschle), former senators can do good and do well, all while absorbing far fewer costs than they would as legislators.

In the end, the attraction of post-Senate careers may increase turnover and make the institution more responsive and democratic. But it may also cost the chamber some of its best lawmakers, who could easily choose to cap their careers not on Capitol Hill, but on K Street or in the Senator X Center for Political Studies—or both. The choice to exit may not be taken, but it will surely be considered.

# References

Bayh, Evan. 2010. http://bayh.senate.gov/news/press/release/?id=2bb190de-ed11-4920-a3bb-fea51fcde0dc, March 2. Accessed

Bernstein, Jeffery, and Jennifer Wolak. 2002. "A Bicameral Perspective on Legislative Retirement: The Case of the Senate." *Political Research Quarterly* 55 (June).

Black, Gordon. 1972. "A Theory of Political Ambition." *APSR* 66 (March).

Burden, Barry C. 2002. "United States Senators as Presidential Candidates." *Political Science Quarterly* 117 (Spring).

Canon, David. 1990. *Actors, Athletes, and Astronauts: Political Amateurs in the United States Congress.* Chicago: University of Chicago Press.

Center for Disease Control. 2010. http://205.207.175.93/HDI/TableViewer/tableView .aspx?ReportId=169. Accessed March 12, 2010.

Chubb, Jerome M. 1994. "The Historical Legislative Career." In Joel Sibley, ed., *Encyclopedia of the American Legislative System,* Vol. I. New York: Scribner's.

Codispoti, Frank. 1987. "The Governorship-Senate Connection: A Step in the Structure of Opportunities Grows Weaker." *Publius* 17 (Spring).

DLA Piper. 2010. press release. http://www.dlapiper.com/global/media/detail.aspx? news=3067/. Accessed March 12, 2010.

Fenno, Richard F., Jr. 1978. *Home Style: House Members in Their Districts.* Boston: Little Brown.

———. 1992. *When Incumbency Fails: The Senate Career of Mark Andrews.* Washington, D.C.: CQ Press.

———. 2000. *Congress at the Grassroots.* Chapel Hill: University of North Carolina Press.

Foley, Michael. 1980. *The New Senate: Liberal Influence on a Conservative Institution, 1959–1972.* New Haven, Conn.: Yale University Press.

Gould, Lewis L. 2005. *The Most Exclusive Club.* New York: Basic Books.

Hess, Stephen. 1986. *The Ultimate Insiders.* Washington, D.C.: Brookings Institution.

Hibbing, John. 1994. "Modern Legislative Careers." In Joel Sibley, ed., *Encyclopedia of the American Legislative System,* Vol. I. New York: Scribner's.

Hirschman, Albert O. 1970. *Exit, Voice, and Loyalty: Responses to Decline in Firms, Organizations, and States.* Cambridge, Mass.: Harvard University Press.

Huitt, Ralph K. 1969. "The Outsider in the Senate: An Alternative Role." In Ralph K. Huitt and Robert L. Peabody, eds., *Congress: Two Decades of Analysis.* New York: Harper and Row.

Leibovich, Mark. 2009. "A Senate Naysayer, Spoiling for Healthcare Fight." *New York Times,* October 29.

Loomis, Burdett. 2003. "Doing Good, Doing Well, and (Shhhhh!) Having Fun: A Supply-Side Approach to Lobbying." Paper presented at the annual meeting of the American Political Science Association, August 28–31, Philadelphia.

Maltzman, Forrest, Lee Sigelman, and Sarah Binder. 1966. "Leaving Office Feet First: Death in Congress." *PS: Political Science and Politics* 29 (December).

Matthews, Donald. 1960. *U.S. Senators and Their World.* New York: Vintage.

Ornstein, Norman J. 1997. *Lessons and Legacies,* Reading, Mass.: Addison Wesley.

Peabody, Robert L., Norman J. Ornstein, and David W. Rohde. 1976. "The United States Senate as a Presidential Incubator: Many Are Called, but Few Are Chosen." *Political Science Quarterly* 91 (Summer).

———. 1996. Need info. cited p. 61.

Rohde, David. 1979. "Risk-Bearing and Progressive Ambition." *AJPS* 23 (February).

Sabato, Larry. 1983. *Good-Bye to Good-Time Charlie,* 2nd ed. Washington, D.C.: CQ Press.

Santos, Adolfo. 2004. "The Role of Lobbying on Legislative activity when Lawmakers Plan to Leave Office." *International Social Science Review* (Spring/Summer).

Schlesinger, Joseph A. 1966. *Ambition and Politics.* Chicago: Rand McNally.

Seelye, Katherine Q. 2009. "Dole, Politics Aside, Pushes for Health Care Plan." *New York Times,* September 12, 2009. http://www.nytimes.com/2009/09/12/health/policy/12dole .html. Accessed March 15, 2010.

Senate Office of Public Records. 2010. http://www.senate.gov/pagelayout/legislative/g_
    three_sections_with_teasers/lobbyingdisc.htm. Accessed March 12, 2010.

Senior, Jennifer. 2010. "Mr. Woebegone Goes to Washington." *New York*, April 4.

Sinclair, Barbara. 1989. *The Transformation of the U.S. Senate*. Baltimore: Johns Hopkins
    University Press.

————. 2006. *Party Wars*. Norman: University of Oklahoma Press.

Theriault, Sean. 1998. "Moving Up or Moving Out: Career Ceilings and Congressional
    Retirement." *Legislative Studies Quarterly* 23 (August).

Treas, Judith. 1977. "A Life Table for Postwar Senators: A Research Note." *Social Forces*
    56 (September).

White, William S. 1957. *Citadel: The Story of the U.S. Senate*. New York: Harper Brothers.

Zeleny, Jeff. 2010. "Political Tide Could Wash Away Utah Senator." *New York Times*,
    March 26.

# 5

# Senate Parties and Party Leadership, 1960–2010

Barbara Sinclair

Were the senators of the early 1960s to revisit their old haunt, they would find a legislative chamber that was not much different in terms of its rules and much of its internal structure, especially its committee system—and yet, one that functions in an almost unrecognizable way. Of course, the United States itself has changed enormously over the course of these fifty years, and the many societal, economic, and technological changes have in major or minor ways impacted the Senate. Everything from the number of women in the Senate to the ubiquitous Blackberry would likely surprise the Dirksens and the Mansfields, but perhaps most of all they would be taken aback by the altered role of the political parties in the chamber and how that has influenced the legislative process.

Here I examine Senate parties and party leadership, how they have changed since 1960 and how the legislative process has been affected. Senate parties are shaped by the political environment external to the chamber as well by internal rules and arrangements. Senate party leadership is itself shaped by the character of the leaders' party membership and the character of the Senate as an institution at a given point in time; at minimum these factors constrain the leaders' styles and set the basics of their task. In this essay, I first describe how the Senate parties and their memberships have changed over this fifty-year period using quantitative data. Next I examine how the Senate as a legislature has changed, with special emphases on the job of its leaders and the challenges they face. I conclude by discussing the contemporary Senate in more depth.

## The Senate Parties and Their Memberships, 1960–2010: A Quantitative Portrait

The 1960s began with big Democratic majorities in the Senate; the Senate membership of the 87th Congress (1961–62) consisted of sixty-four Democrats and thirty-six Republicans. This was, however, a Democratic Party that was sharply split between a conservative and senior southern contingent and a larger, more liberal but junior northern group (Sinclair 1989). The Republican membership was ideologically diverse as well, with its midwesterners, especially those from the upper Midwest and Plains states, tending toward the conservative end of the spectrum and coastal senators from both the East and West leaning moderate. A few Republicans, like Jacob Javits of New York, were clear liberals. By 2010 Democrats again had a sizeable majority—sixty before the special election in Massachusetts— but this was now a different Democratic Party. Although far from monolithic, the Senate Democratic Party of 2010 is not split into distinct wings and is considerably more ideologically homogeneous than its 1960s counterpart. And the opposition Republican Party is even more homogeneously conservative. The result is a Senate membership that is polarized along coinciding partisan and ideological lines, with a liberal and moderate Democratic membership and a Republican membership ranging from moderately to extremely conservative.

Examining the evolution of Senate parties over this fifty-year period is important in providing the essential background for understanding the changing impact of parties on how the Senate has come to function.

Size matters in American legislatures; the majority party organizes the chamber and, other things being equal, a big majority has a better chance of passing its agenda than a small one. From the breakthrough elections of 1958 until the 1980 elections (86th through the 96th Congresses), Senate Democrats had large majorities, averaging sixty-one members; in only two congresses in the early 1970s did the number of Democrats fall below fifty-eight (54 in the 92nd and 56 in the 93rd).

To the surprise of most political observers and the shock of Democrats, the 1980 elections that saw Ronald Reagan win the presidency also brought in a GOP majority in the Senate, with Republicans holding fifty-four seats. A period of narrower margins followed, even after Democrats won back the majority in 1986; the average size of the majority from 1981 through 1990 was fifty-four. The size of Democratic majorities crept up in the early 1990s to fifty-seven in the 103rd Congress (1993–94), President Bill Clinton's first Congress.[1]

The 1994 elections again ushered in a Republican majority and another period of narrow margins. The GOP held the Senate majority from 1995 through 2006, with the exception of a year and a half (June 2001–end of 2002) when Jim Jeffords' party switch gave the Democrats a 51–49 margin. During this period, the average size of the majority was only fifty-three. When Democrats took back the majority in 2006, they had just fifty-one members; in the 2008 elections they increased their majority substantially (first to 58; to 59 when Arlen Specter switched parties; to 60

---

1. Data are from Norman Ornstein, Thomas Mann, and Michael Malbin (2002) and *CQ Almanac*, various years. Senators elected as Independents or from third parties are counted as part of the major party with which they caucus.

when Al Franken was seated after the Minnesota recount; and then back to 59 when Republican Scott Brown won the seat previously held by Democrat Ted Kennedy). These fifty years, then, have seen large and small majorities, Democratic and Republican ones. By and large, majorities since 1980 have been smaller than those in the 1960–1980 period.

In addition to size, the like-mindedness of the majority and the minority matter as well. An ideologically homogeneous majority will more likely agree on a legislative agenda and more likely pass it through the chamber; on the other hand, an ideologically homogeneous minority that opposes the majority is more likely to be able to make use of the extraordinary prerogatives that Senate rules give individual senators, as we shall see.

To portray the change over time in party polarization, I use several measures. Party votes are those recorded votes on which a majority of Democrats vote against a majority of Republicans. Figure 5.1 shows that the proportion of roll calls that were party votes declined a bit from the early 1960s to the early 1970s; more striking is the large increase from the late 1980s on. The party support score measures the percent of party votes on which a party member voted with his or her party colleagues. The average support score for party members in a particular congress provides an indicator of how cohesive the party is on party votes and indicates the

**Figure 5.1**   The Increase in Party Votes in the Senate, 1959–2009

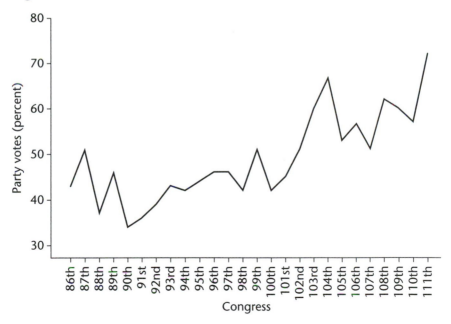

Source: *CQ Weekly* and *CQ Almanac*, various dates.

**Figure 5.2**  The Increasing Distance between Parties in the
Senate, 1959–2009

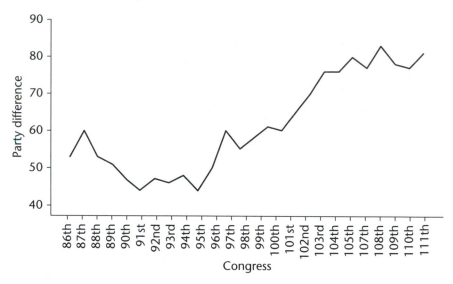

Note: Party difference = Democratic mean party support–Republican mean party support.

Source: Computed by the author from CQ Party Support Scores from *CQ Weekly* and *CQ Almannac*,
various dates.

distance between the parties on party votes. Figure 5.2 displays this measure of the distance between the parties from the 86th Congress (1959–
60) through 2009, the first session of the 111th. The pattern is similar,
though even more dramatic than that of the percent of party votes; there
is a decrease from the early 1960s to the early 1970s, a low plateau through
much of the 1970s, and then a steady, quite dramatic increase to a much
higher level from the late 1980s on. These two figures in combination
show that a majority of Democrats now much more frequently votes in
opposition to a majority of Republicans than in the past and, when such
party votes occur, most Democrats vote together in opposition to most
Republicans.

A final indicator is the Pool-Rosenthal DW-Nominate score, which is
based on all non-unanimous roll calls and can be interpreted as a measure of
liberalism-conservatism (Poole and Rosenthal 1997).[2] Its range is from –1 on
the liberal end of the spectrum to +1 on the conservative end. Figure 5.3
shows the difference in the median score of Democrats and Republicans

2. Data come from Keith Poole's Voteview website at www.voteview.com.

**Figure 5.3**    The Growing Ideological Distance between the Senate Parties, 1959–2008

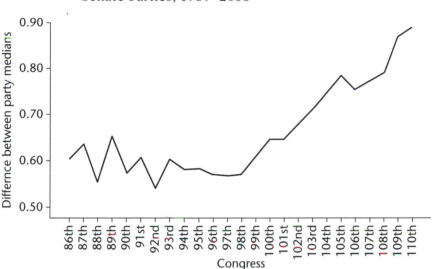

Note: Values computed from Poole-Rosenthal DW-Nominate data.

Source: Computed by the author using data from Keith Poole's Voteview Website at www.voteview.com.

over time and can be interpreted as a measure of the ideological distance between the parties. Again the pattern is similar; from relatively modest differences between the centers of the two parties in the 1960s and 1970s, the distance rises steeply through the 1990s and 2000s.

All these measures tell essentially the same story. The parties were not very polarized in the 1960s, they actually became less so through the early to mid-1970s, but from the late 1980s on polarization rises enormously.

An important cause of the polarization, though not the only one by any means, is a change in the composition of the two parties' memberships as a result of changing regional voting patters. As Figure 5.4 shows, there were no Republican senators from the South in 1960; over the next fifty years, GOP fortunes improved greatly in that region.[3] Thus, over time, conservative southern Democrats were replaced, most often when they retired, with still more conservative Republicans. The proportion of the total Democratic Senate membership from the South has fallen to only around 10 percent, while southerners now make up the single largest regional subset of Senate Republicans, over 30 percent in recent congresses. Among the consequences

---

3. The South is defined as the states of the old Confederacy minus Tennessee.

**Figure 5.4**   The South Becomes More Republican in the Senate, 1959–2009

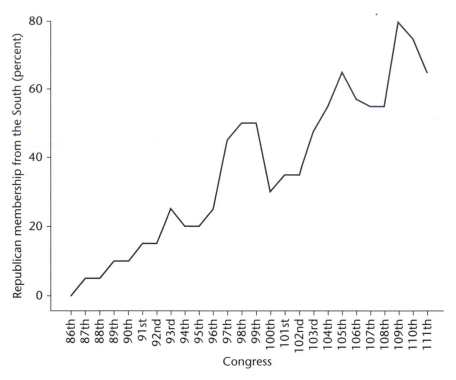

Note: The South consists of the states of the old Confederacy minus Tennessee.

Source: Compiled by the author from data from Norman J. Ornstein, Thomas E. Mann, and Michael J. Malbin, *Vital Statistics on Congress 2001–2002* (Washington, D.C.: American Enterprise Institute, 2002), and *CQ Almanac*, various dates.

of this regional shift are a more liberal Democratic Party and a more conservative Republican Party.

A similar sorting of voters, with those who think of themselves as conservatives increasingly identifying as Republicans while liberals and many moderates increasingly think of themselves as Democrats, occurred in other parts of the country as well; this too contributed to partisan polarization (Abramowitz 2006 and Chapter 2 in this volume; Jacobson 2006; Sinclair 2006). The core voters who elect Republicans even outside the South are likely to be quite conservative. They expect their senators to act and vote consistent with their preferences; similarly, though perhaps to a lesser extent, Democratic core voters in many parts of the country are likely to expect their senators to reflect their liberal inclinations.

# The Transformation of the Senate

The Senate of the 1950s has often been portrayed as the domain of an inner club that ran the institution and enforced the Senate folkways of apprenticeship, specialization, the restrained use of prerogatives, and institutional patriotism (White 1957; see also Matthews 1960 for a more measured analysis). Although the journalists' portrait is certainly an exaggeration, the Senate was, in fact, a body in which conservative southern Democrats held a disproportionate share of the positions of influence (see Chapter 1). Legislative decision making was decentralized in committees, and committee chairs, who were most often southerners, tended to work with their Republican ranking members, who were not so distant from them in policy preferences. Lyndon Johnson, now legendary as a Senate majority leader of unparallel clout, nevertheless held his position by leave of powerful southerners such as Richard Russell (Caro 2002; Shuman 1991).

## Mansfield and the Individualist Senate

By 1960 this Senate had already begun to change. The 1958 elections brought into the Senate a big class of new senators with different policy goals and reelection needs than the generally conservative and electorally secure members who had dominated the chamber. Mostly northern Democrats, they were activist liberals, and most had been elected in highly competitive contests, in many of those defeating incumbents. Both their policy goals and their reelection needs dictated a more activist style than prescribed by Senate folkways. And, as subsequent elections brought in more and more such members, they became increasingly unwilling to defer to senior southern conservatives or support internal arrangements that did so.

Mike Mansfield (D-Mont.) succeeded Johnson as majority leader in 1961. Both his own inclinations and the political context led Mansfield to a very different style of leadership, almost antithetical to Johnson's. For Mansfield, the Senate was an assembly of equals (R. Baker 1991: 277); as his long-time aide Frank Valeo (1999) put it, "he believed in the concept, he expressed it again and again, and he lived it" (37). According to Maine senator Edmund Muskie, Mansfield "felt that the way to make the Senate effective was simply to let it work its will" (R. Baker 1991: 276). Mansfield's light hand was also dictated by his members' changing expectations; junior and more liberal senators had grown resentful of Johnson's hard-charging style and, in the 86th Congress (1959–60), Johnson's last as majority leader and the one in which he had by far his largest majority, the legislative product had been meager. Furthermore, Mansfield was acutely aware that his caucus was deeply split on many major issues and "had given him no carte blanche to put forth a 'Senate Democratic position'" (Valeo 1999: 35). "As Democratic leader in the Senate," Valeo writes, "Mansfield saw his role as harmonizing the various viewpoints held by Senate Democrats. When full orchestration was not feasible, as was often the case, he refused to choose from among the various positions to champion in the name of the leadership" (35).

Mansfield responded to liberals' complaints and made the party committees—the Policy Committee, charged with scheduling legislation, and the Steering Committee, which makes committee assignments—more representative. In the 1950s they had been dominated by senior southern senators. At Mansfield's insistence, both committees operated in a more collegial fashion than under Johnson. He revived the Democratic Conference—often known as the Caucus—that had seldom met when Johnson was leader. For a time it became a forum for policy and political discussion, but attendance gradually declined and it played little role of significance (R. Baker 1991: 277–279).

How the Senate functioned legislatively changed greatly during the 1960s and early 1970s. The Senate floor became a more important decision-making arena as senators became much more active on the floor, offering more amendments to a wider range of bills. No longer were senators content to work in their committees behind closed doors or restrict themselves to the issues within their committees' jurisdictions. Senators exploited extended debate to a much greater extent, and the frequency of filibusters shot up (Binder and Smith 1997; Oppenheimer 1985; Sinclair 1989).

Junior northern Democratic liberals were prominent among these activists, but they were by no means the only senators who began to exploit more fully the prerogatives the Senate gave its members. In the 1960s, the political environment began a transformation that made an activist style attractive to most senators. A host of new issues rose to prominence—first civil rights, then environmental issues and consumer rights; the war in Vietnam and related questions about American foreign and defense policy; women's rights and women's liberation; the rights of other ethnic groups, especially Latinos and Native Americans; the rights of the poor and the disabled; and, by the early 1970s, gay rights. These were issues that engaged, often intensely, many ordinary citizens, and politics became more highly charged. The interest group community exploded in size and became more diverse; many of the social movements of the 1960s acted as or spawned interest groups. So a plethora of environmental groups, consumer groups, women's groups, and other liberal social welfare and civil rights groups joined the Washington political community and made it more diverse. Then, in response to some of these groups' policy successes, for example, on environmental legislation, the business community mobilized. In the 1970s, many more businesses established a permanent presence in Washington, and specialized trade associations proliferated. Finally, the media—especially television—became a much bigger player in politics.

This new environment offered tempting new opportunities to senators (Loomis 1988; Sinclair 1989). The myriad interest groups needed
champions and spokesmen, and the media needed credible sources to represent issue positions and provide commentary. Because of the small size
and prestige of the Senate, its members fit the bill. The opportunity for
senators to become significant players on a broader stage with possible
policy, power, reelection, or higher-office payoffs was there, but to take
advantage of the opportunity senators needed to change their behavior and
their institution.

From the mid-1960s through the mid-1970s, senators did just that.
Working through the leadership, they increased the number of positions on
good committees and the number of subcommittee leadership positions
and distributed them much more broadly. Staff too was greatly expanded
and made available to junior as well as senior senators. Senators were consequently able to involve themselves in a much broader range of issues, and
they did so. The media became an increasingly important arena for participation and a significant resource for senators in the pursuit of their policy,
power, and reelection goals.

By the mid-1970s the individualist Senate had fully emerged. The
Senate had become a body in which every member, regardless of seniority,
felt entitled to participate on any constituency or policy issue. Senators took
for granted that they—and their colleagues—would regularly exploit the
powers the Senate rules gave them. Senators became increasingly outward-
directed, focusing on their links with interest groups, policy communities,
and the media more than on their ties to one another. Mansfield's leadership style facilitated this transformation but, clearly, greater forces were at
work.

How did a legislative chamber, so lightly led and with a majority party
deeply split, produce a mass of significant legislation? Enormously consequential legislation on civil rights, aid to education, and health care for the
elderly passed in the mid-1960s and much environmental and consumer
protection legislation in the late 1960s and early 1970s. Large majorities, a
sense of mandate, and, during the 1960s, effective presidential leadership
were important factors. In Mansfield's view, the Senate majority leader's
job did not entail pressuring committees and their chairs to report the president's program. He "made it clear" to the Kennedy administration that "if
they were impatient for a measure still in committee, it was their responsibility to persuade the chairman to move it" (Valeo 1999: 40). He did, however, move both Kennedy's and Johnson's priorities to the floor expeditiously
once they had been reported. And he was more than willing to delegate the
tasks of negotiating needed compromises and of legislative floor leadership
to others with the requisite skill and desire, as he did with Hubert Humphrey on the 1964 civil rights bill. The Senate Democratic leadership did

not perform whip counts, leaving that task to the administration (R. Baker 1991: 278; Valeo 1999).

An important Mansfield contribution to these enormous legislative achievements was the relationship he established with the minority and its leader, Everett Dirksen. Mansfield's "all senators are equal" philosophy extended to the minority party. His even-handedness, eschewing of procedural tricks, willingness to shift the spotlight, and consequent good working relationship with Dirksen facilitated the key role Dirksen played on the civil rights bill.

Dirksen's own leadership style contributed as well, of course (Loomis 1991, passim). Although toward the conservative side of the GOP spectrum, he maintained cordial and often close working relationships with Democratic presidents and with Democratic senators; the role of the minority as he saw it was to participate in legislating, getting the best deal they could, not simply to oppose.

The political parties in the Senate were much less polarized than they were to become later in the century, as Figures 5.1–5.3 showed. Most of the major legislation enacted passed with considerable support from Senate Republicans—at least on the final passage vote (Mayhew 1991: 122). To be sure, in a number of these cases Senate Republicans voted for weakening amendments but then voted for the bill on final passage whether or not their amendments had won. In some instances, then, some Republicans' votes for final passage probably indicated electoral calculation rather than policy support. However, that itself is indicative of a distribution of voter policy attitudes less polarized along partisan lines than is the case today. Dirksen as Republican leader displayed a restrained partisanship in part because, in Valeo's estimation, "he had a good sense of what could be done and what could not be done by a political opposition and what the public would and would not tolerate in politics on serious national issues" (1999: 45). In sum, the Dirksen style was in considerable part a response to the character of his membership and of the Republican Party of the day.

## The Senate in Transition

Mansfield left the Senate at the end of 1976 and was succeeded by Robert Byrd (D-W.Va.), who had been bearing the bulk of the floor oversight burden since his election as whip in 1971. Hugh Scott (R-Penn.) was elected minority leader in the fall of 1969 after Dirksen's death and was himself succeeded by Howard Baker (R-Tenn.) in 1977. When, surprisingly, Republicans won control of the Senate in the 1980 elections, Baker became majority leader.

This was a period of transition for the Senate and its parties. The Senate was still an arena of 100 individualists, each of whom considered himself entitled to pursue his own agenda and to participate on any issue that interested him. Still, the election of Ronald Reagan as president in 1980 signaled a more ideological turn in American politics, and Senate Republicans, in the majority for the first time in a generation, felt a mandate to deliver policy results. Furthermore, the 1980 elections accelerated the regional realignment of the parties, with the GOP Senate membership becoming more southern and the Democratic membership less so.

Baker, who famously analogized leading the Senate to "herding cats," faced the task of orchestrating the passage of Reagan's program. Although he did not originate the strategy, Baker used reconciliation under the Budget Act to pass Reagan's domestic spending cuts. (See Gold 2003: 44–46; and Chapter 7 in this volume for more on reconciliation.) Doing so made it possible to package the various Reagan proposals into one bill, thus keeping the focus on the whole and not on individual, often unpopular, parts. It also prevented delaying tactics by the minority, though none were threatened. As the first use of reconciliation to effectuate major policy change, the effort set an important precedent. The big Reagan tax cuts passed without the aid of reconciliation. On both of these signature Reagan bills, Democrats offered amendments to meliorate their effect but, even though most were defeated, they voted for passage by considerable margins. The more conservative segment of the Democratic Party, which still had a significant presence, undoubtedly agreed with the legislation's thrust; other Democrats were shell shocked by their loss of the majority and feared for their electoral futures.

Senate Republicans supported Reagan at then-unprecedented levels (*CQ Almanac* 1981). "They were so tickled to be in the majority and gave so much credit to Reagan for helping to put them there," explained Marty Gold (2003, 44), a contemporary Senate GOP staffer. Yet these same senators were unwilling to make rules changes that would increase the power of the majority in the Senate. Gold reports that when Baker first became majority leader his staff prepared a list of options for enhancing majority power. Baker had his staff then consult several prominent Republican senators, who were adamantly opposed. Baker as leader never proposed rules changes (46).

Yet Baker and the other leaders of this era did enhance their own capabilities and that of their parties in other ways. Mansfield and Dirksen had kept their own leadership staffs and those of the party policy committees small. Byrd on the Democratic side and Scott and then Baker on the Republican side expanded the staffs significantly. In 1981 Baker had fifteen leadership aides, compared with two to five for his predecessors; the Policy Committee and the Conference together had twenty-nine, a legacy of Scott's expansion. Over the course of the 1980s both leadership and party committee staffs continued to grow. The Democratic leader chaired the Policy Committee and controlled its staff. Byrd concentrated staff increases at the Policy Committee; in 1975, near the end of Mansfield's tenure, the combined staff totaled nine; by 1981 it had grown to twenty-five and by 1985 to thirty-six (all data from Smith 1993: 275). Staff resources increased the leaders' capacity to participate in policy matters, as was increasingly required of them. With more senators involving themselves on major issues and committees less able to pass their legislation without change, the party leaders more often had to broker agreements on substance as well as process.

The increase in staff resources also made it possible to greatly expand the services the party committees provide to members. Issue research in the form of issue briefs and longer papers, floor schedule information, and media assistance in a variety of forms came to be among the services made available on a routine basis.

The party committees as member organizations did not, however, become consistently more active. Dirksen together with the chair of the Republican Policy Committee had convened weekly lunch meetings to which the full Republican membership was invited, but these were not policymaking meetings. Baker in 1981 turned the committee into a council of standing committee chairs and often used the weekly meetings to push chairs to move the Reagan program. Under Byrd's leadership, the Democratic Policy Committee seldom met, although he did consult its members individually.

The majority leaders of the 1970s and succeeding decades were confronted with leading—or attempting to lead—a chamber that operated, in Howard Baker's words, "under rules that encourage .polite anarchy and embolden people who find majority rule a dubious proposition at best" (H. Baker 1998). Furthermore, the senators of the 1970s and succeeding decades were more inclined than those of the 1950s and early 1960s to exploit those rules aggressively. As filibusters became more frequent, the character of the filibusterers and of the targeted legislation broadened. By the 1970s, with major civil rights legislation on the books, southerners no longer needed to protect the filibuster for their one overriding issue of segregation and using extended debate was no longer a badge of racism. Liberals as well as conservatives frequently used this weapon, and senators used it on all sorts of legislation, parochial as well as momentous.

Senators often operated as individuals or in small groups to pursue their own agendas regardless of the sentiments of their party or party leadership. For example, liberal Democrat Howard Metzenbaum (Ohio) so regularly objected to otherwise noncontroversial bills, which he considered corporate giveaways, that Baker's staff took to consulting him on a routine basis before bringing legislation to the floor (see Gold 2003). Nor did all the trouble come from minority party members. Whether in the majority or the minority, Jesse Helms (R-N.C.) used the Senate's permissive amending rules to offer non-germane amendments and force innumerable votes in every Congress on hot-button issues such as abortion, pornography, and school prayer. And it was his own majority leader, Howard Baker, whom Helms and his North Carolina Republican colleague John East defied when, in 1982, they filibustered a gas tax increase deep into what was supposed to be the Christmas recess.

"Holds"—notices to the party leader that a senator objects to the scheduling of a bill or nomination before being consulted—became an increasing problem. Baker and later majority leaders Robert Dole (R-Kan.) and George Mitchell (D-Maine) publicly announced and then reiterated their position that when a senator placed a hold it entitled him only to notification before the leader scheduled the matter. Thus, a hold was not a veto. Yet the leaders had difficultly making that understanding stick. In a chamber that conducts most of its business through unanimous consent, one member's objection can cause havoc on an often overcrowded floor schedule. Holds were often treated as threats to filibuster and, unless the matter at issue was of great importance, served as individual vetoes. Leading the individualist Senate had become a complex and often frustrating enterprise.

## The Partisan Senate

George Mitchell, elected Democratic leader by his colleagues in late 1988, two years after Democrats had regained the majority, began his tenure by spreading party leadership positions and duties more broadly. He reactivated the Policy Committee as a forum for discussion among senators—all Democrats were invited—and appointed a junior member, Tom Daschle (D-S.D.), as co-chair. Daschle was given control over the domestic and services staffs, thereby allowing the committee to become more active. Unlike his predecessor, Byrd, who had spent most of his time on the floor, Mitchell shared floor oversight duties with party colleagues. Following Byrd's lead, he appointed party task forces on a variety of issues; these groups were variously charged with developing policy proposals that most Democratic senators could support, working out and implementing message strategies, or resolving legislative differences among Democrats. Under Mitchell's guidance, Senate Democrats began to develop explicit policy agendas (Smith 1993; DPC 2007).

These moves were prompted not only by Mitchell's understanding of the requirements of effective leadership in the Senate but also by increasing demands from junior members for more concerted party efforts and for more opportunities to participate. The partisan polarization that was developing in the late 1980s and accelerated in the 1990s made participation through their parties more attractive to senators than it had been when the respective parties were more heterogeneous and the ideological distance between them less. Wise leaders not only gave their members the chance to participate, but also used their efforts to the party's advantage.

Senate Republicans have long spread their party leadership positions broadly. The chairs of the Conference, the Policy Committee, and the Committee on Committees are held by different senators, not by the leader. Robert Dole as majority and minority leader was a harder-edged partisan than Baker had been. Majority leader in the 99th Congress (1985–86), minority leader from the 100th through the 103rd Congresses (1987–1994), and then majority leader again in the 104th Congress (1995–96), Dole led an increasingly conservative membership. Dole was, however, a consummate deal maker, and he and Mitchell regularly worked together to keep the Senate functioning. As Dole explained, "[Mitchell] would catch hell from his conference that 'you're always doing what Bob Dole wants to do,' and I would catch hell: 'Why are you always doing what Mitchell wants to do?' And we knew what we were doing, . . . we'd worked it out" (Rogers 2009b).

Given the Senate's permissive rules, the chamber only works smoothly if the majority leader and the minority leader cooperate—and not always then. The Senate has long done most of its work through unanimous consent agreements (UCAs), negotiated by the leaders or their staffs. Legislation is brought to the floor, debated, and amended and eventually voted on under UCAs, often a series of piecemeal UCAs. In the contemporary Senate, floor scheduling and floor management are necessarily exercises in broad and, in the end, bipartisan accommodation (Davidson 1985; Smith 1993; Sinclair 1989). A single senator can upset the majority leader's legislative plans by refusing to accede to a unanimous consent request, which is why majority leaders so often respect "holds."

With the acceleration of partisan polarization in the early 1990s, it was the minority party that most often exploited Senate prerogatives. In the 103rd Congress (1993–94), the Dole-led minority Republicans explicitly set out to deprive President Bill Clinton and the majority Democrats of policy successes and employed actual and threatened filibusters to do so, seemingly the first time the strategy was used in such a blanket fashion. Clinton's economic stimulus package; campaign finance and lobbying reform bills; and bills revamping the Superfund program, revising clean drinking water regulations, overhauling outdated telecommunications law, and applying federal labor laws to Congress were among the casualties. When they could not kill legislation, Republicans often extracted concessions. The major policy success of the 103rd Congress, the budget package, was accomplished through reconciliation, and the need for a super-majority in the Senate contributed to the demise of the Clinton health care reform effort.

The 1994 elections were read by the Washington political community as showing that this delaying strategy paid off "big time," held the promise of enormous benefits, and entailed little risk of backfiring. Democrats, after losing their majority in the 1994 elections, employed extended debate to kill many Republican priorities, including ambitious regulatory overhaul legislation and far-reaching property rights bills; they used the same strategy to force concessions on much other legislation. To a large extent, partisan use of the Senate's permissive rules has become standard operating procedure for the minority party, with the frequency and intensity having ratcheted up since the early 1990s.

The increasing polarization of the Senate parties combined with frequent switches in party control changed members' expectations of their leaders. As party leaders, they had always been expected to promote the party's reputation, but now members' expectations that leaders pursue partisan advantage and promote their collective partisan interests intensified. With Democrats and Republicans holding highly divergent views as to what constitutes good public policy, policy compromise became ever more difficult.

Trent Lott's rise in the Senate Republican leadership signaled the change. After the 1994 elections, Lott took on and defeated the incumbent whip Alan Simpson (R-Wyo.), Bob Dole's choice. The victory confirmed that "a new generation of aggressively conservative Republicans is exercising more and more influence in the chamber" (*Politics in America* 1995: 721). As Dole himself stated, "if you don't want to carry the flag for the party, there's 20 guys behind you that would grab it" (Rogers 2009b), and carrying the flag required a harder-nosed, more uncompromising approach. Over the following years, junior conservative Republicans made a series of moves aimed at forcing their senior and often more moderate colleagues to toe the party line; they obtained changes in conference rules that required a secret ballot vote on committee chairs both in committee and in the full conference, imposed term limits on committee leaders, and gave the Republican leader more influence over committee assignments. When moderate senators were in line to chair important committees—Jim Jeffords in 1997 and Arlen Specter in 2005—conservative members successfully pressed their leaders to extract promises of good behavior in return for their appointments (Sinclair 2006: chap. 6). (Eventually, both Jeffords and Specter left the Republican Party.)

## Party Wars in the Contemporary Senate

The Senate now often appears to be an arena for partisan warriors, with the party teams willing to use all the available procedural and public relations tools without restraint. As Table 5.1 shows, the frequency of filibusters has skyrocketed.[4] Senators use actual or threatened filibusters for a variety of purposes. Their aim may be to kill legislation, but it may also be to extract substantive concessions on a bill. Presidential nominations as well as legislation may be targeted. Holding up one measure in order to extract concessions on another, sometimes known as hostage taking, has become an increasingly frequent use of extended debate (Sinclair 2009). The impact on the legislative process on major legislation is enormous.[5] If holds and threatened filibusters as well as actual blocking action on the floor are counted, then major legislation is highly likely to encounter an extended debate-related problem in the Senate. In the 1960s only 8 percent of major measures subject to a filibuster, in fact, encountered such a problem; this increased to 27 percent in the 1970s through the 1980s, to 51 percent in the 1990s through the mid-2000s, and to 70 percent in the period 2007–2008. Thus, the frequency increased substantially as the individualist Senate developed; then, as the Senate parties grew more polarized, this sort of trouble for major legislation in the Senate became essentially routine.

The Senate's permissive amending rules have become a party weapon as well. In the 1990s exploiting Senate prerogatives to attempt to seize agenda control from the majority party became a key minority party strategy. The lack of a germaneness requirement for amendments to most bills severely weakens the majority party's ability to control the floor agenda. If the majority leader refuses to bring a bill to the floor, its supporters can offer it as an amendment to most legislation the leader does bring to the floor. The majority leader can make a motion to table the amendment, which is non-debatable. That does, however, require his or her members to vote on the issue, albeit in a procedural guise, and the leader may want to avoid that because minority party amendments are often framed to require some majority senators to cast politically perilous votes. Furthermore, even after

---

4. For a discussion of the cautions with which these data should be regarded, see Richard Beth (1995); also, see Barbara Sinclair (1997: 47–49). Sources for the data are given in the note to Table 5.1. The House Democratic Study Group publication relies on data supplied by Congressional Research Service experts; these experts' judgments about what constitutes a filibuster are not limited to instances in which cloture was sought. For the 103rd through 110th Congresses, instances in which cloture was sought are used as the basis of the "filibuster" estimate. One can argue that this overestimates because in some cases cloture was sought for reasons other than a fear of extended debate (a test vote or to impose germaneness); however, one can also argue that it underestimates because those cases in which cloture was not sought—perhaps because it was known to be out of reach—are not counted. For an estimate based on a different methodology, see below.

5. Major measures are defined as those measures in lists of major legislation published in the *CQ Almanac* and the *CQ Weekly* plus those measures on which key votes occurred, again according to Congressional Quarterly. This yields forty to sixty measures per Congress. Thus, although truly minor legislation is excluded, the listing is not restricted to only the most contentious and highly salient issues.

**Table 5.1**    The Increase in Filibusters and Cloture Votes,
1957–2009

| Year | Congress | Filibusters (per Congress) | Cloture votes (per Congress) | Successful cloture votes (per Congress) |
|------|----------|---------------------------|------------------------------|------------------------------------------|
| 1951–1960 | 82nd–86th | 1.0 | .4 | 0 |
| 1961–1970 | 87th–91st | 4.6 | 5.2 | .8 |
| 1971–1980 | 92nd–96th | 11.2 | 22.4 | 8.6 |
| 1981–1986 | 97th–99th | 16.7 | 23.0 | 10.0 |
| 1987–1992 | 100th–102nd | 26.7 | 39.0 | 15.3 |
| 1993–1998 | 103rd–105th | 28.0 | 48.3 | 13.7 |
| 1999–2002 | 106th–107th | 32.0 | 59.0 | 30.5 |
| 2003–2004 | 108th | 27 | 49 | 12 |
| 2005–2006 | 109th | 36 | 56 | 36 |
| 2007–2008 | 110th | 54 | 112 | 61 |
| 2009 | 111th | 25 | 39 | 35 |

Source: Data for 82nd–102nd Congresses: column 3, Congressional Research Service, comp., "A Look ar the Senate Filibuster," in Democratic Studies Group Special Report, June 13, 1994, app. B; columns 4–5, Norman J. Ornstein, Thomas E. Mann, and Michael J. Malbin, *Vital Statistics on Congress 1993–1994* (Washington, D.C.: CQ Press, 1994), 162. Data for 103rd Congress: Richard S.Beth, "Cloture in the Senate, 103rd Congress," memorandum, Congressional Research Service, June 23, 1995. Data for 104th–107th Congresses: *CQ Almanac* for the years 1995–2007 (Washington, D.C.: Congressional Quarterly). Data for 108th–111th Congresses: CQ Online.

its amendment has been tabled, the minority can continue to offer other amendments, including even individual parts of the original amendment, and can block a vote on the underlying bill the majority party wants to pass. The leader can, of course, file a cloture petition and try to shut off debate, but he or she needs sixty votes to do so.

The minority party can use this strategy to bring its agenda to the floor and, if accompanied by a sophisticated public relations campaign (which the Senate parties are increasingly capable of orchestrating), can gain favorable publicity and sometimes pressure enough majority party members into supporting the bill to pass it. In 1996 Senate Democrats used the strategy to enact a minimum wage increase; since then, when they were in the minority, they forced highly visible floor debate on tobacco regulation, campaign finance reform, gun control, managed care reform, the minimum wage, and the Bush administration's attempt to change overtime rules to decrease eligibility—all issues the Republican majority would have preferred to avoid. In 2001 campaign finance legislation passed the Senate before the Democrats took control of the chamber. John McCain (R-Ariz.) and the Democrats had threatened to use the add-it-as-an-amendment-to-everything strategy, which would have wreaked havoc with the consideration of President George W. Bush's program. Furthermore, Republicans knew that the cost of trying to stop campaign finance from being considered would be terrible publicity. So the Senate Republican leadership capitulated and agreed to bring it to the floor. Since they lost their majority in 2006, Republicans have forced Democrats to vote on all sorts of difficult issues, from bringing Guantanamo inmates to the United States to expanding gun rights.

The majority party and its agent, the majority leader, are not without weapons to combat this strategy. The majority leader's right of first recognition allows him or her to use a tactic called "filling the amendment tree"—that is, offering amendments in all the parliamentarily permissible slots, thus preventing other senators from offering their amendments, and then usually filing for cloture (see Beth et al. 2009). The problem with this maneuver is that, to get to a vote on the underlying measure, the minority must acquiesce or cloture must be invoked. So the result may well be gridlock. Trent Lott used this tactic in the 1990s; when he could not achieve cloture, which was frequently the case, he simply pulled the bill off the floor. Once Bush was elected president, however, Lott needed to pass the Republican administration's legislation and seldom used the ploy.

Under special circumstances the amendment-tree tactic can work. Bill Frist (R-Tenn.) employed it on a gun maker liability bill in 2005. The bill had the support of more than sixty senators, but in the previous congress Democratic opponents had blocked it by offering "killer" amendments—that is, amendments that were anathema to the bill's strongest supporters. By filling the amendment tree, Frist made that tactic impossible. In early 2007, Harry Reid (D-Nev.) filled the amendment tree on the continuing resolution (CR) necessary because Republicans had not passed most of the appropriations bill for FY07; he then filed for cloture, a vote Democrats won. The result was that the CR passed the Senate quickly and in a form identical to the House bill. Reid was able to succeed with such aggressive tactics because the CR was must-pass legislation, the deadline was imminent, and Republicans were leery about calling attention to their own dereliction. Later in the 110th Congress, Reid filled the amendment tree a number of times; doing so allowed him to bring to the floor bills Democrats wanted to spotlight but at the same time protected his members from tough votes on Republican amendments. If cloture failed, as it often did, he would pull the bill from the floor. Little was lost because, even if the bill had passed, President Bush would have vetoed it. But once the president was of his own party, the need to pass legislation constrained Reid's use of the procedure, though not to the same extent it had Lott's in 2001. Reid had a considerably larger majority.

To counter what is now routine obstructionism by the minority party, the contemporary majority leader has limited procedural options. He or she can, of course, file for cloture; if able to muster the necessary sixty votes, he or she can force an up-or-down vote and also bar all non-germane amendments, since Senate rules require that after cloture is invoked all amendments be germane. During the 109th Congress (2005–06), the Senate voted on cloture fifty-nine times; in the 110th Congress (2007–08), the Senate voted on cloture motions 112 times, far more than in any previous Congress. In 2009 the number was thirty-nine. This is the result, Democrats argued, of Republicans' unwillingness to come to unanimous consent agreements of the sort the Senate usually functions under. Republicans contend that Democrats are unwilling to take the time for full debate and amending activity. Cloture was invoked on 64 percent of the cloture votes in the 109th Congress and on 55 percent in the 110th Congress. In both congresses, however, a bipartisan deal usually preceded a successful cloture vote; seldom could the majority party invoke cloture when a majority of the minority party was opposed. With their larger majority in the 111th Congress, Democrats won thirty-five of the thirty-nine cloture votes in 2009, but still often had to make concessions.

The minority party now frequently forces the majority party to muster sixty votes simply to bring a bill to the floor (Sinclair 2008). Unless a unanimous consent agreement is reached, getting a bill to the floor requires a successful motion to proceed to consider the bill, and this motion can be filibustered. In the 109th Congress (2005–06), minority Democrats blocked a number of Republican priorities by this means—most notably, several bills capping malpractice awards and repealing the estate tax. In the 110th Congress (2007–08), fifty-four of the 112 cloture votes were on motions to proceed. These included a bill allowing Medicare to negotiate prescription drug prices; a bill making labor organizing easier; one giving the District of Columbia voting representation in the House; another overturning a Supreme Court decision severely narrowing plaintiffs' ability to sue in job discrimination cases; the Dream Act, which essentially legalized the children of undocumented workers who had graduated from high school in the United States and had never been in legal trouble; and an auto company bailout. All of these died when Republicans filibustered the motion to proceed. In other cases, the majority party had to make significant substantive concessions to get its bills to the floor. The Democrats' bigger margin in the 111th Congress (2009–10) deterred Republicans from using the tactic as frequently; still, in 2009 Republicans used the time-wasting device on eight important bills.

The minority party's ability to maintain high cohesion on cloture votes has emboldened the minority leader to demand that unanimous consent agreements set a sixty-vote requirement to bring bills to the floor and to pass amendments or bills. CRS experts report that sixty-vote requirements can be found in UCAs going back to the early 1990s, but they have become much more frequent in recent years. Because invoking cloture and then getting to a vote on the substance takes time—a cloture petition with sixteen senators' signatures must be filed, it must lay over for a day before it can be voted on, and the possibility looms of up to thirty hours of debate after a successful cloture vote—recent majority leaders have acquiesced in a number of cases. Frist did so in at least nine instances over the course of the 109th Congress, including on two stem cell research funding bills (*CQ Weekly*, August 14, 2006: 2214). In 2007 the stem cell bill again came to the floor under a UCA specifying a sixty-vote requirement. In the 110th and 111th Congresses, Republican leader Mitch McConnell (Ky.) was very aggressive in seeking sixty-vote thresholds. During the 109th Congress (2007–08), with Bush still in the White House, Republicans refused to allow any of the Democrats' Iraq-related amendments to be decided by simple majority votes. In early 2009, the UCA negotiated by Reid on the Lilly Ledbetter Wage Discrimination Act specified that passage would require fifty-nine votes (three-fifths of the total number of senators sworn, which at that time was 98). Democrats were eager to chalk up a legislative accomplishment quickly and had a big agenda awaiting action, so McConnell had considerable bargaining power. For Democrats, the cost was a weaker bill than had passed the House.

The combination of highly polarized parties and chamber rules requiring super-majorities for most significant decisions makes legislating difficult and majority party leadership a thankless task. Most Senate Republicans sincerely oppose most of the Democrats' agenda and decided early in 2009 that Democratic failure to enact their agenda would benefit the Republican party electorally. Consequently, Reid could expect little help from the Republican leadership on major Democratic priorities. Democrats, for their part, believe that Republicans have been "slow walking" business in the Senate. Democrats contend that Republicans are tardy in responding to unanimous consent agreement offers from Democrats, thus slowing the process of reaching agreements. Republicans have placed "holds" not just on legislation but on many of Barack Obama's executive branch and judicial nominations, delaying the staffing of those branches to a crawl. On the floor, they insist on offering multitudinous amendments. Thus bills that have in the past been noncontroversial, such as the transportation appropriations bill, take days on the Senate floor.

From mid-summer 2009 when Al Franken was seated until a Republican won the Massachusetts Senate seat vacated by Ted Kennedy's death in early 2010, Democrats had sixty members and so, theoretically, could cut off debate at will. And this was a Senate Democratic Party that was better organized, more ideologically like-minded, and more inclined to joint action than its predecessor of the early 1990s—as was its GOP counterpart. The party committees and leadership offices are now generously funded, well staffed, and consequently the providers of an increasingly wide range of services and activities (Lee 2009: 15–16). Tasks previously performed informally have been delegated to newly constituted entities. For example, the Democratic Steering and Outreach Committee, formerly the Steering Committee and then the Steering and Coordination Committee, is charged with acting as a liaison with outside groups in order to build support for key Democratic legislative proposals as well as with its traditional committee assignment function. The number of secondary leadership positions has increased so, on both sides of the aisle, a larger proportion of the membership is a part of its party leadership; in 2009, at least sixteen senators on each side held such a position, and this does not count simple membership on party committees. The whips meet to talk strategy and actually do whip counts (Evans, Husband, and Minnichelli 2009). And senators meet as party groups on a frequent basis. Every Tuesday that the Senate is in session, Democrats and Republicans each meet for lunch; these senator-only lunches (staff are usually barred) have become forums for wide-ranging strategy discussions. Republicans meet under the auspices of their Policy Committee; Democrats meet as a caucus. The Democratic Policy Committee also sponsors weekly lunches to which guests— Obama administration cabinet members, for example—are invited. On Wednesday, Republicans have a lunch sponsored by the Senate Steering Committee, a conservative member group, to which all Republicans are invited. When the regular meetings are combined with the many spontaneous one-party-only meetings, senators now spend much of their Washington time with their party colleagues rather than in bipartisan settings. Like-mindedness and a sense of shared electoral fate were major foundations for these developments, but more intra-party interaction also feeds back to breed more like-mindedness.

Still, with the minority forcing the majority to routinely produce sixty votes from its own ranks for action on almost everything, Democrats needed to hold every member; even with more cohesive parties, that was a tall order. Furthermore, a situation in which every member is key is an invitation to Senate individualism, which still exists alongside the partisan warfare. Lacking big carrots or sticks, Reid relies heavily on eliciting cooperation through negotiation and persuasion, especially from his fellow Democrats. Reid generally defers to his committee chairs, though in the end on the agenda items of the highest priority he has had to get deeply and substantively involved, as he did on the health care reform bill in the fall of 2009. Through innumerable meetings with Democratic senators one-on-one, in small groups, and in weekly caucus lunches, Reid keeps members informed and elicits feedback. He tries to reach decisions that all members of the caucus can live with and clears important ones with the caucus before they are finalized.

Yet, even in a period of high partisan warfare, and even when the majority is large, the Senate majority leader has no choice but to deal with the minority leader on a continuous basis. McConnell could make Senate Democrats' lives considerably more difficult by not agreeing to unanimous consent agreements at all. Even now, the Senate does a large part of its business through unanimous consent. While reaching agreements takes more time than previously, and may be tortuous on major legislation, the lack of agreement would bring the Senate to a total halt. Passing the health care reform bill took twenty-five days on the floor of the Senate and five successful cloture votes. That cannot be done regularly. In fact, floor consideration of health care reform—both the big bill in December 2009 and the reconciliation bill "fix" in March 2010—was governed by innumerable unanimous consent agreements that provided some structure and predictability to what seemed on the surface a no-holds-barred battle.

The incentives for the majority leader to reach unanimous consent agreements to allow the business of the Senate to go forward are obvious. If the Senate is paralyzed, the majority party appears incompetent. The committees are controlled by the majority party so the bills they report almost always enjoy majority support; much of the majority leader's efforts are aimed at advancing the party's agenda. So, even if policy concessions to the minority must be made to reach agreements or minority senators must be given the opportunity to offer amendments that some majority senators would prefer to avoid, an agreement to move a bill is almost always a net benefit to the majority party.

Why then does the minority leader agree to unanimous consent agreements? James Wallner, a political scientist and senior Senate aide, argues that "the majority and minority party leaders generally serve a moderating function in the Senate by acting within certain bounds to ameliorate the conflict and instability inherent in the institution" (2010: 16) and calls this pattern of decision making "structured consent" (16). The minority leader is willing to reach agreements because the two parties' and their leaders' goals are "not always mutually exclusive" (16). When the parties were much less ideologically polarized than they are today, the distance between what the median Republican and the median Democrat considered good public policy was considerably narrower and compromise cost less; now more frequently the minority prefers on policy grounds the status quo to any compromise the majority would sign on to. When the parties were more diverse, individual senators, especially minority party senators, were more likely to see a significant advantage in working with the opposition, so the minority leader could not count on holding party members together. It was better to make a deal himself or herself rather than have party mavericks undercut him or her. In addition, the minority leaders of Dirksen's day believed that the public would punish a party that severely and blatantly obstructed the legislative process; with the public—and particularly the activist bases of the parties—more polarized, the minority leaders of today often see an electoral benefit—not a cost—in obstruction.

Yet contemporary minority leaders do not use their prerogatives to create unmitigated obstruction and, in fact, as Wallner points out, often work to prevent their most hard-line members from doing so. It seems reasonable to assume that some of the same incentives for cooperation operate, just at a different point. McConnell needs to protect his party's reputation, so he does not want to chance its being seen as responsible for a complete breakdown. Blocking legislation unpopular with the activist base of the Republican Party may pay off electorally, but if the less-committed partisans and independents come to perceive the Republican Party as the "party of no," the electoral effect may be negative. A Jim Bunning (R-Ky.) blocking the extension of unemployment insurance does not make the Republican Party look good. On an issue such as financial regulation reform, for example, indefinitely blocking legislation and thus risking being seen as on the side of Wall Street was just not tenable; the risk to the party's reputation was too great. Moreover, McConnell could not count on holding enough of his members to prevent consideration much longer than he did. The more ideologically homogeneous parties of today are still not monolithic; if a minority leader cannot make good on a threat to prevent cloture, he or she loses bargaining clout. The minority leader must often calibrate how far to go and what can be gotten from members in terms of policy concessions, or even just votes on so-called message amendments, and then make a deal. Furthermore, his or her members have legislative goals quite apart from the big issues that separate the parties and accomplishing them requires that the Senate be able to function.

Overall, in the Senate, much more than in the contemporary House, advantage goes to those opposed to action. Strong parties that have made it possible for the House to legislate with dispatch have made it harder for the Senate to do so.

# References

Abramowitz, Alan. 2006. "Disconnected or Joined at the Hip?: Comment." In Pietro Nivola and David Brady, eds., *Red and Blue Nation?* Vol. 1. Washington, D.C.: Brookings Institution.

Baker, Howard H., Jr. 1998. "On Herding Cats." Address, United States Senate, July 14.

Baker, Ross K. 1991. "Mike Mansfield and the Birth of the Modern Senate." In Richard A. Baker and Roger Davidson, eds., *First among Equals.* Washington, D.C.: CQ Press.

Beth, Richard. 1995. "What We Don't Know about Filibusters." Paper presented at the annual meeting of the Western Political Science Association, March 15–18, Portland, Ore.

Beth, Richard, Valerie Heitshusen, Bill Heniff Jr., and Elizabeth Rybicki. 2009. "Leadership Tools for Managing the U.S. Senate." Paper presented at the annual meeting of the American Political Science Association, September 3–6, Toronto, Canada.

Binder, Sarah, and Steven S. Smith. 1997. *Politics or Principle? Filibustering in the United States Senate*. Washington, D.C.: Brookings Institution.

Caro, Robert A. 2002. *Master of the Senate*. New York: Knopf.

Davidson, Roger H. 1985. "Senate Leaders: Janitors for an Untidy Chamber?" In Lawrence C. Dodd and Bruce I. Oppenheimer, eds., *Congress Reconsidered*, 3rd ed. Washington, D.C.: CQ Press.

Democratic Policy Committee (DPC). 2007. "A History of the Democratic Policy Committee 1947–2007."

Evans, Larry, David Husband, and Laura Minnichelli. 2009. "The Senate Republican Whip System: An Exploration." Paper delivered at the annual meeting of the Midwest Political Science Association, April 2–5, Chicago.

Gold, Martin. 2003. Interview by Donald Ritchie, Office of the Senate Historian. December 9.

Jacobson, Gary. 2006. "Disconnected or Joined at the Hip?: Comment." In Pietro Nivola and David Brady, eds., *Red and Blue Nation?* Vol 1. Washington, D.C.: Brookings Institution.

Lee, Frances E. 2009. *Beyond Ideology: Politics, Principles, and Partisanship in the U.S. Senate*. Chicago: University of Chicago Press.

Loomis, Burdett. 1988. *The New American Politician*. New York: Basic Books.

———. 1991. "Everett Dirksen: The Consummate Minority Leader." In Richard A. Baker and Roger Davidson, eds., *First among Equals*. Washington, D.C.: CQ Press.

Matthews, Donald E. 1960. *U.S. Senators and Their World*. New York: Vintage Books.

Mayhew, David. 1991. *Divided We Govern*. New Haven, Conn.: Yale University Press, 1991.

Oppenheimer, Bruce. 1985. "Changing Time Constraints on Congress: Historical Perspectives on the Use of Cloture." In Lawrence C. Dodd and Bruce I. Oppenheimer, eds., *Congress Reconsidered*, 3rd ed. Washington, D.C.: CQ Press.

Ornstein, Norman J., Thomas E. Mann and Michael J. Malbin. 2002. *Vital Statistics on Congress 2001–2002*. Washington, D.C.: CQ Press.

Poole, Keith, and Howard Rosenthal. 1997. *Congress: A Political Economic History of Roll Call Voting*. New York: Oxford University Press.

Rogers, David. 2009a. "The Lost Senate." Politico.com. October 9.

———. 2009b. "Dole: Success Tied to Keeping Word." Politico.com. October 9.

Shuman, Howard E. 1991. "Lyndon B. Johnson: The Senate's Powerful Persuader." In Richard A. Baker and Roger Davidson, eds., *First among Equals*. Washington, D.C.: CQ Press.

Sinclair, Barbara. 1989. *The Transformation of the U.S. Senate*. Baltimore: Johns Hopkins University Press.

———. 1997. *Unorthodox Lawmaking*. Washington, D.C.: CQ Press.

———. 2006. *Party Wars: Polarization and the Politics of the Policy Process*. Julian Rothbaum Lecture Series. Norman: University of Oklahoma Press.

———. 2007. *Unorthodox Lawmaking*, 3rd ed. Washington, D.C.: CQ Press.

———. 2008. "Orchestrators of Unorthodox Lawmaking: Pelosi and McConnell in the 110th Congress." *The Forum* (Issue 3).

————. 2009. "The New World of U.S. Senators." In Lawrence C. Dodd and Bruce I. Oppenheimer, eds., *Congress Reconsidered*, 9th ed. Washington, D.C.: CQ Press.

Smith, Steven S. 1993. "Forces of Change in Senate Party Leadership and Organization." In Lawrence C. Dodd and Bruce I. Oppenheimer, eds., *Congress Reconsidered*, 5th ed. Washington, D.C.: CQ Press.

Wallner, James. 2010. "The Death of Deliberation: Popular Opinion, Party, and Policy in the Modern United States Senate." Paper delivered at the annual meeting of the Midwest Political Science Association, April 22–25, Chicago, Ill.

White, William. 1957. *Citadel: The Story of the U.S. Senate.* New York: Harper and Brothers.

Valeo, Frances R. 1999. *Mike Mansfield Majority Leader.* Armonk, N. Y.: M. E. Sharpe.

# 6

# Individual and Partisan Activism on the Senate Floor

## Frances E. Lee

We've abandoned any discipline. We end up with 100 Proxmires in the Senate. One Proxmire makes a real contribution. All you need is 30 of them to guarantee that the place doesn't work.

Sen. Joseph R. Biden Jr. (D-Del.), 1982[1]

I value my independence. I am not motivated by strident partisanship or ideology. These traits may be useful in many walks of life, but unfortunately they are not highly valued in Congress.

Sen. Evan Bayh (D-Ind.), 2010[2]

It is remarkable that an institution that moves as slowly as the U.S. Senate can change so quickly. In 1982 Sen. Joseph Biden located the problems of the Senate of his era in the undisciplined activism of individual senators. In Biden's view, widely held at the time, the Senate's failures stemmed from the difficulty of leading a fractious body of individuals, all vigilantly guarding their senatorial prerogatives. In 2010 Sen. Evan Bayh bade farewell to a party-polarized Senate that he felt no longer valued his independence. In remarks announcing his retirement, he voiced the conventional wisdom of his era criticizing a Senate that is "not operating as it should" because of "too much partisanship . . . too much narrow ideology, and not enough practical problem solving." In Bayh's portrait, the current Senate has no place for even one individualist, while by Biden's earlier account, independent activists largely populated the chamber of the early 1980s.

---

I thank Sina Esfahani for excellent research assistance with this paper, along with the support of University of Maryland's Undergraduate Research Assistantship Program.

1. Quoted in Alan Ehrenhalt (1982).

2. "Remarks by Senator Evan Bayh Announcing His Retirement from the Senate," Federal News Service, February 15, 2010.

In less than thirty years the conventional critique of the Senate has shifted from that of a body plagued by excessive individualism to one suffering from excessive partisanship. The Senate of 2010 is a body in which an independent-minded senator complains of feeling lonely and undervalued, unable to find a place amidst warring parties and ideologies. The Senate of the 1970s and the early 1980s, by contrast, was characterized as atomized and unpredictable, an egalitarian institution in which party and committee leaders received little deference (Ehrenhalt 1982; Foley 1980; Loomis 1988; Sundquist 1981: 395–402). Sen. Philip Hart (D-Mich.) captured the spirit of the time, observing in 1974: "We are all constructively free-wheeling individuals."[3] Similarly, freshman senator Gary Hart (D-Colo.) could say of the Senate of 1977, "I don't feel pressure to go along with the party position."[4] In the space of a single generation, the Senate traveled from its postwar nadir in partisan roll-call voting cohesion to its apex (Ornstein, Mann, and Malbin 2008: 151).

For its part, the Senate of the 1970s and 1980s was a remarkable shift from the Senate of the 1950s and early 1960s. This earlier Senate imposed a different kind of conformity than the one Bayh chafed against. Individual senators' behavior was regulated by a set of folkways, enforced through social pressure and institutional sanctions (Matthews 1960). These norms facilitated institutional performance and, according to the complaints of nonconformist senators, served the interests of a particular governing coalition, sometimes referred to as the "inner club" (White 1957) or the "Senate establishment" (Clark 1963). Barbara Sinclair (1989) documents the breakdown of these norms during the 1960s, under pressure from a growing number of senators who rebelled against a system that frustrated the achievement of their individual goals.

All these remarkable changes have occurred in a legislative institution that has seen little modification in its formal rules. The most significant revision in Senate rules since the 1960s was the 1975 change to the cloture process that allowed sixty senators, rather than two-thirds of those present and voting, to force a measure to a final vote. In addition, the adoption of the 1974 Budget Act and subsequent amendments made the consideration of budget-related policy more majoritarian. Beyond those, there have been no changes to Senate rules that either restrict or expand the rights of individual senators to speak, to propose amendments, or otherwise to have input on the legislation considered on the Senate floor.

At all points throughout this period, individual senators have enjoyed the most expansive rights available to legislators anywhere in

---

3. Quoted in Burdett Loomis (1988).

4. Quoted in Richard Cohen (1977).

the world. Most close observers of the Senate, both present and past, emphasize the need for senatorial self-restraint if the Senate is going to function at all (see, e.g., Matthews 1960: 116; Sinclair 2006: 232). Nevertheless, with a constant set of rules as a backdrop, the Senate was transformed from an inner-directed club ruled by a bipartisan "establishment" (Matthews 1960; Swanson 1969) to an open egalitarian institution in which all individuals demanded input and received accommodation (Sinclair 1989; Smith 1989) and then to a party polarized body divided down the middle into cohesive partisan blocs (Lee 2009; Sinclair 2006; Theriault 2008).

Although it is possible to sketch the outlines of Senate change over the past fifty years in this manner, one inevitably risks exaggeration in doing so. Legislative scholars have thus sought systematic data to get beyond impressionistic characterizations and to rest any conclusions about Senate operations and behavior on a solid empirical foundation. One of the most important systematic indicators of Senate individualism has long been senators' activism on the Senate floor. Drawing on such data, Sinclair (1989) documented just how much the senator of the 1980s differed stylistically from the senator of the 1950s. She found an explosion of floor participation, a "pervasive change in senators' behavior" (1986: 878), reflecting a new prevailing strategy for goal achievement. Senators took advantage of wider opportunities in an expanded Washington policy community to be active on a much broader array of issues, leading to a new political system "characterized by a greater diversity of significant actors, more fluid and less predictable lines of conflict, and, consequently, a much more intense struggle over agenda space" (Sinclair 1986: 904). Similarly, Steven Smith (1989) analyzed shifts in floor amending activity, concluding that the Senate floor had become a more important policymaking arena and the Senate a more unpredictable, collegial, and inclusive institution.

Below I take a new look at Senate floor amending activity, expanding on earlier work to include the most recent two decades. How has the role of the individual senator changed in a Senate riven by party conflict? How important is the Senate floor in such an environment? After examining the substantial changes that have occurred in floor politics since the mid-1980s, I then advance an admittedly speculative account of the shifts that have occurred in floor politics. I will argue that the freewheeling individualism characteristic of the 1970s rested, in part, on the fact that senators tended to take for granted continued Democratic control of the Senate. But after majority party control of the Senate was put into question during the early 1980s—and it has remained in question since—the excessive Senate individualism of the 1970s began to be brought to heel.

## Declining Floor Activism

Figure 6.1 displays the number of floor amendments that received roll call votes on the Senate floor in each Congress from the 86th through the 110th (1959–2008). Because the focus is on the activism of individual senators, I exclude committee-sponsored amendments and amendments co-sponsored by the floor leaders of the two major Senate parties. Two lines are displayed: one showing the number of recorded votes on all amendments and motions to table amendments; a second line displays only votes directly on the merits of amendments (in other words, excluding amendments handled with tabling motions).

The data reveal a significant drop in floor amending activity since the highly individualistic Senates of the 1970s and early 1980s. Although there had been explosive growth in the amount of amending activity from the mid-1960s through the mid-1970s, the peak number of amendments

**Figure 6.1**    Senate Amending Activity, 1959–2008

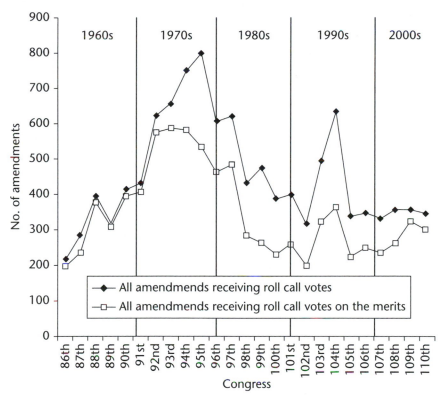

receiving roll call votes was reached in the 96th Congress, in the first two years of the Carter presidency and the majority leadership of Robert C. Byrd (D-W.Va.). Subsequently, the number of amendments considered on the Senate floor dramatically declined over the course of the 1980s. So, by the end of that decade all the increase in amending activity since the mid-1960s had been reversed. With the exception of a burst of floor activism in the 103rd and 104th Congresses, the number of amendments considered on the floor of the contemporary Senate is closely comparable to that of the mid-1960s. Indeed, the level of amending activity almost appears to have reached an equilibrium in the most recent decade, holding steady at around 350 votes on amendments per Congress between the 105th and the 110th Congresses (1997–2008), a lower level than at any point since the 88th Congress (1963–64).

If one focuses only on amendments that received up-or-down votes on the merits, the maximum number ever considered was in the 93rd Congress (1973–74), in a Senate led by Mike Mansfield (D-Mont.), a "laissez-faire" leader extraordinarily tolerant of Senate individualism (Baker 1991). After that point, it became more common for amendments to be summarily tabled, rather than fully debated. As measured by the number of amendments considered on the merits, the contemporary Senate has settled into a level of floor activism that is almost half that of the 1970s. The number of amendments receiving up-or-down votes has averaged 271 per Congress between the 98th and 110th Congresses (1983–2008), compared to an average of 504 between the 90th and 97th Congresses (1967–1983).

These overall patterns are the aggregate result of individual senators' behavior.[5] Figure 6.2 displays trends in the number of amendments offered by the typical senator over the time period. Because a small number of highly active senators always skews the average upward, both the mean and the median are displayed. The median senator in the contemporary Congress is no more active in forcing roll call votes on floor amendments than the median senator of the 90th Congress (1967–68). Although the typical senator of today is about twice as active as a senator of the late 1950s and early 1960s, Senate behavior is no longer characterized by the intense floor activism of the 1970s and early 1980s.

Figure 6.3 highlights changing patterns in the number of senators who engage in markedly high and low levels of floor amending activity. The figure displays the number of senators in each Congress who offered

---

5. The drop in floor amending activity cannot be attributed to the decline in the number of days the Senate was in session. The Senate took around 40 percent fewer votes per day in session during the 1990s and 2000s as it took during the 1970s.

**Figure 6.2**   Average Floor Activism per Capita, 1959–2008

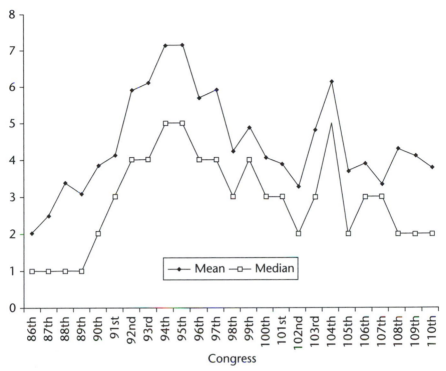

ten or more amendments receiving roll call votes and the number who offered zero or only one amendment on which a roll call vote was taken. Contemporary senators exhibit more deference toward (or acceptance of) legislation brought to the floor than did senators of the 1970s. On average, over the course of the 1970s only twenty-one senators fell into the "most restrained" category by offering fewer than two amendments per Congress. But since the start of the 2000s, an average of thirty-eight senators per Congress has largely eschewed floor activism, a 73 percent increase since the 1970s.

There is no question that a transformation in Senate behavior and floor politics occurred during the 1960s, in that the breadth of participation in floor amending activity today is considerably greater than in the early 1960s. But in light of subsequent changes, the 1970s look exceptional in both the breadth and intensity of senators' floor activity. Since that time, there has been a growing share of senators who largely refrain from offering floor amendments. At the same time, there are just not nearly as many senators in the contemporary era who engage in extremely

**Figure 6.3**   Deference and Extreme Activism on the Senate Floor, 1959–2008

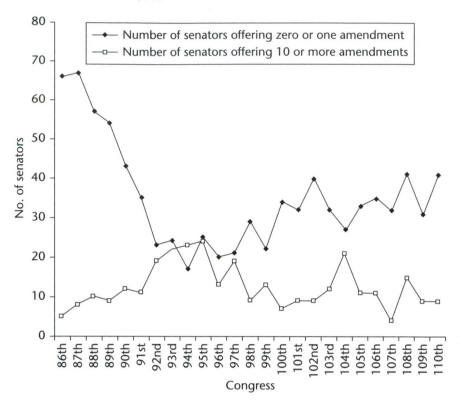

high levels of floor activism, senators Sinclair (1986; 1989) termed "hyperactives." During the 1970s, fully one-fifth of the Senate offered at least ten amendments per Congress; by contrast, less than one-tenth of the Senate of the 2000s falls into this category.

Taken together, the Senate floor of the 1990s and, especially, the 2000s has become a less freewheeling policymaking arena than the floor of the 1970s and early 1980s. The typical senator today makes fewer attempts to amend legislation on the floor, at least with amendments important or controversial enough to warrant a roll call vote. The number of highly activist senators on legislation has dropped by three-quarters. The number of senators who largely forgo attempts to modify bills on the floor has been trending upward, with nearly one-fifth of the Senate on average between 2001 and 2008 declining to offer a single amendment requiring a recorded vote over the course of a Congress.

## Ideological Activism

A highly activist style has always been more attractive to some types of senators than others. Floor activism, of course, reflects dissatisfaction with the legislation reported to the floor. It also permits individual senators to force attention to pet issues, allowing members to shape debate and force other senators to go on the record. As such, floor activism is a tactic traditionally associated with self-styled "Senate outsiders" who champion positions outside the Senate mainstream (Huitt 1961). As Sinclair (1989) documents, the most activist senators of the 1950s and 1960s tended to be liberal northern Democrats, reflecting their frustration with a Senate in which key positions of power were disproportionately claimed by conservative southern Democrats. During the 1970s, this activist style was adopted by a growing group of senators in both parties and across the ideological spectrum.

Figure 6.4 gauges the relationship between ideology and floor activism over the 1959–2008 period. This figure displays the difference between the mean number of amendments offered by "extremist" and "moderate" legislators. Extremist legislators are defined as those to the left of the

**Figure 6.4**    Ideological Extremism and Senate Amending Activity, 1959–2008

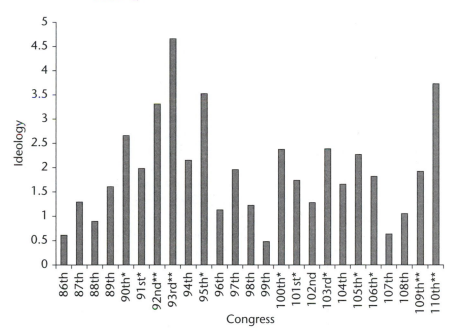

Note: *$p < .05$; **$p < .01$, t-test of difference of means.

Democratic Party's median and to the right of the Republican Party's median (as measured by Poole and Rosenthal's DW-Nominate scores); "moderates" are those to the right of the Democratic median and to the left of the Republican median.[6] As is immediately apparent from this figure, extremists always offer more floor amendments on average than moderate senators. Although the difference between the activism of the two groups is only statistically significant a little more than half the time over the time series,[7] the relationship between extremism and floor amending activity became more stable after the late 1980s. The difference in activism between extremists and moderates reached statistical significance in seven of the eleven Congresses since 1987, as compared to only five of fourteen Congresses between 1959 and 1987.

In the 1990s and 2000s, there is a more consistent correspondence between extremism and floor activism than in earlier periods. In the late 1970s and 1980s, as Sinclair (1989: 81) reports, highly active senators emerged from the ideological extremes, such as James Buckley (R-N.Y.), Jesse Helms (R-N.C.), Howard Metzenbaum (D-Ohio), and Edward Kennedy (D-Mass.), as well as from the ideological center, such as Robert Packwood (R-Ore.), Daniel Patrick Moynihan (D-N.Y.), and John Melcher (D-Mont.). By comparison, there are fewer highly active moderates in the 1990s and 2000s. Notable floor activists of the recent era included liberal stalwarts Tom Harkin (D-Iowa), Russ Feingold (D-Wis.), and Paul Wellstone (D-Minn.). Helms and Kennedy maintained a consistently high level of floor amending activity throughout their careers, remaining prominent through the 1990s and into the 2000s. In the 110th Congress, hard-line conservatives Jim DeMint (R-S.C.) and Tom Coburn (R-Okla.) set a remarkable standard, each securing at least thirty-four recorded votes on amendments they sponsored.

Contemporary Senate moderates are disproportionately represented among senators who engage in little or no floor activism. For example, Sen. Jim Jeffords (Vt.), whose party switch in 2001 transferred Senate control from the Republican to the Democratic Party, offered no floor amendments between 2001 and 2007. Sen. Ben Nighthorse Campbell (Colo.), another moderate party switcher, offered a single floor amendment across five Congresses of Senate service between 1995 and 2004. With fourteen Congresses of service between them, moderates Lincoln Chafee (D-R.I.), Ben Nelson (D-Neb.), and Tim Johnson (D-S.D.) collectively offered a grand total of ten amendments between 1991 and 2008. This is not to deny that there are

---

6. Data on party medians for the 86th–110th Congresses downloaded from the website graciously maintained by Keith T. Poole and Howard Rosenthal, www.voteview.com.

7. Statistical significance in this case was assessed by simple t-tests of the difference of means.

quite a few staunch liberals and conservatives who take minimal interest in floor activism. Among these, for example, were Barbara Mikulski (D-Md.), Daniel Akaka (D-Hawaii), Bob Bennett (R-Utah), Mike Crapo (R-Idaho), and Pat Roberts (R-Kan.).

Overall, it appears that an activist style tends to be a better fit for legislators with sharply defined ideological profiles. There has not been a great deal of change over time in this regard. Throughout the 1959–2008 period, ideologues were more likely to be floor activists, and this correspondence became more pronounced in the post-Reagan era.

## The Rise of Partisan Floor Activism

Senators' floor amending activity reflects more than their own stylistic preferences and personal policy agendas. The Senate's wide-open amending process permits the minority party to systematically contest the majority party's control of the floor agenda. To the extent that Senate floor amendments are used to advance a partisan agenda, one would expect to see minority party senators offering more amendments than majority party senators. However, scholarship on the Senate of the 1960s, 1970s, and 1980s did not find floor activism to be distinctively partisan. Although minority party senators have always been fully empowered under Senate rules to use the floor amendment process to advance a partisan message, majority party senators themselves frequently sponsor floor amendments for their own purposes. As a result, Senate scholarship has tended to characterize the floor amending process as an arena in which individual senators wield influence (Sinclair 1989; Smith 1989) rather than as a battlefield for "party wars" (Sinclair 2006).

Figure 6.5 displays the difference between the average number of floor amendments offered by majority and minority party senators over the 1959–2008 period. The figure reveals a striking rise in partisan floor activism since the start of the Reagan presidency. Although minority party senators almost always offered more amendments than majority party senators over the entire time period, the relationship was only statistically significant in one Congress between 1959 and 1979. Since 1980, however, the difference between the level of majority and minority party amending activity is statistically significant for every Congress except the 107th. (The 107th Congress, it should be noted, was distinguished not only by the majority's one-vote margin of control, but also by the switch of party control as a result of the Jeffords defection.) Furthermore, the differential between majority and minority activity has widened. Despite some variation, minority party senators have engaged in progressively more floor activism relative to their majority party counterparts.

This means that the Senate floor has become more partisan, not just in terms of voting alignments, but also in the types of amendments being

**Figure 6.5**   Amending Activity of Majority and Minority Party
Senators, 1959–2008

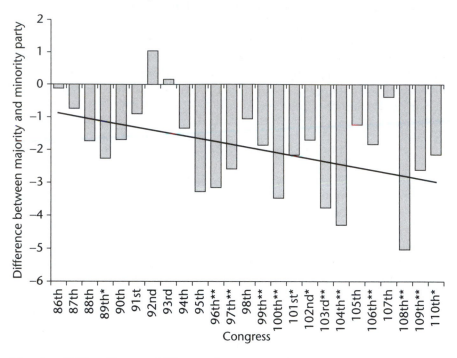

Note: *$p<.05$; **$p<.01$, t-test of difference of means.

considered. To a much greater extent than in the past, legislative initiatives brought to the Senate floor come under a barrage of amendments
sponsored by members of the minority party. At the same time, members
of the majority party appear to exercise more self-restraint in offering
amendments. While overall levels of amendments have remained generally
stable over the two most recent decades (see Figure 6.1), minority party
senators have stepped up their amending activity, while majority party
senators have reduced theirs. The result is apparent in Figure 6.6, which
displays the share of all floor amendments offered by majority and minority
party senators.

Figure 6.6 reveals that a solid majority of floor amendments considered
in the contemporary Senate are offered by minority party senators. Even
though there are obviously fewer senators affiliating with the minority party,
amendments sponsored by members of the minority party have made up on
average 60 percent of all floor amendments receiving roll call votes since
1987. In the 108th Congress, minority party amendments constituted more

**Figure 6.6**  Share of Floor Amendments Receiving Roll Call Votes, by Party, 1959–2008

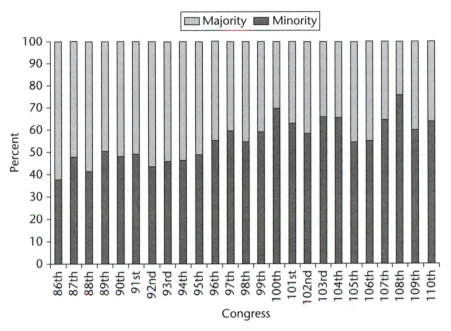

than three-quarters (75.4 percent) of all amendments receiving recorded votes. This pattern represents a sharp departure from the 1960s and 1970s. During the earlier period, the majority of floor amendments were offered by majority party senators. In the 86th Congress, for example, not even 40 percent of contested amendments were offered by minority party senators. But since the 95th Congress (1977–78), minority party senators have always offered a larger share of contested floor amendments.

Although Senate rules have not been altered, the contemporary minority party uses the Senate floor to much greater effect than in the past. In the 1960s and 1970s, amending activity on the Senate floor did not have a strong partisan edge. Today's Senate minority party heavily exploits the chamber's open amending process to vent its objections. Indeed, minority party senators often offer floor amendments as part of coordinated "amending marathons" (Sinclair 2000) designed to obstruct or discredit the majority party's legislative agenda.

To illustrate how differently floor amending unfolds in the contemporary Senate relative to that of the 1970s, consider floor action on two important presidential initiatives. In 1979 President Jimmy Carter proposed a "windfall profits tax" to capture some of the increased profits that would flow to domestic oil producers once oil price controls were lifted with the implementation of the 1975 Energy Policy and Conservation Act. In 2003 President George W. Bush proposed a new prescription drug benefit for seniors on Medicare in an effort to deliver on one of the central promises of his 2000 election campaign. In both cases, the president enjoyed unified party control of Congress. Both proposals were complex, highly salient initiatives subject to large-scale lobbying efforts, and both created substantial divisions within the president's party.

The windfall profits tax was one of Carter's top legislative priorities and a popular idea with a public suffering from energy shortages and outraged by record oil industry profits. Over the course of a month of floor consideration in November and December 1979, the Senate considered thirty-five amendments to the bill, twenty-two of which were sponsored by senators of the majority party. Divisions in the Democratic Party played out openly on the Senate floor as the bill came under attack by oil-state senators, liberals, conservatives, and moderates. Individual senators showed no hesitation to use the bill as a vehicle for varied ideological, policy, and parochial purposes. Sen. David Boren (D-Okla.) offered an unsuccessful amendment to reduce the tax rate. Sen. Lloyd Bentsen (D-Texas) sponsored a successful amendment to exempt independent producers from the tax. Sen. Warren Magnuson (D-Wash.), chair of the Appropriations Committee, led a successful effort to abolish the transportation and low-income fuel assistance trust funds that the administration supported. Sen. George McGovern (D-S.D.) secured $1 billion for railroad improvements from revenues generated by the tax. Sen. Howard Metzenbaum (D-Ohio) offered an amendment that would make the new tax permanent. Sen. Daniel Patrick Moynihan (D-N.Y.) sought to delay the phase-out of the tax. Senator Patrick Leahy (D-Vt.) offered an amendment that would cap independent producers' depletion allowance. The list goes on.

Many of these Democrat-sponsored amendments dealt with contentious matters, exposing rifts in the majority party in the full light of public floor debate and recorded votes. All of this intra-Democratic amending activity unfolded before an alliance of conservative Democrats and Republicans launched a filibuster in mid-December. After protracted negotiations and three unsuccessful cloture attempts, a compromise was reached; however, final passage was delayed by further amending efforts on the part of both majority and minority party senators after cloture had been obtained. Thirteen amendments in all were successful, and the bill originally reported from the Finance Committee had been substantially modified before Senate passage on December 17.

Like Carter's windfall profits tax, President Bush's Medicare prescription drugs initiative was a test of a majority party's ability to deliver on its promises. Prescription drugs costs had become a much more significant component of seniors' health care costs since the 1960s, but Medicare had not been revised to offer any coverage of out-patient prescription drugs. Despite the popularity of the proposal with the broad public, the policy was the subject of significant controversy within the Republican Party, with many conservatives objecting to the idea of adding a new entitlement benefit to a Great Society social welfare program. Fiscal conservatives feared that program costs might balloon with the retirement of the Baby Boomer generation. House passage of the bill would prove to be a heavy lift because of conservative opposition.

In addition to these ideological disputes and fiscal concerns, the bill's policy complexity afforded ample opportunity for individual issue entrepreneurs. There were many controversial questions to be resolved, such as how to structure incentives to ensure that private health plans participated, whether to impose higher premiums for high income beneficiaries, how to guarantee the availability of private plans in all parts of the country, whether the federal government could negotiate with pharmaceutical companies to lower drug prices, and what funding levels to grant hospitals and other providers in rural areas, among others. Given all these issues, senators had many grounds on which they might offer floor amendments. Individual senators could make use of this high salience bill to raise their personal visibility, to forge ties with constituents or organized interests, to force debate on important matters, and to shape the legislation on the Senate floor.

The Senate took up the Medicare prescription drug bill on June 27, 2003, with a negotiated committee substitute supported by both Finance Committee chair Chuck Grassley (R-Iowa) and ranking minority member Max Baucus (D-Mont.). After the committee substitute was adopted, the bill was then subject to thirty-two amendments, twenty-seven proposed by minority party Democrats and only five by Republicans. Twenty-three of the Democratic amendments sought to make the benefits more generous by reducing co-payments, lowering deductibles, and providing more comprehensive coverage; another Democratic amendment would have permitted re-importation of prescription drugs from Canada. In other words, Democratic amendments centered on only a small slice of the policy issues under consideration. But taken together, the amendments they sponsored allowed Democrats to advance a single, coherent, collective message: that Republicans were stingy with benefits for seniors. Only a single Democratic amendment, proposed by Sen. Diane Feinstein (D-Calif.), contradicted this Democratic message by proposing a means test for the benefit. Meanwhile, four of the six Republican amendments were entirely uncontroversial proposals both within the Republican Party and the chamber as a whole. One of the two controversial amendments, offered by Sen. Jeff Sessions (R-Ala.), dealt with benefits for legal immigrants under Medicaid and the State Children's Health Insurance Program, a matter not central to the Medicare prescription drug debate.

There was only one Republican-sponsored amendment considered during Senate floor debate on the Medicare prescription drugs benefit that spoke to the divisions within the Republican Party about a new government entitlement program. Sen. Chuck Hagel (R-Neb.) proposed to replace the large-scale reform with a modest prescription drug discount and some special assistance for seniors with low incomes or catastrophic drug costs. According to Sen. John Ensign (R-Nev.), who spoke on its behalf, the amendment only received "20-30 minutes' worth of debate."[8] Although the Hagel amendment garnered support from twenty other Republicans, the fact that his was the only amendment registering any significant intraparty dispute on the important question of entitlement expansion suggests a great deal of restraint on his part, as well as among other Republicans who shared Hagel's concerns about the long-term cost of this new federal government commitment.

Compared to the full flowering of 1970s Senate individualism on display in the consideration of Carter's windfall profits tax, Senate individualism was in short supply during the 2003 debate over the Medicare prescription drug benefit. Although the bill's wide-ranging and controversial effects would seemingly have presented many opportunities for individual senators to raise questions and force debate, there was limited amending activity, especially among Republicans. The amendments proposed by senators of both parties largely seemed to serve partisan, not individual purposes.

These two examples reflect the broad patterns in the aggregate data. In the 1970s, there was no statistically significant difference in the number of amendments offered by majority and minority party senators. Majority party Democrats in the 1960s and 1970s did not hesitate to bring up and force open floor votes on controversial issues that divided the party internally. In the post-Reagan era, Senate parties appear to handle more of their disputes internally. Majority party senators force fewer votes on the floor than their minority counterparts. Meanwhile, the Senate minority party uses floor amendments to launch sustained attacks on the majority's legislative initiatives. In short, floor activism appears to have become more of an arena for partisan combat than for individual entrepreneurship.

## Accounting for the Trends

These post-1970s changes in Senate behavior have occurred even though many of the factors that facilitated the growing activism of individual senators remain as powerful as ever. The individualism that characterized the

---

8. *Congressional Record*, 108th Cong., 1st sess., June 26, 2003, S8672–S8673.

Senate of the 1970s and early 1980s developed in the context of more intense national media scrutiny and an expanding universe of contentious political issues (Sinclair 1989). In addition, senators of the 1970s were empowered to take more individual initiative because they enjoyed far more personal staff resources than senators of the 1950s and 1960s (Sundquist 1981: 402–414). Given their new resources and opportunities, more senators could aspire to command media coverage, to drive national policy agendas, and to lead a national constituency.

The new issues that swelled the national political agenda during the 1970s—such as the environment; abortion; consumer protection; and rights for women, the disabled, Latinos, and immigrants—did not disappear from the agenda during the 1990s and 2000s. The size and scope of the federal government did not diminish, whether measured by spending or regulatory activity. The business community that mobilized during the 1970s remained on the scene. As gauged by the number of lobbyists and the amount of money spent on lobbying, the size of the Washington policy community continued to mushroom.[9] The issues before the contemporary Congress are no less multifarious and contentious as those in the 1970s.

The contemporary media environment presents senators with ample means and opportunity to seek national attention. If anything, senators' ability to find an audience is even greater now than it was in the 1970s and early 1980s. C-SPAN began broadcasting Senate floor proceedings in 1986. In 1996 the Fox News Channel and MSNBC joined CNN in offering twenty-four-hour news broadcasting. Technological advances now make it easy for senators to send messages to constituencies outside the Senate. Official Senate websites, along with Twitter and Facebook, enable senators to communicate instantly to external audiences. An activist senator can offer a floor amendment and make a speech, and then immediately make a video clip or text available to constituents, advocacy organizations, and local or national media outlets. Senators' personal staff resources have not declined over the past thirty-plus years.[10] Taken together, the contemporary Senate remains an unparalleled platform for individual political ambition. There has certainly been no shortage of senators aspiring to the presidency since the 1970s.

All these considerations would point to a level of Senate individualism at least equal to that of the 1970s. But earlier accounts of changing Senate behavior were unable to assess an additional factor that probably contributed to the explosion of individual issue entrepreneurship on the Senate floor during that era: a perception among both minority and majority party

---

9. See the lobbying database maintained by the Center for Responsive Politics at http://www.opensecrets.org/lobby/.

10. See Table 5-1 in Norman Orstein, Thomas Mann, and Michael Malbin (2008: 110).

senators that control of the chamber was not in doubt. Once the Senate entered an era of tight competition over majority status, the undisciplined individualism of the 1970s began to be reined in, even while many of the other factors that encourage senators to adopt an activist style remained in force.

When floor activism was at its peak in the late 1970s, Democrats had controlled the Senate for eight straight Congresses and for forty-two of the preceding forty-six years. By contrast, party control of the Senate shifted seven times between 1980 and 2010, with Democrats in the majority for six Congresses and Republicans in the majority for eight.

It is easy to see how individual senators of the 1970s might have evaluated the risks and rewards associated with rampant activism differently than they do in the 1990s and 2000s. In the 1970s it might well have appeared that there was little senators could do as individuals to affect party control of the body one way or another. Under such circumstances, senior Democrats could view their chairs as secure entitlements; junior Democrats could enjoy the perquisites of majority status with little fear of their loss. Minority party Republicans were free to choose whatever style better suited their individual goals: policy influence through bipartisan cooperation or voice through protest and criticism. On both sides, if forcing a vote on a controversial matter could help a 1970s senator gain visibility or have a desired effect on public policy, what was the potential downside of doing so? Such freewheeling activism might make one's party look ineffective or embarrass its leadership, but politicians who could not remember a time when Democrats did not control the Senate could easily take Democratic majorities for granted. Offering attention-grabbing amendments that could win individual influence and media attention is likely to be a more attractive tactic for members in an environment where Senate control is viewed more as a fact of life than an achievable goal.

Since the 1980s, however, senators have been locked in tight competition for majority party control of the chamber. This intensely competitive environment probably affects members' calculus when they consider whether to offer floor amendments that might divide their fellow partisans, embarrass their own party leadership, or burnish their individual reputation at the expense of their party. Of course, there will be many occasions when an individual senator's policy concerns or constituency interests will take precedence or be worth the tradeoff. But the fact that the Senate majority, and all its contingent benefits, potentially hangs in the balance may well lead senators to see greater value in team cooperation. Reflecting on the impressive party unity of Republicans in the 111th Congress, Senate minority leader Mitch McConnell (R-Ky.) explained the logic succinctly: "I think the reason my members are feeling really good is they believe the reward for playing team ball this year was the reversal of the political environment and the possibility that we will have a bigger team next year."[11]

Of course, there have been other important political changes that have made it easier for Senate partisans to cooperate with one another. In particular, regional and ideological realignments since the 1970s have made the two parties more internally homogeneous and more distinct from one another in ideological terms (see Chapter 2 in this volume). The Senate of the 2000s contains few moderate Republicans or conservative Democrats. But the greater ideological homogeneity of Senate parties cannot fully account for the shifts in floor amending activity documented here. Although it is undoubtedly easier today for majority party–controlled committees to craft legislation that will be acceptable to majority party senators, shared ideology does not settle the many diverse political and policy questions that can allow an individual senator to cut a figure in Senate floor debate. To return to the 1979 windfall oil profits tax example, liberal Democrats took many opportunities to offer their own favored policy alternatives during this debate. Even though liberals agreed among themselves that an oil profits tax was desirable, it could take many different forms, generate revenue for different policy purposes, apply for different lengths of time, or to different types of producers. Ideology alone doesn't resolve such questions. Regardless of ideology, a senator seeking policy influence and media attention can find many points to distinguish himself or herself as an individual during floor debate, especially if unconcerned about how activism might make life difficult for the leaders or affect the party's image as a whole.

Individual senators who want to display their own policy ideas and to differentiate themselves as individual lawmakers in the public eye can use the Senate floor to seek a spotlight for themselves in the current era, just as in the past. What has changed since the 1970s is that senators are less aggressive in doing so. To a greater extent, majority party senators in the recent era work out their disagreements in pre-floor settings and then refrain from offering amendments on the floor. Meanwhile, the amending that occurs appears largely designed to advance partisan aims. Minority party senators are considerably more active in offering amendments, and the minority proposes a much larger share of the amendments considered on the Senate floor. Often these amendments are strategically crafted to advance a broader partisan "narrative" rather than to draw attention to minority party senators' individual concerns. This kind of team spirit probably takes at least some of its roots in senators' perception of the possibility for team rewards.

---

11. Quoted in Carl Hulse and Adam Nagourney (2010).

# Implications

> The Senate of the 1980s should be characterized, still, as somewhere between the communitarian and individualistic modes—and still moving. Its members have not yet found an equilibrium.
>
> Richard F. Fenno (1989)

Richard Fenno was surely right to perceive the Senate of the 1980s in a state of transition. Indeed, the "slow institution" has been in a state of constant evolution since the 1960s. Examined in the broad sweep of five decades of change, the 1980s appear to be, along with the 1960s, an important turning point in Senate floor politics.

Since the 1970s, the Senate floor has become a markedly less active policymaking arena. The typical senator of the 1990s and 2000s proposes considerably fewer contested amendments on the Senate floor than the typical senator of thirty years' before. Furthermore, patterns in floor amending activity have taken a sharply partisan tilt, as minority party senators now dominate the floor amending process, while majority party senators make fewer efforts to revisit legislative proposals developed in pre-floor settings. Compared to the 1970s, floor debate seems designed more to advance partisan purposes than individual senators' personal objectives.

These developments have implications for Senate leadership and for the role of individual member action. As David Mayhew (2008) writes, "exceptionally strong political parties are probably not good news for the realm of member action. For the American public sphere to function as it has traditionally done . . . members need to perform as individuals, and the public needs to be able to witness them performing as individuals" (264). If senators are using floor amendments to convey partisan messages—one team opposed to the other—then the Senate floor has become less of a public sphere in which senators perform as individuals.

For many senators in the contemporary Congress, floor activism may be less a function of their personal stylistic choice than of their majority or minority party status. More systematic investigation is needed to ascertain precisely how shifts in party control affect individual senators' involvement in floor amending activity. Nevertheless, even an impressionistic look at the most active senators over recent Congresses reveals a lot of variability depending on party control. Rather than maintaining a consistent level of floor activism as part of a distinctive Hill style—like Helms and Kennedy over long decades of service—many senators now leap into action as partisan foot soldiers when their party is in the minority, while falling into relative quiescence when in the majority. Some contemporary senators—such as DeMint or Feingold—maintain an activist style that transcends transitions from majority to minority status. But these senators' individualism stands out in a Senate where parties are demarcated not just by voting behavior but by the nature of the amendments on which votes are taken.

These post-1980s shifts in the way senators use floor amendments also have implications for Senate leadership. Contemporary Senate leaders appear to enjoy more cooperation from their co-partisans. Majority party senators have been more willing to "go along with the team" by offering fewer troublesome amendments on the Senate floor. This undoubtedly aids the majority party in presenting a unified message to the public, as majority party senators increasingly refrain from forcing votes on issues that expose internal party divisions.

Even so, as difficult as it was for Majority Leader Byrd to contain the fractious, individualistic senators of his era, his job was probably easier than the contemporary Senate majority leader's. A majority leader in the Senate of the 1990s and 2000s must do more than coordinate his fellow partisans, he must then face down a party opposition determined to deploy all the Senate's expansive prerogatives in concerted efforts to embarrass the majority and frustrate its aims.

In the face of these difficulties, contemporary Senate leaders have been more aggressive in attempting to control floor proceedings. They often seek cloture before encountering any specific problems with extended debate in order to ensure that amendments will be germane (Evans and Oleszek 2002; Oleszek 2007). They have also developed a variety of creative, albeit cumbersome, procedural techniques to limit amending activity (Beth et al. 2009; Schiller 2000). The Senate majority leader's arsenal remains limited, however, and such devices have been entirely insufficient to reverse an increasing ability of the minority party to dominate floor debate by forcing votes on amendments. Whatever leverage Senate majority leaders gain by virtue of procedural mechanisms or through the process of bargaining over unanimous consent agreements (Ainsworth and Flathman 1995; Smith and Flathman 1989), the Senate majority party nevertheless has found that it must devote a significantly greater share of floor time to considering amendments sponsored by the minority party, a reality that has made the difficult task of leading the Senate even more onerous.

# References

Ainsworth, Scott, and Marcus Flathman. 1995. "Unanimous Consent Agreements as Leadership Tools." *Legislative Studies Quarterly* 20: 177–195.

Baker, Ross K. 1991. "Mike Mansfield and the Birth of the Modern Senate." In Richard A. Barker and Roger H. Davidson, eds., *First among Equals: Outstanding Senate Leaders of the Twentieth Century*. Washington, D.C.: CQ Press.

Beth, Richard S., Valerie Heitshusen, Bill Heniff Jr., and Elizabeth Rybicki. 2009. "Leadership Tools for Managing the U.S. Senate." Paper presented at the annual meeting of the American Political Science Association, September 3–6, Toronto.

Clark, Joseph S., and Other Senators. 1963. *The Senate Establishment*. New York: Hill and Wang.

Cohen, Richard E. 1977. "Byrd of West Virginia—A New Job, A New Image." *National Journal*, August 20.

Ehrenhalt, Alan. 1982. "In the Senate of the '80s, Team Spirit Has Given Way to the Rule of Individuals." *Congressional Quarterly Weekly Report*, September 4, 2175–2182.

Evans, C. Lawrence, and Walter J. Oleszek. 2002. "Message Politics and Senate Procedure." In Colton C. Campbell and Nicol C. Rae, eds., *The Contentious Senate: Partisanship, Ideology, and the Myth of Cool Judgment*. New York: Rowman and Littlefield.

Fenno, Richard F., Jr. 1989. "The Senate through the Looking Glass: The Debate over Television." *Legislative Studies Quarterly* 14: 313–348.

Foley, Michael. 1980. *The New Senate: Liberal Influence on a Conservative Institution, 1959–1972*. New Haven, Conn.: Yale University Press.

Huitt, Ralph K. 1961. "The Outsider in the Senate: An Alternative Role." *American Political Science Review* 55: 566–575.

Hulse, Carl, and Adam Nagourney. 2010. "Senate G.O.P. Leader Finds Weapon in Unity." *New York Times*, A1.

Lee, Frances E. 2009. *Beyond Ideology: Politics, Principles and Partisanship in the U.S. Senate*. Chicago: University of Chicago Press.

Loomis, Burdett. 1988. *The New American Politician: Ambition, Entrepreneurship, and the Changing Face of Political Life*. New York: Basic Books.

Matthews, Donald. 1960. *U.S. Senators and Their World*. Chapel Hill: University of North Carolina Press.

Mayhew, David R. 2008. *Parties and Policies: How the American Government Works*. New Haven, Conn.: Yale University Press.

Oleszek, Walter J. 2007. *Congressional Procedures and the Policy Process*. Washington, D.C.: CQ Press.

Ornstein, Norman J., Thomas E. Mann, and Michael J. Malbin. 2008. *Vital Statistics on Congress, 2008*. Washington, D.C.: Brookings Institution.

Schiller, Wendy J. 2000. "Trent Lott's New Regime: Filling the Amendment Tree to Centralize Power in the U.S. Senate." Paper presented at the annual meeting of the American Political Science Association, August 31–September 3, Washington, D.C.

Sinclair, Barbara. 1986. "Senate Styles and Senate Decision Making, 1955–1980." *Journal of Politics* 48: 877–908.

———. 1989. *The Transformation of the U. S. Senate*. Baltimore: Johns Hopkins University Press.

———. 2000. *Unorthodox Lawmaking: New Legislative Processes in the U.S. Congress*. Washington, D.C.: CQ Press.

———. 2006. *Party Wars: Polarization and the Politics of National Policy Making*. Norman: University of Oklahoma Press.

Smith, Steven. 1989. *Call to Order: Floor Politics in the House and Senate*. Washington, D.C.: Brookings Institution.

Smith, Steven S., and Marcus Flathman. 1989. "Managing the Senate Floor: Complex Unanimous Consent Agreements since the 1950s." *Legislative Studies Quarterly* 14: 349–374.

Sundquist, James L. 1981. *The Decline and Resurgence of Congress*. Washington, D.C.: Brookings Institution.

Swanson, Wayne R. 1969. "Committee Assignments and the Nonconformist Legislator: Democrats in the U.S. Senate." *American Political Science Review* 13: 84–94.

Theriault, Sean M. 2008. *Party Polarization in Congress*. New York: Cambridge University Press.

White, William S. 1957. *Citadel: The Story of the U.S. Senate*. New York: Harper and Brothers.

# 7

## The Senate Syndrome

### Steven S. Smith

The United States Senate, known for the stability of its rules, exposed its procedural fragility in the first decade of the twenty-first century. The parliamentary arms race between the parties that has unfolded in the Senate in recent decades eventually brought the Senate to the brink of chaos in 2005. Tensions had been building for years—minority obstructionism motivated majority countermoves, generated partisan incrimination, and led to more obstruction and preemptive action. In the spring of 2005, the majority leader promised to change the application of the Senate's most distinctive rule, Rule XXII, by a ruling of the presiding officer, rather than suffer more delay in acting on several judicial nominations. The minority promised to retaliate by "going nuclear"—making the Senate ungovernable by obstructing nearly all Senate action—but a small group of senators negotiated an arrangement for either the majority or the minority to follow through on their threats.

Since early 2005, majority leaders have taken steps to avoid or control debate and amending activity. The result is a Senate, long known for the flexibility and informality of its floor proceedings, that is more bound by formal rules and precedent than at any time in its history. In today's Senate, each party assumes that the other party will fully exploit its procedural options—the majority party assumes that the minority party will obstruct legislation and the minority assumes that the majority will restrict its opportunities. Leaders are expected to fully exploit the rules in the interests of their parties. The minority is quick to obstruct and the majority is quick to restrict. Senators of both parties are frustrated by what has become of their institution.

This obstruct-and-restrict syndrome is new to the Senate. This chapter is about that syndrome.

## Essential Background

The distinctive feature of Senate parliamentary procedure is the ability of a large minority of senators to block votes on most legislative matters. Consequently, the most important developments in the Senate's modern procedural history concern adaptation to, circumvention of, or reform of the super-majority requirement for cloture under Rule XXII, which requires a super-majority of senators to support a cloture motion in order to impose limits on debate and amendments. The possibility of obstructionism and the details of Rule XXII provide the foundation for much of the Senate's decision-making machinery. Exploitation of Rule XXII by minorities and majority responses have forced strategists to be far more expert in parliamentary rules and precedents; this in turn has encouraged more gamesmanship by senators and their parties and has intensified frustration with the Senate among both insiders and outsiders.

The Senate of the mid-twentieth century had settled into a fairly stable procedural pattern. The cloture rule, Rule XXII(2), was modified in 1949 to clarify that cloture may be applied to procedural motions (such as the motion to proceed), thereby making it possible to limit debate with the requisite number of votes and get a vote on a bill. In 1959 the Senate changed the majority required for cloture from two-thirds of senators duly chosen and sworn (67, when 99 or 100 seats are filled) to two-thirds of senators present and voting. The 1959 rule also explicitly provided that cloture may be applied to motions to consider changes in Senate rules. With the 1959 rule in place, the Senate enacted the major civil rights legislation of the 1960s and early 1970s. In 1975 the threshold for cloture was reduced to three-fifths of senators duly chosen and sworn, except for measures that change Senate rules, for which the threshold at two-thirds of senators present and voting was retained. The 1975 thresholds remain in place.

Rule XXII, with its cumbersome cloture process and super-majority threshold, forces floor leaders to rely on unanimous consent agreements to give some order to floor decision making. Over the years, in response to senators' demands and leaders' efforts to close loopholes, unanimous consent agreements became quite complex and required considerable attention from the floor leaders. But reliance on unanimous consent created opportunities for individual senators to delay Senate action. Holds and clearance practices emerged in tandem in the early 1970s (Smith 1989). Holds are requests to the floor leader asking that a measure not be considered on the floor. The practice became regularized in the 1970s as the leadership instituted informal clearance processes to avoid surprises on the floor. Senators found that a hold could be used to take a bill hostage for some unrelated purpose, such as to get a committee chair to commit to considering another measure.

The 1970s witnessed an increase in the use of obstructionist tactics by Senate minorities, which is reflected in the more frequent use of cloture (Figure 7.1). Several temporally overlapping and mutually reinforcing developments contributed to the emergence of the Senate's new procedural condition. First, the passing of the civil rights era of the 1960s freed conservatives, particularly southern Democrats, to use the filibuster to oppose the broader

**Figure 7.1**    Frequency of Cloture Petitions, 1961–2008

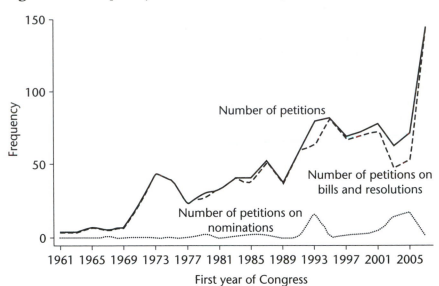

Source: U.S. Senate, available at http://www.senate.gov/pagelayout/reference/cloture_motions/clo-tureCounts.htm.

legislative agenda of the liberal majorities of the 1970s. Second, the incentives for individual senators and the minority party to exploit their procedural prerogatives amplified as the lobbying community expanded, electioneering pressures intensified, and time became scarce as the Senate agenda expanded through the 1960s and 1970s. Third, minority strategies from the House of Representatives, where minority party Republicans adopted all-out opposition strategies as standard operating procedure in the late 1980s, were adapted to the Senate as House members were elected to the Senate. Fourth, movement from a pluralistic Senate, one in which voting coalitions shifted from issue to issue, to a polarized Senate, one in which the parties are sharply divided on most issues, has encouraged elected party leaders to more aggressively use the procedural tools at their disposal (see Chapter 6).

It was in this context of intensifying obstructionism and a stronger but frustrated liberal faction within the majority Democratic conference that the Senate began to take steps to limit debate. Debate limits were adopted for budget measures as a part of the Budget Act of 1974, which was enacted in the midst of budget battles with the Nixon administration (Schick 2000). The Budget Act created expedited procedures for implementing a schedule under which budget resolutions and reconciliation measures are considered, procedures that include a fifty-hour debate limit for budget resolutions, a twenty-hour debate limit for reconciliation measures, debate limits for conference reports, and a prohibition on non-germane amendments.[1] The Budget Act created points of order to preserve the fiscal purposes of budget measures. Most notable about the enforcement mechanisms is that a point of order can be waived, or a ruling of the presiding officer overturned, only with a three-fifths majority. These mechanisms include the "Byrd rule," which provides for a point of order for violation of limits on the content of reconciliation bills.[2] Thus, for this class of legislation, the Senate not only accepted limitations on debate and amendments, but also bound itself more tightly to formal rules than it generally does.

In 1975, with a cooperative presiding officer in Vice President Nelson Rockefeller, liberals again pushed for cloture reform. Rockefeller, initially backed by a Senate majority, ruled that a simple majority could close debate on a rules resolution at the start of a Congress, creating the possibility that a simple majority could reform Rule XXII.[3] Delays in acting on the resolution caused by a variety of dilatory motions orchestrated by southerners threatened a serious rupture in the party. Majority Leader Mike Mansfield (D-Mont.), who opposed Rockefeller's ruling but favored some reform, negotiated a compromise. He persuaded conservative Democrats to accept a threshold of three-fifths of senators duly chosen and sworn (60 if 100 or 99 seats are filled) for most legislation and, in order that the conservatives would not have to fear additional reform in the foreseeable future, persuaded liberal Democrats to accept retention of the old threshold of two-thirds of senators present and voting for measures changing the Senate rules.

## The Flowering of the Polarized Senate, 1989–2000

As the parties became more polarized in the late 1980s, Senate floor leaders became more centrally involved in negotiating the details of major bills, building the required floor coalitions to pass or block legislation, and shepherding legislation through negotiations with the House. Obstruction by minority parties became more common as cohesive minorities became quite capable of blocking the majority party's agenda in most Congresses. In

---

1. The process usually takes longer than twenty hours because motions and amendments may be voted upon without debate at the end of the period, yielding what has been labeled a "vote-a-rama" as the last step in considering a budget measure.

2. For background on the Byrd rule, including a review of points of order and waivers considered under the rule, see Robert Keith (2008).

3. A motion to table the appeal of Rockefeller's ruling was adopted 51–42. A subsequent motion to table a point of order, raised by Mansfield, against a motion to consider the reform resolution was adopted 46–43.

response, majority leaders continued to innovate in their procedural strategies, but their frustration with floor proceedings intensified.

## Intensifying Obstructionism

Democrat George Mitchell (D-Maine), elected majority leader in late 1988, sought to improve relations with minority Republicans with more transparency about the schedule, a greater willingness to tolerate debate and votes on key amendments, and, perhaps as a consequence, holding fewer cloture votes (Hook 1989b). Better relations between the parties did not last. The number of cloture petitions receiving votes jumped from an average of fewer than twenty-five per Congress in the 1970s and 1980s to over fifty for the five Congresses starting in 1991 (Figure 7.1). The percentage of major measures (key vote measures; see Figure 7.2) subject to cloture had been trending upward since the 1970s and continued to ratchet upward in the 1990s.

Long before his first Congress as leader ended, Mitchell expressed exasperation with the difficulty of gaining unanimous consent to gain votes and expedite business. He struggled with colleagues who failed to inform bill managers of their intended amendments and who often were slow to come to the floor to offer amendments that they had submitted. He resorted to Monday, Friday, and long sessions to overcome obstructionism,

**Figure 7.2** Key Vote Measures Subject to Cloture Petitions, 1961–2008

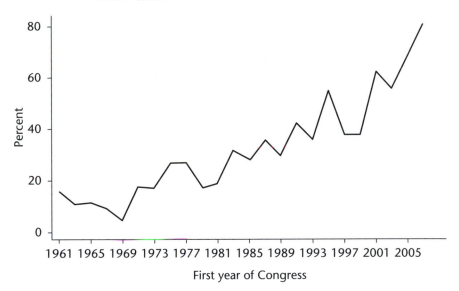

Source: *CQ Almanac*, annual editions.

and, predictably, pursued more cloture votes (Alston 1990; Hook 1989a).[4] Although it is difficult to document, it appears that Republicans deliberately resisted time agreements to slow action on the Democrats' legislative agenda. The Senate has been in procedural turmoil ever since.

The 1980s Republican minorities confronting Byrd and Mitchell made it difficult for the majority leaders to obtain unanimous consent to structure debate before a bill was brought up for consideration. After a bill made it to the floor, the leaders battled, amendment by amendment, to gain time limits on debate, which yielded a highly unpredictable, stop-and-go, floor process. By necessity, majority leaders continued the long-term trend of attempting to structure floor activity with detailed unanimous consent agreements.

Obstructionism on executive and judicial nominations contributed to inter-party tensions (see Chapter 9). Senators of both parties expanded the use of holds to block action on nominees in order to gain some leverage with the administration (Hook 1993), but, as is reflected in Figure 7.1, Republicans forced Majority Leader Mitchell to seek cloture on an unusually large number of executive branch nominees in President Bill Clinton's first two years in office (Doherty 1994; Palmer 1993). Republicans used some nominations to gain leverage on a Justice Department investigation, but others were obstructed for no publicly announced reason.

### Changing Cloture Practices

Like all leaders, Mitchell looked for ways to move legislative business while struggling with minority obstructionism. Mitchell was the first majority leader to frequently seek cloture on motions to proceed once he discovered resistance from the minority party to unanimous consent to bring up significant legislation (Hook 1990). In a few cases, Mitchell withdrew the motion to proceed once the cloture process was initiated so that the Senate could consider other matters while waiting for the cloture vote two days later. If cloture failed, Mitchell had lost little time. Cloture on the motion to proceed now is the most common motion on which to file for cloture, which reflects minority willingness to oppose legislation at every stage and, at times, the insistence of majority leaders to test the strength of the minority at the start of floor action on legislation.

In 1993, at the start of his last Congress in the Senate, Mitchell proposed reforms of Rule XXII that he hoped would be endorsed by the

---

4. In September 1989, the Senate Committee on Rules and Administration approved a resolution, sponsored by David Pryor (D-Ark.) and John Danforth (R-Mo.), to require the third reading of a bill (that is, move a bill to final passage) if fifteen minutes have passed since the disposition of the last amendment considered or the conclusion of other debate on a bill. Most Republicans, the minority party, opposed the resolution, which was not considered on the floor.

Joint Committee on the Organization of Congress. His proposals included a two-hour debate limit for motions to proceed, a three-fifths majority to overturn a ruling of the chair under cloture, counting the time for quorum calls under cloture against the senator who suggested the absence of a quorum, and allowing the Senate to go to conference with only one debatable motion. With minority Republicans opposed, the Mitchell proposals went nowhere.

Soon after the Republicans won a Senate majority in the 1994 elections, Democrats Tom Harkin (Iowa) and Joseph Lieberman (Conn.) again advanced their proposal to ratchet down the number of votes required for cloture from sixty to fifty-one over a series of votes. The proposal was defeated in a 76–19 vote that was opposed by more than half of the Democrats, including Byrd and Democratic leader Tom Daschle, who saw no need to disarm now that they were in the minority. The majority Republicans opposed reform because they distrusted the Democratic sponsors of the reform and foresaw a long filibuster over the matter that would obstruct action on their Contract with America legislation.

## New Uses for Reconciliation

The Republican majority leaders of the late 1990s and 2000s found minority obstructionism as debilitating as their Democratic predecessors did. While Republican leaders were limited to the same set of procedural tools as their predecessors, they exploited the reconciliation process, provided in the Budget Act, for the purpose of imposing the debate and amendment limitations on the consideration of tax-cut legislation. In doing so, they successfully avoided minority filibusters on measures that were high on their list of priority legislation.

The precedent for passing measures that reduce revenues as reconciliation bills was established in 1996, when a Republican majority rejected a point of order raised by Senator Daschle, then the minority leader, on a party-line vote (*Congressional Record*, 104th Cong., 2nd sess., May 21, 1996, S5419). The result was the consideration of three reconciliation bills, one a tax bill. In practice, reconciliation has been used for a wide variety of legislation, including the creation of federal nursing home standards in 1987 (Democratic congressional majorities) and the Children's Health Insurance Program in 1997 (Republican congressional majorities).[5] Tax bills taken up as reconciliation measures were vetoed by President Bill Clinton in 1999 and 2000, apparently sanctioned by the Republican-appointed parliamentarian, Bob Dove. Democrats voiced only token opposition to the use of reconciliation for tax measures in those years.

---

5. See Thomas Mann, Molly Reynolds, and Norman Ornstein (2009).

## Rising Obstructionism in a Polarized Senate, 2001–2010

As sharply partisan as the 1990s turned out to be, the Lott-Daschle battle was mere child's play in comparison with what was to come in the first decade of the twenty-first century. As Figure 7.1 shows, more bills, including more minor matters, were subject to cloture petitions and votes. At the same time, a much higher proportion of major bills felt the sting of obstructionism (Figure 7.2).[6] In the most recent years, the majority Democrats resorted to cloture for the vast majority of important measures.

The surge in obstructionism since the election of 2006, when the Democrats regained Senate and House majorities in the second midterm election of President George W. Bush, deserves special notice. Following the 2006 elections, Democrats had a small fifty-one-seat majority and lost half of the cloture votes. Republicans noted, correctly, that some of Majority Leader Harry Reid's use of cloture was intended to block non-germane amendments or to set up opportunities for filling the amendment tree (see below). But Republicans forced Reid to find sixty votes for cloture on a wide range of bills on which the parties were divided—minimum wage, 9/11 Commission recommendations, immigration reform, energy, children's health insurance, domestic intelligence, climate change, and others.

Since the Democrats regained a majority in 2006, daily floor action has resembled hand-to-hand combat. As Figure 7.3 shows, the frequency of minority objections to majority party unanimous consent (UC) requests reached a high level in the new century. The number skyrocketed in the 110th Congress (2007–08) when objections to majority party UC requests averaged more than one per day when the Senate was in session.[7] The new level of obstructionism continued into the 111th Congress (data not shown). The evidence seems to confirm the majority party complaint that they faced record levels of obstructionism. Combined with the record of cloture petitions and votes, the evidence certainly supports the claim that the Senate has reached a new plateau in the minority's exploitation of its procedural prerogatives.

Before the recent period, the majority leader, whip, or bill manager made most UC requests, and objections, if any, were made by their minority counterparts. In the first decade of the twenty-first century, objections to UC requests by rank-and-file minority party members became far more

---

6. Figure 7.2 reports the number of "key vote" measures subject to cloture petitions. *CQ Almanac* identifies 20–30 votes per Congress that Congressional Quarterly deems to be the most important votes on the most important issues. Budget measures, which are subject to debate limits, and resolutions to reform Rule XXII are excluded from the count in Figure 7.2.

7. The count in Figure 7.3 excludes objections under Rule XIV that place legislation on the Senate *Calendar*.

**Figure 7.3**    Objections to Unanimous Consent (UC) Requests, by Party of Author and Objector, 1991–2008

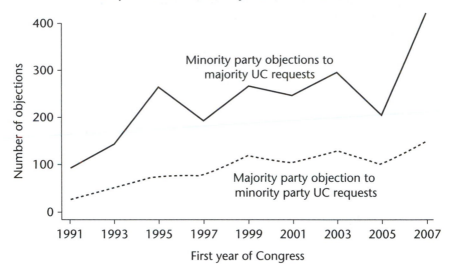

Source: *Congressional Record.*

common. Moreover, minority party members made far more UC requests, sometimes to slow down or disrupt the proceedings and often to show the unwillingness of the majority party to treat them fairly by prompting an objection to a request. At times, there have been dueling UC requests with each party trying to prove a point about the other side's partisanship. As Figure 7.3 illustrates, the result is that the minority UC requests spurred a corresponding increase in majority party objections.

The heat from inter-party friction intensified. Majority leaders complained bitterly that silent (quietly refusing clearance for bills or nominations) and overt obstructionism had reached a new level, a level that necessitated that they bring up matters on the floor without clearance—generating more objections to unanimous consent requests and more cloture petitions on bills and nominations. Minority leaders insisted that the majority party leaders had a quick trigger when it comes to filing cloture petitions and seeking unanimous consent to bring up minor bills and nominations. The frequency with which a cloture petition is withdrawn or vitiated was cited by both sides: the majority party claiming that they are calling the bluffs of an obstructionist minority effectively and the minority claiming that their willingness to let matters go forward without a cloture vote shows that they are not obstructing. To the outsider, it looked like both sides were more fully exploiting their procedural prerogatives. Among minority party senators, there seemed to be fewer and fewer dissenters to obstructionism; among majority party senators, there seemed to be fewer dissenters to procedural manipulations by the majority leader.[8]

Cloture petitions and objections to UC requests are like a geologic history. They are the formal record of more complicated interaction between the majority and minority parties, much of which does not get recorded. The need to create some kind of a schedule forces the majority leader to check with the minority leader on a regular basis. When the minority leader reports that there is a hold on his side or that he is not receiving timely responses from his party colleagues, the majority leader must either delay action on some matters or risk objection to a UC request to bring up a bill on the floor. These informal interactions and the record of cloture petitions and objections to UC requests reflects the expansive use of obstructionist strategy on the part of the minority party in response to the majority party agenda.

## Reconciliation Revisited

Republicans began the decade by using reconciliation for large tax measures proposed by the Bush administration, which would allow them to avoid a filibuster on the top legislative item on their agenda. At Byrd's urging, the Democrats did not raise a point of order against the use of reconciliation again in 2001 so as to avoid reinforcing the 1996 precedent. Confusing matters, the parliamentarian, Bob Dove, appeared to change his views about whether revenue-cutting bills could be treated as reconciliation measures under the Budget Act (Taylor 2001a), which created tensions between the Republican leadership and "their" parliamentarian. Although there was precedent for such a move, the Democrats objected and argued that the reconciliation process was intended to balance in *one* bill the spending and revenue decisions to be made before the start of a new fiscal year. With the Senate split 50–50 between the parties and the Republican vice president

8. A curiosity: In early 2001, before James Jeffords (Vt.) changed parties in late May to give the Democrats a Senate majority, Republicans had to struggle with the implications of the 50–50 split. One consequence was giving up the majority's longstanding reliance on motions to table to expeditiously dispose of minority amendments. Because a 50–50 tie would defeat a motion to table, Vice President Richard Cheney would have had to be present whenever the Republicans wanted to use motions to table to defeat unfriendly amendments. To spare him the need to be available to preside at all times, the Republicans simply voted directly on the amendments, although this meant tolerating more debate on the amendments than would happen with use of the non-debatable motion to table (Parks 2001). It also is noteworthy that a direct vote on an amendment may create more of a political problem for a senator than the procedural motion to table. In this case, however, forcing the vice president to cast a vote on popular Democratic amendments may have caused more political problems for the Republicans.

giving the Republicans official majority status, the Republicans authorized separate reconciliation bills for tax cuts in the budget resolution (the key vote was 51–49, with one Democrat, Georgia's Zell Miller, voting with the Republicans).

The reconciliation process was used for tax legislation again in 2003. An important feature of the 2003 episode was a Senate Republican effort to authorize oil drilling in the Alaskan National Wildlife Refuge (ANWR) through budget measures. Drilling in ANWR would have been defeated in legislation that could be filibustered, as it was on a cloture vote in 2002. The Republicans included in the 2003 budget resolution a separate provision that assumed future revenue from oil and gas leases. If approved, the provision would have allowed ANWR drilling provisions to be included in a subsequent reconciliation bill, also subject to debate limitations. An amendment to strip the provision from the resolution was approved with the support of Democrats and a handful Republicans (Goldreich 2003).[9]

## Nuclear Option

The most spectacular procedural episode of the recent period was the 2003–2005 confrontation over judicial nominations. By the spring of 2003, Republicans had become deeply frustrated with Democrats' obstruction on several judicial nominations (see Figure 7.1) and anticipated having the same problem with a Supreme Court nomination in the near future. Majority Leader Bill Frist proposed use of a mechanism similar to the one proposed by Harkin and Lieberman a decade earlier but applied only to presidential nominations. Not all Republicans were supportive of the proposal, with some of them wondering about the possibilities of future minority status, but Republicans were beginning to recite Democratic constitutional arguments from earlier decades about the right of a simple majority to change the Senate rules, at least at the start of a Congress. Frist's proposal was not considered on the floor, but the proposal stimulated a very sharp exchange of words between the parties, with senators of both parties indicating a willingness to go to any length to get their way (Stevens and Perine 2003). The term "nuclear option" was invented by Trent Lott (R-Miss.), then chair of the Committee on Rules and Administration, to describe a scenario in which the Republicans gain a new cloture threshold through a ruling of the chair (Vice President Richard Cheney) backed by a simple-majority motion to table an appeal. Lott's nuclear reference was to

---

9. With no Republican votes, Democrats approved a contingent use of reconciliation in the 2009 budget resolution so that reconciliation was authorized for health care reform legislation if the Senate failed to pass the regular legislation by a specified date. Democrats did not avail themselves of the opportunity to do so.

the possibility of massive obstructionism by the Democrats in response, which some Republicans doubted would follow.

In early 2005, when the confirmations of several appeals court nominees were being blocked by the Democrats, Republicans shifted arguments but again threatened the "reform-by-ruling" option. By that time, the Senate was divided 55–45 in favor of the Republicans. Frist and many Republicans called their possible procedural move the "constitutional option" and insisted that the Constitution's "advise and consent" provision required the Senate to vote up or down on every judicial nomination.[10] This was a dubious argument (see Binder, Madonna, and Smith 2007), but Republicans found it to be a credible basis for a ruling of the chair that would allow cloture by a simple majority on judicial nominations. As Frist's May deadline for breaking the impasse approached, fourteen senators—seven Democrats and seven Republicans—announced their intention to both oppose a constitutional option (thereby creating a majority in favor of an appeal) and support Senate action on some of the nominations in dispute (thereby creating more than sixty votes for cloture). The "Gang of 14" announcement diffused the situation and the senators in both sides backed away from the precipice. Frist appeared to be frustrated with the way the Gang of 14 pulled him away from triggering the nuclear option.[11]

## The Syndrome Takes Hold: Filling the Amendment Tree

Majority leaders have pursued old procedural tactics more frequently in their efforts to influence outcomes. One such tactic is filling the amendment tree. Due to the precedent that gives the majority leader the right to be recognized before other senators, the majority leader may offer a sequence of amendments to exhaust the amendments that may be pending at one time. The result is that no other amendment may be offered while the majority leader's amendments are pending or he or she seeks to offer another amendment. When combined with cloture, which sets a limit for debate and a time for a passage vote, this tactic can prevent amendments unfriendly to the majority leader's cause from being considered.[12]

---

10. The term, "constitutional option," was borrowed from a law review article written by a former Senate Republican leadership aide (Gold and Gupta 2005).

11. The technical feasibility of the reform-by-ruling strategy did not seem to be in doubt, but it would have represented the most radical use of the strategy and involved a constitutional ruling by the presiding officer, a matter usually left for the Senate to decide.

12. Without cloture, the majority leader's opposition can simply delay action on a bill until they have an opportunity to offer amendments, which may force the majority leader to take the bill off the floor. The impasse created by filling the amendment tree has sometimes created an opportunity for the parties to attract votes, perhaps to win a cloture vote, or to negotiate a compromise on the associated issues.

Senate majority leaders have filled the amendment tree with greater frequency in recent Congresses (Taylor 2000a, 2000b, 2000c; Beth et al. 2009). Partisan arguments became particularly intense in 1999 and 2000, when Majority Leader Lott appeared to fill the amendment tree to avoid votes on politically sensitive issues. He learned that the practice encourages the minority party to oppose cloture so that filling a tree does not cut off minority opportunities for amendments altogether and extends the length of time required to take action on bills. The uproar over Lott's practices led him to announce a change as that Congress ended. The issue remained so sensitive that the "power-sharing" agreement between the parties for the period in which each party had fifty members in 2001 included a provision that neither party leader would fill the amendment tree (Taylor 2001a). Lott's successor, Democrat Tom Daschle, disavowed the practice, but used it once.

Daschle's successors, Frist and Reid, used the technique many times, usually by carefully pairing it with cloture.[13] Reid observed in the summer of 2005 that Majority Leader Frist began, uncharacteristically, to fill the amendment tree following the nuclear option episode.

## The Syndrome Intensifies: Place-Holding Amendments

The floor amendment process has changed in a fundamental way in recent Congresses. It has become common for a majority leader or bill manager, using their right to be recognized first, to offer a first-degree amendment to a bill and leave the amendment pending. Another senator seeking to offer amendment must gain unanimous consent to temporarily set aside the pending amendment, which gives the floor leader or bill manager the opportunity to object to the consideration of the amendment. This tactic gives the majority leader some leverage with colleagues who want to offer or vote for amendment, and to do so at a convenient time, in negotiating a unanimous consent agreement to structure the amendment process. Senators regularly complain that they cannot get their amendments considered.

At some point, of course, the Senate must dispose of the place-holding amendment and create an opportunity for other amendments to be considered. By that time, the floor leadership hopes, a unanimous consent agreement can be negotiated to manage remaining amendments or cloture can be invoked. If a unanimous consent agreement can be negotiated, a sixty-vote threshold for an amendment guarantees the amendment sponsor a vote but,

---

13. In 2007 frustration with filling amendment trees motivated Republican senators Arlen Specter (Penn.) and Tom Coburn (Okla.) to introduce a resolution to prohibit a senator from offering a second degree amendment to his or her own first degree amendment. Specter's floor statement provides a useful summary of many senators' complaints about "abusive procedural actions taken by both Republican and Democratic majority leaders" (*Congressional Record*, 110th Cong., 2nd sess., September 24, 2008, S9378).

for the bill manager, effectively removes the threat of the adoption of the amendment. If cloture can be invoked, the thirty-hour debate limit, the rule limiting senators to two amendments, and the possibility of filling the amendment tree give the majority leader even more bargaining leverage with amendment sponsors.

One consequence of the place-holding amendment strategy is that there is less need to exploit the motion to table an amendment. As Figure 7.4 shows, motions to table have been used far less frequently in recent Congresses. With more amendments considered with the approval of the majority leadership or bill manager until a unanimous consent agreement is achieved or cloture is invoked, the efficiencies gained by quick, non-debatable motions to table are not as important.

It bears observing that the majority party's amendment tactics have motivated minority party members to insist that they will more resolutely obstruct the majority. The majority party surely takes that threat into account. In the highly polarized context of recent Congresses, the majority leadership may correctly predict that no additional votes for cloture are lost by this pre-cloture strategy. It is noteworthy that majority party members express frustration with this strategy, too, but, in most circumstances, they seem tolerant of an approach that suits the collective interests of their party.

## Sixty-Vote Thresholds in Unanimous Consent Agreements

Perhaps the most curious procedural development in the Senate in the 109th and 110th Congresses (2005–2008) is Frist's and Reid's inclusion of sixty-vote thresholds for votes on motions under unanimous consent agreements.[14] This became a near-standard feature of Reid unanimous consent requests for major legislation. The approach, essentially new to recent Congresses, provides that a motion or an amendment is considered adopted if supported by at least sixty senators; in most cases, the subject of the provision is an amendment, which is considered withdrawn if the sixty-vote threshold is not reached. The effect of such a provision is to force motion or amendment proponents to demonstrate sufficient votes for cloture without taking the time for a three-day process of filing a cloture petition, voting on cloture, and completing thirty hours of debate. When applied to amendments, most of the amendments failed to achieve the required sixty votes (Beth et al. 2009).

The rationale for the sixty-vote threshold in unanimous consent agreements is seldom articulated, but some inferences about the tradeoffs are reasonable. The majority leader gets a quick vote on an amendment without

14. A few, but very few, precedents have been found in previous congresses. Richard Beth and colleagues (2009) find nine votes under the terms of such a unanimous consent agreement in the 109th Congress and a surge to fifty-one such votes in the 110th Congress.

**Figure 7.4**   Disposition of Senate Floor Amendments Subject to a
Recorded Vote, 1991–2008

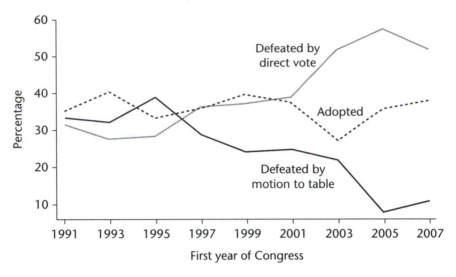

Source: Senate vote record.

suffering a filibuster (on the amendment or the bill), which expedites action
on the legislation. In fact, most of the recent bills were high priority legislation with substantial time sensitivity for the majority leader (Beth et al.
2009). Naturally, for senators who oppose the amendment, primarily majority party members, the sixty-vote threshold is no problem. For senators who
support the amendment, the unanimous consent agreement must offer
some advantage, too. They, too, may favor expeditious action on important
legislation but appreciate that the majority is not imposing cloture, filling
the amendment tree to avoid votes on the amendment, and allowing senators to vote on the record (as opposed to facing a motion to table). Still, like
the practice of holds, it is reasonable to speculate the frequency with which
Reid uses the sixty-vote threshold may alter senators' expectations about
the management of amendments.

## Holds

When Trent Lott resigned as majority leader in late 2002, he remained
frustrated with the practice of holds and, after taking over as chair of the
Committee on Rules and Administration in 2003, conducted a hearing on
reform proposals. The proposal, offered by Charles Grassley (R-Iowa)
and Ron Wyden (D-Ore.), would mention holds in the standing rules (and
precedents, for that matter) for the first time, but Grassley, Wyden, and
Lott deemed this necessary to deal with a troublesome practice that more

than a quarter century of complaints had not changed. By the time Lott's hearings took place, senators realized that holds reflected the leadership's need to be observed and held confidential, and that the minority leader sometimes used a hold as a way to obscure partisan purposes for objecting to the majority leader's plans. They also complained that some senators would continue to abuse the process. Abuses cited by senators included using a hold on one bill to gain favorable action on another matter (for example, to get a hearing on another bill or gaining a presidential nomination for a political friend), rolling holds (senators taking turns placing holds on a bill to frustrate efforts to clear a bill for floor action), and retaliatory holds (placing a hold in response to another hold).[15] To be sure, holds were often used for innocent purposes, such as getting notice in order to offer an amendment in a timely way, but Lott and others believed that the efforts of a half dozen floor leaders to limit the practice had failed.[16]

The Lott hearing produced no action on reform at that time, but a modified version was incorporated in the 2007 ethics reform bill.[17] The rule does not ban holds but rather is intended to make public the identity of senators placing holds under certain circumstances. It provides direction to majority and minority floor leaders that they recognize a "notice of intent" to object only if a senator, "following the objection to a unanimous consent to proceeding to, and, or passage of, a measure or matter on their behalf, submits the notice of intent in writing to the appropriate leader or their designee," and then "submits for inclusion in the Congressional Record and in the applicable calendar" a notice not later than six session days.

The 2007 rule establishes a convoluted process full of ambiguity, which reflects the difficulty of regulating what has been an informal, intra-party process for three decades.[18] Disclosure is not required until after objection to taking up a bill is made publicly on the floor. The identity of the senator placing the hold need not be publicly disclosed for a minimum of six days (the rule does not specify how quickly the leader must be notified in writing and when the six-day clock starts). Until actual objection is made to a unanimous consent request, the hold remains secret and a private matter between a senator and the leader, as it always had been.

Experience with the new rule is still limited. Just a few days after the 2007 bill was signed into law a Republican senator objected to a motion to

---

15. See Janet Hook (1993), Carroll Doherty (1998), Albert Eisele and JoAnn Kelly (1998), Brian Friel (2007), and Emily Pierce (2007).

16. For a review of leaders' efforts and reform proposals, see Walter Oleszek (2007). I am ignoring the practices of the Senate Committee on the Judiciary with respect to blue slips and holds on judicial nominations that are registered with the committee. See Sarah Binder and Forrest Maltzman (2009) and Betsy Palmer (2005).

17. The Honest Leadership and Open Government Act of 2007 (P.L. 110-81), Section 512.

18. For a review of ambiguities in the rules, see Walter Oleszek (2008).

proceed on a bill on which a hold was known to exist. The senator's staff insisted that he had not previously placed a secret hold and that was the end of the matter, at least for that bill (Pierce 2007). Some senators have long had a policy of disclosing their holds, but it is clear that confidential communications with leaders have not been disclosed. A majority leader would not object to his own request to bring up a bill so a hold placed by a majority party member is unlikely to yield the objection that triggers publication in the *Record*. The effect of the rule should be greatest for the minority leader, but the minority leader is seldom too concerned about the scheduling problems of the majority and, in any case, can privately discourage the majority leader from proceeding with a bill. In the 110th Congress (2007–08) and first session of the 111th Congress (2009), four notices of intent to object to proceeding were printed in the *Record*. No one believes that exhausts the holds placed on bills.[19] When President Barack Obama called for an end of holds on executive nominations in his 2010 State of the Union Address, many senators' responses were quite negative and cynical (Shanton 2010).[20]

## Avoiding Conference

Senate leaders also have become more involved in managing relations with the House. Senate leaders, who may need to overcome a filibuster to go to conference and appoint conferees, were not so quick as House leaders to manipulate the conference process, but Senate rules played a role in motivating leaders to approach negotiations with the House in new ways.[21]

---

19. In late 2009, the watchdog group Citizens for Responsibility and Ethics in Washington wrote the leadership of the Senate Committee on Ethics to investigate the enforcement of Section 512. It is noteworthy that Section 512 is directed to the floor leaders. Section 512 becomes relevant only when an objection to a unanimous consent request is voiced on the floor, but that hardly exhausts the ways in which a hold could affect floor action (see Yachnin 2009). There is some evidence that Section 512 stigmatized holds and may have reduced their frequency (Stanton 2007).

20. In early 2010, Majority Leader Harry Reid informed his colleagues that Alabama senator Richard Shelby had placed a hold on most pending executive branch nominations. An MSNBC report indicated that Shelby was unhappy that the administration was not moving to build an FBI facility in his home state (http://firstread.msnbc.msn.com/archive/2010/02/05/2195404.aspx, accessed).

21. House Democrats, it has been reported, were the first to exclude the minority from conference discussions. Republican Speaker Newt Gingrich became far more assertive by more carefully manipulating the composition of conference committees, assigning a leader to oversee the work of each conference, inserting himself in inter-cameral negotiations, successfully suggesting non-conference methods for working through House-Senate differences among Republicans, and frequently excluding Democrats from a role in the negotiations (Allen and Cochran 2003).

Minority Democratic frustrations about being excluded from a meaningful role in conference negotiations came to a head in 2003 and 2004, when Democrats said that they were shut out of meetings on Medicare reform and energy legislation, to which the House and Senate majority leaders were appointed. Democrats responded by objecting to unanimous consent requests to take other bills to conference (Allen and Cochran 2003; Cohen, Victor, and Baumann 2004; Stevens 2004). Partisan tensions were heightened in mid-2004 when Frist became the first floor leader to campaign against his opposite floor leader—Tom Daschle—in the latter's home state. Daschle lost his seat.

Objections to the usual unanimous consent requests to go to conference are potentially costly to the majority, particularly near the end of a session, because they can delay the move to conference. Three motions—a motion to disagree with the House, a motion to request a conference, and a motion to authorize the appointment of conferees—are required for the Senate to go to conference, and all three are debatable and subject to filibusters. Gaining cloture three times is time consuming, which creates an incentive for Senate majority leaders to advocate non-conference approaches to resolving House-Senate differences. Informal discussions among majority party committee and party leaders can produce either an exchange of amendments between the chambers or the incorporation of new legislative language in other bills. Frist began to pursue these alternatives more frequently.

In fact, non-conference approaches to managing inter-chamber relations have been used with increasing frequency in recent Congresses. The percentage of enacted bills sent to conference fell from thirteen in the 103rd Congress (1993–94) to nine in the 106th (1999–2000) to just two in the 110th Congress (2007–08) (Jansen 2009; Rybicki 2010). For "major" measures, the percentage of enacted legislation going through conference fell from seventy-five in the 1961–1990 period to fifty-six in the 1993–2008 period (Sinclair 2009). The stratagem of avoiding conference comes in a variety of forms. One approach is to have committee and party leaders in the two chambers coordinate their action in a way that allows a bill (or parts of bills) to be passed in both houses without the creation of differences that must be resolved through an exchange of amendments between the houses or conference. The percentage of bills managed in this way has increased from sixty-three to eighty between the 103rd and 110th Congresses and ticked up a few percentage points for major bills (Jansen 2009; Sinclair 2009).

Tensions about conferences lingered so that by the time Harry Reid was about to become majority leader after the 2006 elections he wrote the new Republican leader, Mitch McConnell, that he intended to convene "real" conference committees with minority participation (Kady 2006).[22] Of course, this is not something a Senate leader can really promise because inter-cameral processes have to be arranged with House leadership. In fact, the commitment did not last as Reid, particularly in 2008, again worked with House leadership to avoid the conference process on several important bills.

Frist and Reid went a step farther. When the majority leader fills the amendment tree in conjunction with invoking cloture on a House amendment to a Senate bill or amendment, he or she eliminates the opportunity for the opposition to offer amendments and delay a vote on the House amendment. Thus, in combination with cloture, a majority leader's use of an exchange of amendments between the houses and filling the amendment tree can streamline the process of resolving House-Senate differences and minimize the opportunities for votes on unfriendly or politically sensitive amendments. Frist appears to have been the first to fill the tree on a House amendment, doing so twice, and Reid did so eight times (Beth et al. 2009). Effectively, this makes House amendments non-amendable, like conference reports.[23]

Contingent on having sixty votes for cloture at each stage, these developments complete a loop in the majority leader's procedural toolbox. If a majority leader can invoke cloture on the motion to proceed and on the bill, the leader can fill the amendment tree to get an up-or-down vote on his or her version of the bill. Then, a majority leader can either invoke cloture on a conference report or invoke cloture on a House amendment, followed by filling the amendment tree. He or she is now in a position to get an up-or-down vote on a House-Senate compromise he or she favors. Sixty votes for cloture at each stage is a necessary condition for realization of this legislative scenario, but it is a possibility from time to time in a polarized Senate.

## Unorthodox Appropriating—Exploiting the Conference Process, Part 2

A second wave of omnibus appropriations bills occurred in the first decade of the twenty-first century, and again election years proved the most difficult.

---

22. In January 2007, the House of Representatives adopted a new rule that requires conference committees to be open to all conferees.

23. It also bears notice that the Senate rules limiting a conference report to the scope of the differences between the House and Senate versions of a bill and requiring it be available online for forty-eight hours before a floor vote do not apply to amendments between the houses (Beth et al. 2009). It also is noteworthy that Senate Republicans adopted a standing order as a part of a 1996 bill that provides that conference reports are not required to be read. House amendments are not exempt so a reading of an amendment could consume considerable time.

The decade began much like the Congresses of the mid-1980s. In 2002, with divided party control, divisions between and within the parties made a budget resolution and non-defense spending difficult issues—so difficult that the Senate's slim Democratic majority did not consider a budget resolution or ten of the thirteen regular appropriations bills on the floor. Instead, all ten were folded under a series of continuing resolutions, the last of which authorized spending only through January 11, 2003, when a new Republican majority would control the Senate (*CQ Almanac* 2002).

After the Republicans won a Senate majority in the 2002 elections and enjoyed unified control of the White House, House, and Senate, the new strategic circumstances allowed the majority party leadership to orchestrate the process in the party's interest. In 2004 politically unpopular domestic spending cuts were approved after the elections—only the defense, military construction, and homeland security bills were enacted as separate bills before the elections while the other ten bills were included in an omnibus bill. Only the District of Columbia, defense, military construction, and homeland security were considered on the Senate floor. Technically, the 2004 legislation was not a continuing resolution but instead a bill, which reflected the fact that the full text of regular appropriations bills was included and many non-appropriations subjects were addressed in the bill. In 2006 the Republican Senate majority passed only the defense and homeland security appropriations bills and, after the elections established that the next Senate would have a Democratic majority, wrapped all others (nine of the now eleven regular appropriations bills) in a more standard continuing resolution that extended spending authority to only early the next year. As in the 1980s, the conference reports were the only opportunities for senators to consider and vote on the appropriations bills folded into the omnibus appropriations measures (*CQ Almanac* 2004, 2006). But, with unified party control during the 2003–2006 period, the Democratic minority complained that Republicans were deliberately exploiting the conference process to prevent serious debate or floor amendments to appropriations bills.

With the Democrats in the majority in both houses after the 2006 elections, confrontations with a Republican president led to stalemate on most domestic spending bills. In 2007 the Senate considered and passed seven of the twelve regular appropriations bills, but only the defense spending bill was enacted and signed by the president as a separate bill. In 2008, seeking to avoid veto showdowns with the president altogether, the Democrats brought no appropriations bills to the Senate floor; placed the text of the defense, homeland security, and military construction bills in one bill; and treated all other bills in a temporary continuing resolution to allow the next Congress, under a Democratic president, to complete action for fiscal 2008 (*CQ Almanac* 2007, 2008).

## Bad Rules or Misbehaving Senators?

Many observers find the Senate dysfunctional. In early 2010, a Google search of "dysfunctional Senate" returned 7,190 hits. This is an old but deserving theme that resurfaces whenever one party or the other engages in a filibuster on a major piece of legislation. Reasonably, the target of the complaints always is obstructionism associated with the super-majority threshold for cloture and often the practice of holds. Defenders of the cloture threshold usually come from minority party senators and outsiders, who cite Senate tradition, the need to protect the rights of the minority, and the extremism of the majority. The majority, for its part, seldom finds these arguments about procedure sufficient justification for denying the majority the right to act on policy.

Another perspective is that the problem is not the rules. Rather, the problem is senators. Selfishness, catering to outside interests, and mean-spirited partisanship are the problems, not the rules of the Senate. What we need, this argument goes, are public-spirited, problem-solving senators who will not let the rules stand in the way of getting the nation's work done.

Assigning blame to the rules or to senators' character is tempting—truly tempting. The Senate could (and should) have different rules and could (and should) have senators who allow institutional norms to trump their policy interests, but neither analysis is complete. Both credible accounts—the Senate as a bad set of rules and the Senate as misbehaving senators—miss a more important element of the story: Senators' policy preferences, dictated by their political circumstances and personal views, are sharply polarized by party. There are few centrist senators who can successfully demand a deliberative, consensus-building process that produces constructive and successful compromises. Few minority party senators withhold support for obstructionist maneuvers and few majority party members resist efforts to limit amending activity and invoke cloture. Each party's leaders, guided by a consensus view among their fellow partisans, pursue strategies that perpetuate the partisanship.

## What Reforms Have Been Proposed?

Three dimensions to "filibuster reform" deserve notice: the threshold for cloture, the motions with debate limits, and the measures with debate limits. Rules affecting any of three may be modified to alter the advantage between the majority and minority. From the majority's perspective, any change that saves time for its agenda is a step in the right direction.

The most obvious way to reform Rule XXII is to reduce the threshold for cloture from three-fifths of senators duly chosen and sworn (or from two-thirds of senators present and voting for changes in the rules) to some lower number, such as fifty-five or a simple majority of either all senators or senators voting. I favor such reform. There are compromises on that approach that have received considerable attention. One is the Harkin-Lieberman proposal, reintroduced in early 2010 by Harkin and Senator Jeanne Shaheen (D-N.H.), to ratchet down the number required for cloture from three-fifths, or sixty, to fifty-seven, to fifty-four, and finally to fifty-one in steps over a period of two or three weeks.

Another is the approach recommended by former majority leader George Mitchell in which debate is limited on the motion to proceed and motions to go to conference so that super-majority cloture is restricted to the legislation itself. While a bill could still be blocked by filibuster, a majority leader with the required number of votes could more rapidly dispose of a measure and reduce the harm of obstructionism to his or her larger agenda. It is fair to assume that Senate minorities have recognized that filibusters and threatened filibusters gain some of their effectiveness by the collateral damage that delays cause for majorities' larger agenda.

Finally, limitations on debate might be adopted for specific categories of legislation. The executive calendar (nominations and treaties), appropriations bills, and tax measures have been mentioned as categories that majority parties and presidents might be especially interested in protecting from obstructionism. In the case of appropriations and tax bills, it might be feasible to add them to the Budget Act's provisions that limit debate on budget resolutions and reconciliation bills.

A recent wrinkle is the proposal by Sen. Jeff Merkley (D-Ore.) to approve reform of the rule but to make the reform effective at some future date (Klein 2009). Merkley argues reform will be possible only when neither party can predict whether it will be advantaged or disadvantaged under the reformed rule. At this writing, the proposal has not been formally introduced as a Senate resolution, and no other senators have publicly expressed views on this intriguing proposal.

## Force "Real" Filibusters?

One of the most commonly proposed solutions to the problem of obstructionism is to force the minority to take the floor and conduct extended debate. After all, it is noted, failure of minority senators to seek recognition leads to a vote on the motion at hand. Allowing a minority to keep a bill off the floor altogether makes obstructionism painless for the minority. Moreover, the argument continues, exposing a filibustering minority to the C-SPAN audience will pay a price in public opinion for its obstructionism. If the majority would increase the cost of obstructionism, obstructionism will melt away.

This argument is appealing, but, unfortunately for Senate majorities, the promise of this approach as a strategy for generally reducing obstructionism is limited. We must consider the calculations of both the minority and majority.

First, the majority must consider whether forced filibustering is likely to persuade at least some senators, or perhaps the leadership of the whole minority party or faction, who have already decided to oppose cloture to change their minds. They usually conclude that it will not. In most cases, minority senators already have decided that obstructionism is popular at home. And, while there is a chance the some voters will think ill of an obstructionist minority party, there is little evidence that voters' view of the minority procedural moves have an effect on vote intentions independent of their policy views. Moreover, minority senators can conduct extended debate one senator at a time with little inconvenience to themselves. It is true that a filibuster may delay action on other legislation favored by some members of the minority, but minority senators bet, usually correctly, that the majority wants action on the backlogged legislation even more than they do.

Second, the majority—especially a majority party—pays a high price for truly extended debate. A lengthy debate forces the majority party to produce a quorum on the Senate floor and makes it difficult for senators to conduct business in committees or at home during the filibuster. Inevitably, the majority party is subject to criticism by its opponents and commentators for its unwillingness to compromise with the minority, whether or not the minority is willing to consider compromise, and for its misplaced priorities as other legislation—important reauthorizations, essential appropriations—is held up. Inevitably, some majority party or faction members, facing a cohesive minority, begin to demand that the leaders move on to other matters.

Finally, filibusters gain real bite at the end of session or Congress when must-pass legislation and election campaigns are awaiting senators' attention. The price of failing to pass essential measures or attend to campaigns makes the advice of forcing real filibusters seem foolish. The minority knows this and obstructs more often and with greater effect as time constraints intensify.

In fact, history is not kind to majority leaders who insist on real filibusters. The last time a majority forced extended "real" filibustering was in 1987 when a Democratic majority wanted to pass campaign finance reform. Majority Leader Byrd interrupted consideration of a defense bill—also subject to a filibuster for most of that summer—to bring up the campaign finance bill and kept the Senate on the campaign finance bill for nearly two weeks. He forced seven cloture votes. Despite the fact that Byrd had at least a five-vote majority for the bill and showed remarkable determination, the largest vote in favor of cloture came on the first vote, with absentees diminishing his count on subsequent votes. Byrd set aside the campaign finance bill when another important measure was ready for floor consideration.

## Why Doesn't the Senate Majority Change Rule XXII?

The obvious answer—that the majority is blocked by a minority that will filibuster a change in the rule—is correct but incomplete. It is correct that there have been several occasions in which a majority of senators sought to create or change the cloture rule and were blocked by a minority of senators who prevented a vote on the reform resolution (Binder and Smith 1997). It also is correct that judging whether a majority favors a change in the rules is difficult because a filibuster can block a vote that would confirm the existence of a majority for reform. But certainly it is not clear that cloture reform is always or generally favored by a Senate majority. Senators in the majority may fear minority status in the foreseeable future. It also may be true that some or many senators favor a super-majority cloture rule because it enhances their *individual* power to delay and obstruct. Certainly, both majority and minority senators exploit opportunities to speak at length and on any subject on the floor, to offer non-germane amendments, and to object to the consideration of legislation through holds or other means, all of which rests on Rule XXII.

The history of the Senate, both distant and recent, leaves reformers pessimistic about the chances of changing Rule XXII through means implied by the standing rules. The two-thirds majority threshold for cloture on a measure changing the standing rules is very high. Since the initial adoption of Rule XXII in 1917, the majority party in only five Congresses— four in the New Deal era when precedent held that the rule did not apply to the motion to proceed—exceeded two-thirds of the Senate's membership. The other Congress was the 89th (1965–66), in which many members of the majority party (the southern Democrats) would not have supported reform of the rule.

Significant change seems likely only if a majority party is committed to making them and has the support of a presiding officer who, through rulings on points of order, is willing to assist that majority gain a vote on new rules. That is likely to happen only when there is consensus within the majority party about the reforms to be adopted, the president and vice president support the move, and the time required to take up reform has little impact on the party's legislative agenda. Those conditions are most likely to be realized at the beginning of a new Congress when members of the majority party are persuaded that minority obstructionism will continue to undermine their public mandate to enact their legislative agenda.

# References

Allen, Jonathan, and John Cochran. 2003. "The Might of the Right." *CQ Weekly Online*, November 8, 2761–2762. http://library.cqpress.com/cqweekly/weeklyreport108-000 000899550. Accessed January 6, 2010.

Alston, Chuck. 1990. "Legislative Agenda: Reputation of 101st Congress at Stake in Coming Weeks." *CQ Weekly Online*, July 7, 2123–2123. http://library.cqpress.com/cqweekly/WR101409794. Accessed January 2, 2010.

Beth, Richard S., Valerie Heitshusen, Bill Heniff Jr., and Elizabeth Rybicki. 2009. "Leadership Tools for Managing the U.S. Senate." Paper prepared for delivery at the annual meeting of the American Political Science Association, September 3–6, Toronto, Canada.

Binder, Sarah A., and Forrest Maltzman. 2009. *Advice and Dissent: The Struggle to Shape the Federal Judiciary*. Washington, D.C.: Brookings Institution.

Binder, Sarah, and Steven S. Smith. 1997. *Politics or Principle: Filibustering in the Senate*. Washington, D.C.: Brookings Institution.

Binder, Sarah, Anthony Madonna, and Steven S. Smith. 2007. "Going Nuclear, Senate Style." *Perspectives on Politics* 5 (December): 729–740.

Cohen, Richard E., Kirk Victor, and David Baumann. 2004. "The State of Congress." *National Journal*, January 10. http://www.nationaljournal.com.libproxy.wustl.edu/njmagazine/nj_20040110_5.php. Accessed

*CQ Almanac*. Various years. Washington, D.C.: CQ Press.

Doherty, Carroll J. 1994. "NOMINATIONS: Brown's Prospects Dimmed by GOP Filibuster." *CQ Weekly Online*, May 28, 1409. Accessed

———. 1998. "Senate Caught in the Grip of Its Own 'Holds' System." *Congressional Quarterly Weekly Report*, August 15, 2242.

Eisele, Albert, and JoAnn Kelly. 1998. "Texas-Minnesota Senate Feud Blocks Measure Honoring LBJ Foe Former Sen. McCarthy." *The Hill*, October 7, 6.

Friel, Brian. 2007. "Wrestling with Holds." *National Journal*, January 13, 47.

Gold, Martin, and Dimple Gupta. 2005. "The Constitutional Option to Change Senate Rules and Procedures: A Majoritarian Means to Overcome the Filibuster." *Harvard Journal of Law and Public Policy* 28: 205–272.

Goldreich, Samuel. 2003. "Vote against ANWR Drilling Hits Core of Bush Energy Plan." *CQ Weekly Online*, March 22, 698–701. http://library.cqpress.com/cqweekly/weekly report108-000000638270. Accessed January 7, 2010.

Hook, Janet. 1989a. "Mitchell Learns Inside Game." *CQ Weekly Online*, September 9, 2293–2296. http://library.cqpress.com/cqweekly/WR101407218. Accessed January 2, 2010.

———. 1989b. "New Leaders Felt Their Way Gingerly through Session." *CQ Weekly Online*, December 2, 3284–3286. http://library.cqpress.com/cqweekly/WR101408039. Accessed January 2, 2010.

———. 1990. "Dole Outburst Shows Frustration over More than Civil Rights Bill." *CQ Weekly Online*, July 21, 2314–2315. http://library.cqpress.com/cqweekly/WR101409915. Accessed January 2, 2010.

———. 1993. "Busting the Silent Filibuster." *Congressional Quarterly Weekly Report*, November 13, 3095.

Jansen, Bart. 2009. "Capitol Hill's Conferences: Can They Be Revived?" *CQ Weekly*, January 5, 2009, 18.

Kady, Martin, II. 2006. "Reid Will Be Quieter Hand at Senate's Helm." *CQ Weekly Online*, November 13, 2972–2972. http://library.cqpress.com/cqweekly/weeklyreport109-000 002401311. Accessed January 6, 2010.

Keith, Robert. 2008. "The Budget Reconciliation Process: The Senate's 'Byrd Rule.'" *CRS Report for Congress*. Congress Research Service RL30862.

Klein, Ezra. 2009. "Fixing the Filibuster: An Interview with Sen. Jeff Merkley." *Washington Post* (online), December 26. http://voices.washingtonpost.com/ezra-klein/2009/12/ fixing_the_filibuster_an_inter.html. Accessed

Mann, Thomas E., Molly Reynolds, and Norman Ornstein. 2009. "Truth and Reconciliation." *The New Republic*, April 20. http://www.tnr.com/article/politics/truth-and -reconciliation. Accessed

Oleszek, Walter J. 2007. "Proposals to Reform 'Holds' in the Senate." *CRS Report for Congress*. Congressional Research Service RL31685 (December 20).

———. 2008. "Senate Policy on 'Holds': Action in the 110th Congress." *CRS Report for Congress*. Congressional Research Service RL34255 (March 14).

Palmer, Betsy. 2005. "Evolution of the Senate's Role in the Nomination and Confirmation Process: A Brief History." *CRS Report for Congress*. Congressional Research Service, RL31948.

Palmer, Elizabeth A. 1993. "Nominations: Senate Confirms Diplomats as McConnell Relents." *CQ Weekly Online*, November 6, 3062. Accessed

Parks, Daniel J. 2001. "Senate GOP Spares Cheney, Tables Tabling." *CQ Weekly Online*, April 14, 816. http://library.cqpress.com/cqweekly/weeklyreport107-000000237901. Accessed January 3, 2010.

Pierce, Emily. 2007. "Mystery Still Surrounds Filing Hold." *Roll Call*, September 26, 1.

Rybicki, Elizabeth. 2010. "Amendments between the Houses: Procedural Options and Effects." *CRS Report for Congress*. Congressional Research Service RL41003 (January 4).

Schick, Allen. 2000. *The Federal Budget: Politics, Policy Process*, rev. ed. Washington, D.C.: Brookings Institution.

Shanton, John. 2010. "Senators Won't Fold on the Hold." *Roll Call*, February 1. http:// www.rollcall.com/issues/55_84/news/42806-1.html. Accessed

Sinclair, Barbara. 2009. "Resolving Differences: Party Leaders and Procedural Choice." Paper presented at the Conference on Bicamerlism, Vanderbilt University, October 23–24.

Smith, Steven S. 1989. *Call to Order: Floor Politics in the House and Senate*. Washington, D.C.: Brookings Institution.

Stanton, John. 2007. "Without Time for Review, Coburn Will Block Bills." *Roll Call*, December 6. http://www.rollcall.com/issues/53_67/news/21249-1.html. Accessed

Stevens, Allison. 2004. "Will Conference-Blocking Tactic Come Back to Bite Democrats?" *CQ Weekly Online*, January 31, 266. http://library.cqpress.com/cqweekly/weekly report108-000000989512. Accessed January 6, 2010.

Stevens, Allison, and Keith Perine. 2003. "Bid to Curb Nominee Filibusters Tests Limits of GOP Risk-Taking." *CQ Weekly Online*, May 17, 1185–1186. http://library .cqpress.com/cqweekly/weeklyreport108-000000697091. Accessed January 3, 2010.

Taylor, Andrew. 2000a. "Congressional Affairs: Senate Leaders' Parliamentary Ploys." *CQ Weekly Online*, February 26, 394–399. http://library.cqpress.com/cqweekly/weekly report106-000000039618. Accessed January 5, 2010.

————. 2000b. "A Different Sense of Urgency." *CQ Weekly Online*, September 30, 2255–2256. http://library.cqpress.com/cqweekly/weeklyreport106-000000145680. Accessed January 5, 2010.

————. 2000c. "Republicans Expected to Welcome Back Floor Votes." *CQ Weekly Online*, October 21, 2449–2449. http://library.cqpress.com/cqweekly/weeklyreport106-000000157215. Accessed January 5, 2010.

————. 2001a. "Senate GOP to Share Power." *CQ Weekly Online*, January 6, 21–22. http://library.cqpress.com/cqweekly/weeklyreport107-000000193017. Accessed January 5, 2010.

————. 2001b. "Law Designed for Curbing Deficits Becomes GOP Tool for Cutting Taxes." *CQ Weekly Online*, April 7, 770. http://library.cqpress.com/cqweekly/weeklyreport107-000000235233. Accessed January 3, 2010.

Yachnin, Jennifer. 2009. "Watchdog Wants Investigation of Senate 'Holds.'" *Roll Call*, December 2. http://www.rollcall.com/news/41085-1.html. Accessed

8

# The Filibuster Then and Now: Civil Rights in the 1960s and Financial Regulation, 2009–2010

Gregory Koger

One of the most significant changes in the Senate from 1960 to 2010 has been a revolution in the practice and influence of filibustering. In 1960 it was rare for senators to drag out debate on a bill or nomination in the hope of blocking the measure or gaining some concession. In 2010, on the other hand, senators commonly threaten filibusters against bills and nominations and share the expectation that any major legislation that passes the Senate will need the support of at least sixty votes—the number required to limit debate.

In recent work, I have explained that the Senate changed because of a shift in senators' tactics. Filibustering used to be a public spectacle as a senator (or team of senators) occupied the Senate floor continuously; this required senators to make a serious commitment of their time and political reputations in taking a stand against the will of the majority of the Senate. During the 1960s, Senate majority leaders eschewed these "wars of attrition" in favor of quick cloture votes to determine if they had the backing of a cloture-sized majority (Koger 2010).

This chapter provides a snapshot of this transformation by describing filibusters that occurred in 1960 and 2010. For each of these years, I review one filibuster related to a nomination, one appropriations cycle, and one piece of major legislation. While I explain my reasons for choosing each case, I should note that the nominations and major bills are chosen to provide interesting examples that are, in my view, typical of their eras. These cases are drawn from recent work (Koger 2010) in which I provide a more systematic analysis of twentieth-century Senate filibustering.

For each case, I seek to answer the same basic questions: Are the obstructionists primarily members of a party, ideological faction, region, or something else? Why are they filibustering? What tactics do they use to obstruct? How do their opponents respond? And finally, what is the critical element that explains the outcome of the filibuster?

As we shall see, one of the essential differences between the 1960 Senate and the 2010 Senate lies in the tactics used to respond to a filibuster. In 1959 the rules of the Senate allowed a super-majority of two-thirds of those present and voting to invoke cloture, or limit debate, on a bill or nomination. Alternatively, senators could wage a "war of attrition"—senators who wished to overcome a filibuster would try to keep the obstructed measure on the Senate floor until the obstructionist senators were too exhausted or embarrassed to continue. By 2010 the threshold for cloture was slightly lower: three-fifths of the entire membership of the Senate, voting or not. More important, senators in the 111th Congress can still wage wars of attrition, but they almost never do.

## I. Filibustering in the 86th Congress, 1959–60

It is not difficult to select filibuster case studies for the 86th Congress. Using the methodology described in Koger (2010), I identified seven filibusters for these years, which are listed in Table 8.1. We shall discuss the only nomination on the list, the defeated nomination of Lewis Strauss for secretary of commerce, as well as the 1960 Civil Rights Act. While the 1960 act was comparatively minor relative to the 1957 act—the first in decades—and the landmark 1964 Civil Rights Act and 1965 Voting Rights Act, it marks a turning point in the development of the U.S. Senate. The doomed attempt to outlast the southern filibuster against the bill soured senators on the marathon gabfests and led to a transformation of Senate decision making.

### Lewis Strauss Nomination for Secretary of Commerce

On November 13, 1958, President Dwight Eisenhower gave Lewis Strauss a recess appointment as secretary of commerce. Strauss had previously served as the chair of the Atomic Energy Commission, and in that position he had made some enemies in the Senate. Clinton Anderson (D-N.M.) and the Democratic leadership rallied these opponents to fight the nomination.

**Table 8.1**    Filibusters in the 86th Congress

Cloture reform
Mutual Security Aid appropriations—Civil Rights Commission extension
1960 Civil Rights Act (HR 8315)
Strauss nomination to be secretary of commerce
Diversion of Lake Michigan water to Chicago sewage project (HR 1)
School Construction—Powell amendment
Republican Civil Rights Bill

The battle over Strauss's nomination began on June 18, 1959, when Senate Majority Leader Lyndon Johnson (D-Texas) noted that several Republicans were absent. Seeking to take advantage of this weakness, Johnson sought a unanimous consent agreement to debate Strauss's nomination for eight hours, and then vote. Republicans objected, and Johnson announced his intention to keep the Senate in continuous session until a vote was held. This meant that the Senate would continue working night and day without a break. Republicans then began to filibuster, fielding a series of speakers to occupy the floor while their leaders scrambled to fly the missing senators back to Washington. Mischief managed, the filibuster ended around midnight and a close vote ensued; the Senate voted to reject Strauss, 46–49 (Drury 1959; Krock 1959; "This Sad Episode" 1959).

Three points about this case are worth noting. First, the timing of the vote highlights the variable attendance of senators during the mid-twentieth century. Faced with ever-longer sessions, senators took advantage of improved transportation options to leave Washington, D.C., for their home states or speaking opportunities around the country. The contingent attendance of senators continues to limit Senate leaders to this day, as increasingly the Senate meets three days a week (or fewer) so that senators are free to travel over four- or even five-day weekends (Koger 2010). Second, the Senate's schedule was highly contingent; Johnson decided to bring up Strauss's nomination on a moment's notice and proposed unanimous consent requests (UCAs) to limit debate to eight (later five) hours. This is similar to the 2010 Senate, which also has a fluid schedule based on unanimous consent agreements. The critical difference, however, is Johnson's reaction when the Republicans rejected his unanimous consent proposals: Johnson committed to keep the Senate in session until it held a vote on Strauss. In recent years, UCAs usually have been negotiated in advance and rarely rejected on the Senate floor, unless a senator is trying to highlight obstruction against a bill or nomination by proposing UCAs and forcing opponents to publicly object. Moreover, it is extremely rare in the modern Senate for a rejected UCA to be followed by a sustained effort to wait out a filibuster. Third, the "filibuster" in this case was strictly short term, and only to buy time for absent senators to arrive. Even though the outcome of the vote was uncertain, Strauss's opponents did not wage a filibuster against him; they allowed an up-or-down vote on the nomination rather than forcing a cloture vote that they were certain to win. In this critical sense, the 1959–60 Senate was still a majority rule institution.

## The Fiscal Year 1960 Appropriations Cycle

One of the most fundamental tasks of Congress is to enact annual appropriations bills to pay for the activities of the federal government. Congress divides this task into several bills and, by tracing the progress of these bills for a given year, we get a sense of how well Congress is functioning. For this chapter I look at fiscal year (FY) 1960 (beginning July 1, 1959) and, later, fiscal year 2010.

During the 86th Congress, there were fifteen regular appropriations bills and, in FY 1960, a major supplemental bill to fund the National Aeronautics and Space Administration. Overall, Congress did a mediocre job: of the sixteen bills, only two were enacted by the deadline of July 1, with another five in July, four in August, and five in September. However, there is little evidence that this delay is attributable to Senate obstruction. Only one of the filibusters listed in Table 8.1 is linked to an appropriations bill. The Mutual Security Aid appropriations bill was slowed when senators attached a non-germane amendment, or rider, that extended the authorization for the Civil Rights Commission for two years. This provoked a short filibuster that delayed the bill by a couple days, but dissent soon faded so the Senate could finish for the year.

It is also possible, however, that covert threats to filibuster legislation (known as "holds") could have delayed appropriations bills, or that the bills lingered on the Senate calendar while other filibusters occupied the attention of the Senate. To test for this, I gathered data on how long it took each chamber to pass each appropriations bill after the Appropriations Committee of each chamber reported it to the chamber. For example, the House Appropriations Committee reported the Defense Appropriations bill on May 28, 1959, and the House passed the bill on June 3 (six days); the Senate Appropriations Committee reported its version on July 7, and the full Senate approved the bill on July 14 (seven days). By comparing the House and Senate we have a natural experiment that holds the policy issues and budgetary environment constant and compares the House, a majority rule chamber, with the 1960 Senate.

The bill-by-bill comparisons are shown in Figure 8.1. Overall, there is very little difference in how quickly each chamber passed its bills. In fact, the House lagged slightly behind the Senate; on average, 4.4 days elapsed in the House and 3.3 in the Senate, with a median of 3.5 days for the House and 2.5 days for the Senate. These differences are not statistically significant, but the fact that the Senate was, if anything, no less efficient than the majority-rule House suggests that obstruction did not keep the 1960 Senate from performing this basic task.

## The 1960 Civil Rights Act

Finally, the 1960 Civil Rights Act provides a case of obstruction against a major bill. In the course of civil rights policymaking, the 1960 act is generally considered a half-measure between the 1957 Civil Rights Act (which

**Figure 8.1**  Days Elapsed between Committee Approval and
Chamber Passage, Fiscal Year 1960 Appropriations

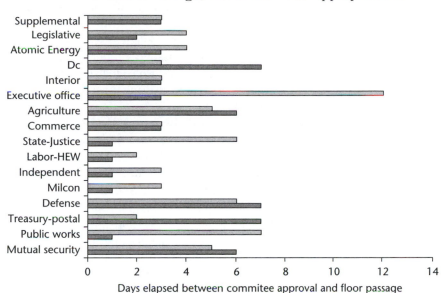

Days elapsed between commitee approval and floor passage

House    Senate

was ineffective but renewed congressional action on civil rights (Caro 2002) and the landmark Civil Rights Act of 1964 and Voting Rights Act of 1965. Substantively, the 1960 act was a reaction to reports that the 1957 act was not accomplishing its stated goal of increasing the registration and participation of African American voters in southern states. Politically, it was motivated by the complex partisan strategies of the mid-twentieth century: each party sought to appeal to African American swing voters in northern states without losing the support of southern whites (Frymer 1999; Valelly 2004); a significant faction of each party wanted to at least *appear* to support civil rights as the 1960 elections approached without enacting major changes that would provoke a short-term defeat or a long-term realignment.

The 1960 act, however, plays a central role in Senate history. It marks the last sustained effort to outlast a filibuster by a major faction of the Senate. The failure of this effort, combined with the elevation of Mike Mansfield (D-Mont.) to Senate majority leader after Lyndon Johnson became vice president, sparked a transition from attrition contests to votes on cloture as the dominant response to obstruction (Koger 2010). After 1960, Senate leaders would occasionally threaten prolonged sessions—even invite the press to take pictures of Senate workers wheeling in cots for overnight debates—but the default responses would be compromise and cloture votes.

Action on civil rights started slowly. After a flurry of proposals by Johnson, President Dwight D. Eisenhower, and a coalition of liberals, there was little action for most of 1959. In September, as Congress was preparing to end its session, the Civil Rights Commission issued a report detailing the ineffectiveness of the 1957 act and calling for additional legislation. Johnson and Republican leader Everett Dirksen agreed to bring up civil rights legislation early in 1960 (Mann 1996: 242–245).

On February 15, 1960, Johnson cleverly bypassed the southern-dominated Judiciary Committee by announcing that the Senate would use a minor House bill as a vehicle for civil rights legislation and inviting senators to offer their proposals as amendments (Mann 1996: 248–249). A team of southern senators responded by filibustering on the Senate floor.

After ten days of debate on the Civil Rights Act, Johnson attempted to exhaust the southerners with round-the-clock sessions. While they had been well organized during previous filibusters, this time they adopted a sophisticated rotation scheme to ensure that there were always two southerners on the Senate floor at any given time, working eight-hour shifts (Mann 1996: 251–257). The southern obstructionists maximized the costs for the majority by calling for a quorum while absenting themselves from the chamber, which forced supporters of the bill to appear in the Senate at any time, day or night. From February 29 to March 8, 1960, the Senate was in session for 157 hours, held thirteen roll call votes and fifty quorum calls, and filled over 650 pages of the *Congressional Record* ("Statistical Summary" 1960). During this marathon, Wayne Morse (D-Ore.) made an attempt to collect signatures for a cloture petition that met an abrupt end. After Morse announced that he had a petition to sign, Thurston B. Morton (R-Ky.), who was acting as the floor monitor for pro–civil rights Republicans, crossed the chamber and ripped the petition into dozens of pieces ("Morton Rips Up Petition" 1960). Morton believed that a cloture vote, if held too soon, would doom the bill by locking in senators' positions before the bill's supporters had formed a two-thirds majority. Eventually, however, a faction of the pro–civil rights group filed a cloture petition, and Johnson, angry at the premature move, called off the twenty-four-hour sessions ("Senate Calls Off" 1960). The cloture attempt failed 42–3.[1]

Weeks later, the Senate renewed the civil rights debate with a just-passed House bill as the base text. The Democratic Policy Committee (DPC) discussed attempting a cloture vote prior to this debate and decided that it was a no-win strategy. If a cloture attempt failed, there would be

---

1. This paragraph and the next two paragraphs are drawn from Gregory Koger (2010).

"another heated debate on the Senate rules in January [1961]." If cloture was invoked, "it would certainly be succeeded by a number more petitions for cloture," but it was unlikely because "there were many Senators outside of the South who did not like to invoke cloture" (Democratic Policy Committee 1960). In the end, no cloture votes were held on the House civil rights bill, and, after ample debate, it passed 71–18.

The contest over the 1960 Civil Rights Act illustrated the futility of attrition against a phalanx of southern senators. It was unrealistic to expect a majority of the Senate to remain in the chamber indefinitely while obstructionists killed time in two-man teams. The world of the 1960s Senate was a different place: increasing workload, globe-trotting membership, and growing dissatisfaction with the racial status quo. Over the next decade, senators gradually accepted the necessity of using the Senate's dormant cloture rule to respond to a rising tide of filibusters.

## II. The Contemporary Senate, 2009–10

Between 1960 and 2010 the Senate experienced a dramatic escalation of obstruction. In 1960 filibusters tended to be rare and significant events; by 2010 the ability of every senator to delay bills or nominations had been institutionalized into the daily routines of the Senate. The key to this evolution was that senators could no longer afford prolonged floor battles like the one over the 1960 Civil Rights Act and, during the 1960s, transitioned to attempting cloture (or negotiations) as the default response to a filibuster threat (Koger 2010). And, as our first case illustrates, Senate leaders developed a system for cataloging and, when possible, resolving filibuster threats.

### Hold Everything: Richard Shelby's Power Play

On February 5, 2010, the office of Senate majority leader Harry Reid leaked the news that Richard Shelby (R-Ala.) had placed a "hold" on dozens of pending executive nominations. Shelby hoped that, by stalling these nominations, he would force the Obama administration to pay attention to two critical issues—critical to Shelby, that is. First, Shelby was disappointed by the draft "request for proposals" issued by the Air Force as part of its plan to re-bid a contract for air refueling tanker planes; Shelby thought the draft proposal was biased against a European company that had promised to assemble its planes in Alabama. Second, he was unhappy that the administration had not begun building a new Terrorist Explosive Device Analytical Center in Alabama with funds earmarked for that purpose in a 2007 omnibus appropriations bill (Shiner and Raju 2010).

Shelby was taking advantage of an informal practice that developed alongside the growth in filibustering on the Senate floor. Beginning as early as the 1950s, Senate party leaders collected requests to "hold" legislation off the Senate floor, either for a defined or indefinite period of time (Koger 2010). Some of these requests were benign: senators merely wanted a chance to read about a bill, prepare amendments, question a nominee, offer amendments to a bill, or ensure that they would be present for the debate on a proposal. Other holds, however, were de facto threats to obstruct. For party leaders, this is useful information, because it helps them avoid surprises; if they know that a bill or nomination faces a filibuster, they will schedule enough time to overcome it or keep the proposal off the floor. The latter outcome, in turn, leads to criticism of the hold system. Bills and nominations are killed or delayed by private threats, so bill sponsors, nominees, and the media may never know why certain bills or nominations fail. There have been several attempts to ensure that dilatory holds are revealed to the public, including a 2007 law that compels party leaders to reveal the identity of senators who are "holding" a bill or nomination if six days elapse after a party leader objects to a request to debate a bill or nomination and a 2011 revision that prevents senators from holding legislation on behalf of another senator. It is still unclear if senators and leaders will consistently implement this mandate, which can be evaded with little difficulty (see Chapter 7 in this volume).

Shelby probably wished that his blanket hold had remained private. It was entirely impractical to overcome Shelby's holds on a case-by-case basis using the cloture process, as Reid lamented on the Senate floor: "There isn't enough time in the world—the Senate world, at least—to move cloture on every one of these" (Wilson and Murray 2010). But if the Democrats could raise the political costs of obstructing the Senate, he might relent. The White House immediately blasted his ploy, and liberal blogs and media heaped scorn on the wholesale gridlock inflicted by Shelby's parochial concerns. Obama escalated the showdown by threatening to bypass the Senate and appoint delayed nominees to "recess appointments" (Philips and Zeleny 2010).

After a weekend of public criticism, Shelby relented, reducing his holds to a few targeted Air Force nominations pertaining to the aircraft contract. Thirty nominations passed the Senate over the next few days (Shiner 2010; Stern and Hunter 2010). Shelby's blanket hold, however, was just a single battle in a broader contest over judicial and executive nominations during the 111th Congress. There were cloture votes on over a dozen nominations, and Democrats complained that the Republicans are deliberately slowing down the confirmation process (see Chapter 9 in this volume).

The Fiscal Year 2010 Appropriations Cycle

In 2009 Congress struggled to enact its FY 2010 appropriations bills. In the end, three out of twelve passed as individual bills. Another seven were

**Figure 8.2**  Days to Complete Legislative Stages for Fiscal Year 2010 Appropriations Bills

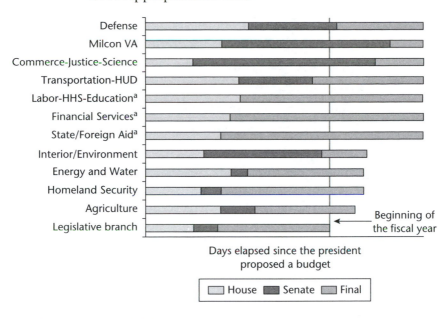

Note: The x-axis begins at 100 days after submission of president's budget.

[a]Senate did not approve a version of this appropriations bill.

enacted as part of an omnibus bill, that is, they were bundled with other appropriations bills or policy proposals, while the remaining two were attached to resolutions to continue funding at the current level while Congress negotiated. Even though Congress had moved its fiscal year back by three months in the 1974 Budget Control and Impoundment Act, only one appropriations bill was finished by the October 1 deadline. Figure 8.2 illustrates the days elapsed for each stage of each bill. Notably, three bills are never passed by the Senate, and another three bills do not pass the Senate until *after* the October 1 deadline.

How much of this dysfunction is attributable to Senate filibustering? The Senate invoked cloture on five of the nine bills that made it to the Senate floor, while cloture petitions were filed and withdrawn for another two bills. Although cloture votes are not used exclusively to respond to filibusters, this record suggests that the majority faced difficulty in limiting debate on FY 2010 appropriations bills. Furthermore, as above, we can compare the number of days that elapsed between committee approval and chamber passage for each bill. Figure 8.3 illustrates this metric for the FY 2010 cycle. If we ignore the three bills that never passed the Senate—Financial Services, Labor-HHS-Education, and State Department/Foreign

**Figure 8.3**   Time Elapsed between Committee and Floor
Approval for Fiscal Year 2010 Appropriations Bills

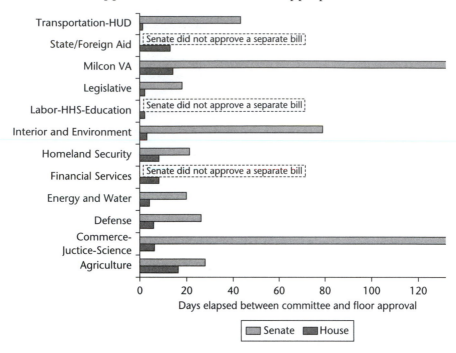

Aid—*every* bill waits longer for Senate approval than House passage. On average, House Appropriations Committee–approved bills waited 6.75 days for chamber approval, while the mean wait in the Senate was 55.7 days. Not surprisingly, this difference is statistically significant (p < .02 two-tailed for a t-test of two samples with unequal variances). Putting these patterns together, there is evidence that appropriations bills did face obstruction on the Senate floor, and that this obstruction significantly slowed the progress of FY 2010 spending bills, thereby contributing to an overall delay in passing these essential measures.

Finally, I might highlight that FY 2010 was a comparatively successful appropriations cycle. The previous year, the Democratic majority minimized compromise with outgoing president George W. Bush by bundling three national security bills into an omnibus package that passed September 30, 2008, and reserving the rest until Barack Obama had taken office. No bill passed either chamber. In FY 2008, only seven of twelve bills passed the Senate, and three of those passed after the October 1 deadline. All twelve bills were late, with eleven bills passing in an omnibus measure on December 26, 2007. The modern Congress struggles to enact its spending bills, and Senate obstruction is a major source of delay.

## Financial Reform Legislation

In 2008 the United States suffered a financial crisis that led to a worldwide recession. In response, Congress enacted the Troubled Asset Relief Program in October 2008 to shore up the credit markets with $700 billion of federal loans, while the Federal Reserve intervened to prevent the collapse of major corporations like AIG and to maintain liquidity in the banking system. Once the crisis was ameliorated, legislators of the 111th Congress began crafting legislation to revamp federal regulation of the financial system to ensure its long-term stability.[2]

The House passed its financial reform bill on December 11, 2009, after two days of speaking and votes on fourteen amendments and a motion to recommit. The final passage tally was 223–202 (D 223–27; R 0–175)—a close vote that attracted zero minority party Republicans despite the appeal of financial reform in the wake of a profound crisis. House Republicans blasted the bill as a "job killer" that would lead to future bailouts. They were also concerned about the inclusion of a new Consumer Financial Protection Agency (CFPA) (Mattingly and Davidson 2009).[3] In addition, financial regulation promised to be a major achievement for the Democratic Party, which meant that the Republicans had little political incentive to assist its passage. Finally, to the extent that some financial interests were opposed to provisions of the bill (e.g., the CFPA), they appear to have donated heavily to opponents of the bill, helping to lower the size of the winning coalition.

The Senate, on the other hand, was slowed by a long debate over health care that began in November 2009 and (although the bill passed in December 2009) did not truly end until March 2010. In the background, however, Senate Banking Committee chair Chris Dodd (D-Conn.) tried to lay the foundation for a broad reform bill. But Dodd could not rely on the Rules Committee, in contrast to the House, to guarantee access to the Senate floor, nor would a narrow majority be sufficient to pass the bill. The easiest way to minimize the time and effort required to overcome a filibuster on the

---

2. The obstruction against health care reform was probably the best known filibuster of the 111th Congress, but it had several unique features—its political salience, the Democrats' sixty-vote majority when health reform first passed the Senate, and the final resolution using the budget reconciliation process—that make it unique. Financial regulatory overhaul is more typical of modern filibusters.

3. Although the bill increased regulations on a private industry, members of both parties seemed to agree on the supervisory role of government and the goal of avoiding future government-funded bailouts, with many of the key differences stemming from the choice of means to achieve this end. The CFPA did tap into the general "more vs. less government" divide, however, since it extended the scope of the bill from banking and high finance to consumer loans and protection.

Senate floor was to craft a bipartisan (or at least sixty-vote) compromise before the bill came to the Senate floor.

Dodd's efforts to build a compromise were ultimately fruitless. In early 2009, the Senate Republicans had adopted a strategy of solid opposition to the Democratic agenda, including financial reform (Hulse and Nagourney 2010). Dodd attempted to negotiate with the ranking Republican on the Banking Committee, Richard Shelby (R-Ala.), but these discussions repeatedly broke down. By mid-February, Bob Corker (R-Tenn.) had become the lead Republican negotiator, although Shelby continued to be indirectly involved. After another month of talks, however, Dodd and the Democrats grew impatient and marked up Dodd's bill in committee. As *Politico* reported, "Democrats . . . praised Dodd for learning the painfully earned lesson from health care reform negotiations in the Senate: More time does not guarantee Republican support, and in the meantime the legislative window may close" (McGrane 2010). The Banking Committee reported the bill on a 13–10 party-line vote after the Republicans on the committee refused to offer any of the over 200 amendments they had prepared. According to Corker, negotiations broke down because other Republicans were unlikely to support any compromise bill—in part due to party strategy, and in part because they did not want to support Dodd's circumvention of the ranking member to negotiate with a junior Republican (McGrane 2010; McGrane and Lerer 2010; Packer 2010).

**Senate Floor Action.** Three weeks later, Reid announced that the Senate Democrats were resolved to begin debate on Dodd's financial reform, with or without Republican support.[4] Minority Leader Mitch McConnell (Ky.) then released a letter from all forty-one Republican senators pledging their opposition to Dodd's bill (Brown 2010b). Democrats, however, pressed on, expecting that public pressure would help them peel off at least one Republican. Dodd also continued to meet with Shelby and Corker in the hopes of eventually reaching agreement on the few remaining issues.

The showdown began on April 26, when senators voted on cloture on the motion to begin debate on financial regulation—that is, the Republicans were not obstructing the Democrats' bill but the question of whether to bring up the bill at all. From April 26 to April 28, senators voted on cloture daily. Each time, the motion came up short against united Republican opposition: 57–41, 57–41, and 56–42, with Ben Nelson (D-Neb.) and a united Republican conference voting against cloture on each case and Reid voting

---

4. One source of delay was the effort of Agriculture Committee chair Blanche Lambert Lincoln (D-Ark.), backed by a veto threat from President Obama, to add regulations of financial derivatives to the bill (Brown 2010a). The Agriculture Committee reported a derivatives bill on April 21 by a vote of 13–8, including the support of Chuck Grassley (R-Iowa).

against cloture on the first and third votes so he could move for a re-vote immediately (the vote on April 27 occurred after such a motion).

However, Democrats expected that the Republicans' opposition was unsustainable. By bringing the bill up on the Senate floor, they could effectively "expand the game" (as E. E. Schattschneider phrased it in 1960) by taking the bill out of the committee hearing room and into the court of public opinion. As Barbara Sinclair (2006) has noted, the recent increase in party polarization in the Senate means that senators often view major legislation as a zero sum game, since major legislation amounts to a "win" for the majority party and bolsters its reputation. Thus the majority party must convince some or all of the minority party members that blocking the bill will have adverse effects on their individual or collective electoral fortunes. Consequently, the Senate wages simultaneous debates on major bills—a legislative debate over the content of the bill and a public relations effort to shape general opinion.

In this case, the Democrats hoped that by increasing media attention to financial reform and highlighting the Republicans' opposition to debating the bill, the minority would be more accommodating in the legislative sphere by accepting some of the more controversial Democratic proposals. Polls generally reported public support for financial reform, by margins of 50–36 percent (Gallup), 63–29 percent (ABC/Washington Post), and 69–20 (Fox News). And, polls showed more support for the Democratic effort on this issue by a margin of 42–34 percent (Gallup), 52–35 percent (ABC, pitting Obama against the "Republicans in Congress"); and 47–34 percent (Fox).[5] Also, a concurrent news story was the revelation that the investment firm Goldman Sachs (which had received and paid back TARP funds) had engaged in questionable practices, such as selling bundles of home mortgages to investors while betting that the investments would fail. By early May, a Fox poll (see above) reported that Goldman Sachs' public approval ratings had slipped to 7 percent approve/55 percent disapprove. This parallel news story (a Senate subcommittee grilled Goldman Sachs executives for 11 hours on April 27) probably increased public disapproval of the status quo regulations, further complicating the Republicans' effort to push for changes in the bill without causing its failure.

---

5. All polls were accessed at pollingreport.com/business.htm on June 17, 2010. The number of respondents and margin of error were: ABC/Washington Post (1,001 adults, ± 3.5, 4/22–25/2010), Fox (900 registered voters, ±3.5, 5/4–5/2010), Gallup (1,024 adults, ±4, 4/17–18/2010). Gallup and ABC used a split sample to ask about support for financial reform. Gallup found 4 percent higher support for regulating "Wall Street banks and Wall Street financial institutions" compared to "large banks and major financial institutions," while ABC found little difference between these phrasings.

After three days of negative headlines and a third cloture vote (and the threat of a fourth when Reid moved to reconsider the failed cloture vote), the Republicans caved. Although Dodd granted a few concessions, "The standoff ended with a whimper, as Republicans agreed to proceed to the bill on a voice vote, declining an opportunity to put their position on the record" (Brown and Shiner 2010a). Beginning on April 28, the Senate debated financial reform under a series of unanimous consent agreements negotiated between the leaders of both parties. Republicans refused to allow any votes on amendments until Dodd and Shelby had finalized a compromise on a section of the bill that provided for the dissolution of failing banks; on May 4, Reid blasted the Republicans' blockade on floor votes and urged the completion of the bill by May 14. Finally, a deal was struck on the dissolution section and voting began.

Over the next sixteen days, the Senate voted on twenty-eight amendments, including one vote to table an amendment and another to waive budgetary rules and allow an amendment. Democrats offered twelve amendments and Republicans sixteen. Fourteen of the amendments passed, including five offered by Republicans. Eighteen of these votes meet the standard definition of a "party vote," pitting a majority of the Democrats against the position of a majority of the Republicans. This pattern, illustrated more clearly in Figure 8.4, portrays the percent of each party voting in support of each amendment. Figure 8.4 distinguishes between amendments proposed by Republicans (triangles) and Democrats (circles); not surprisingly, Republican support is high for amendments offered by their own members, and Democratic support is high for Democrat-sponsored amendments. Interestingly, all the near-unanimous amendments were offered by Democrats. But almost all of the amendments are nearly unanimous or highly polarized, highlighting the partisan nature of Senate voting even when the issue content is not obviously ideological (Lee 2009; Theriault 2008).

While House floor debate was structured by a pair of resolutions from the Rules Committee, the Senate's debate and amending was guided by ongoing negotiations and a series of unanimous consent agreements. On May 13, for example, the morning schedule was set by a UCA announced the previous afternoon, with two other UCAs scheduling votes on amendments announced during floor debate. Although the 1960 Senate did rely on UCAs to structure its schedule, the number and complexity of UCAs has increased over time (Smith and Flathman 1989). One very recent innovation is the imposition of sixty-vote thresholds on amendments by unanimous consent (Lynch 2009). Three amendments in this series faced this threshold—two sponsored by Democrats, one by a Republican—but the threshold was not critical for any of them, since two garnered less than a majority and the third received sixty-four votes.

**Figure 8.4**    Roll Call Voting on Amendments to Financial
Regulation Reform, May 2010

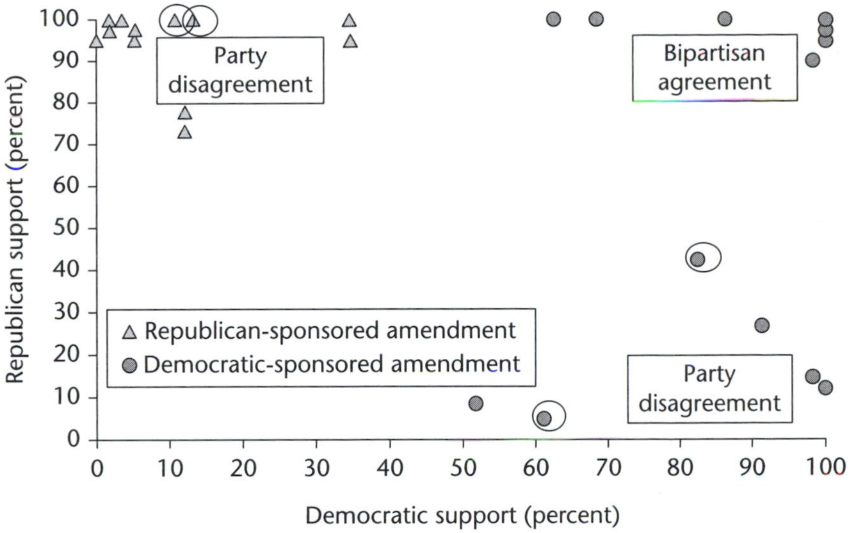

Note: Votes with 60 percent thresholds for approval are circled.

Even after voting began on floor amendments, Dodd and Shelby continued to negotiate on a manager's amendment that would combine several noncontroversial amendments with revisions to some of the bill's most controversial, anti–Wall Street provisions, particularly Sen. Blanche Lincoln's strong restrictions on derivatives. Dodd and Shelby never came to an agreement, however, and after three weeks Reid insisted that the Senate needed to move on to other issues and filed for cloture. Reid expected that a few moderate Republicans would vote for cloture, but did not appreciate how strongly several Democrats felt about voting on their own pending amendments to increase regulations on Wall Street before imposing cloture on the bill. The Republicans were able to exacerbate this situation by blocking unanimous consent requests for several of these amendments (Shiner and Brown 2010).

The final phase of the debate began on May 19, when the first cloture attempt failed 57–42. Two Republicans—Susan Collins and Olympia Snowe, both of Maine—voted for cloture, with the rest opposed. The real surprise was that two Democrats, Maria Cantwell (Wash.) and Russ Feingold (Wis.) voted against cloture. Cantwell was holding out for votes on a couple key amendments, while Feingold simply considered the bill inadequate. Reid also voted against cloture, so he could move to reconsider the vote on the following day. Reid complained bitterly that Scott Brown (R-Mass.) had reneged on a promise to vote for cloture. The next day, however, Reid eked out a 60–39 vote with the support of Brown and the previously absent Arlen Specter (D-Penn.). The bill then passed swiftly, 59–39, with Cantwell and Feingold still opposed and Chuck Grassley (R-Iowa) joining in support (Brown and Shiner 2010b).

In the end, this "filibuster" was a far cry from the general opposition of southern Democrats against any civil rights bill; after the initial partisan skirmishing, Reid's push for cloture stemmed from pressures to move on to other issues, a large number of controversial amendments, and the necessity of obtaining unanimous consent to actually vote on these amendments in the face of minority party recalcitrance. Cloture was not simply a proxy for passing the bill; it was a mechanism for cutting short a floor debate that was reasonably open and productive but moved too slowly.

**Conference Stage.** The House and Senate developed a compromise bill in "textbook" fashion by holding a series of open meetings to discuss and resolve their differences. This was remarkable in itself, since there has been a trend toward resolving differences by "ping-ponging" bills back and forth between chambers, or by holding sham conferences with backroom negotiations among majority party members and a few minority party senators (Epstein 2010). After eight meetings over the course of June, the conference finalized its agreement on June 29. This involved reconvening the conference to make a final change in the bill to attract a few Senate Republican votes: removing an assessment on large banks to finance a bank liquidation fund and substituting an increase in deposit fees (Sloan 2010).

The House approved the report on June 30 by a vote of 237–192 (D 234–19, R 3–173), but Senate approval remained uncertain. There was no guarantee the four Republicans would support the report, or that Cantwell or Feingold would continue to oppose the bill, and the death of Robert Byrd (D-W.Va.) further complicated the vote counting. This uncertainty delayed the bill for two weeks, but on July 15 the Senate approved cloture on the conference report 60–38 with the support of Republicans Collins, Snowe, and Brown and Democrat Cantwell. In the end, the need to get sixty votes to invoke cloture on the conference report led to delay and modification of the funding mechanism for the liquidation fund.

## III. Comparison and Conclusion

This comparison of the 86th and 111th Congresses has illustrated one of the most dramatic changes in the Senate over the last fifty years. In 1960 filibusters were rare and required active effort on the Senate floor and, consequently, the risk of public criticism. In the two 1960 filibuster cases, obstruction was used to delay a final vote on a nomination for a few hours and to prevent the passage of a civil rights bill—perhaps the most contentious issue of the era. Filibusters did not prevent the Senate from passing its appropriations bills as efficiently as the House, which suggests that this core function of Congress was not directly or indirectly affected.

The modern Senate, on the other hand, operates on the basis of supermajority rule. The default assumption is that bills and nominations can only pass if supporters can muster sixty votes to invoke cloture on them. Each individual senator gains immense power from the ability to threaten a filibuster against any bill or nomination, as illustrated by Senator Shelby's blanket hold on all nominations; even if the rest of the Senate supports a measure that faces a filibuster threat, party leaders may not want to invest time and effort into overcoming a threatened filibuster. And it is cheap to threaten a filibuster because the Senate no longer wages classic attrition marathons; faced with a threatened filibuster, Senate leaders schedule a cloture vote, negotiate, or give up. This creates a general climate of delay that hinders the Senate's ability to pass its appropriations bills.

The 2010 Financial Regulation bill illustrated both the impact of modern filibustering and the ability of the Senate to overcome its challenges and pass landmark legislation. The Republican minority opposed the bill at each stage, forcing the Democrats to muster a sixty-vote majority to bring the bill to the floor, pass it, and approve the conference report. The Democrats, for their part, employed the power of shame; in the wake of a financial meltdown, Republicans did not want the responsibility for killing the bill and backed off on their first-stage filibuster after Reid threatened to force them to actively filibuster through the night. In the end, the Democrats were able to pass major legislation with the aid of a few Republican moderates, but at the cost of weeks of Senate floor time. Consequently, other Democratic priorities like climate change, immigration, and economic stimulus were put off into the summer of an election year, when they were less likely to pass.

## References

Brown, Carrie Budoff. 2010a. "Obama Threatens Reg Reform Veto." *Politico*, April 16. http://www.politico.com/news/stories/0410/35926.html. Accessed June 10, 2010.

———. 2010b. "United GOP Front against Wall St. Bill." *Politico*, April 17. http://www.politico.com/news/stories/0410/35938.html. Accessed June 10, 2010.

Brown, Carrie Budoff, and Meredith Shiner. 2010a. "GOP Relents, Wall St. Debate Opens." *Politico*, April 28. http://www.politico.com/news/stories/0410/36470.html. Accessed June 10, 2010.

———. 2010b. "Senate Passes Sweeping Wall St. Bill." *Politico*, May 20. http://www.politico.com/news/stories/0510/37569.html. Accessed June 10, 2010.

Caro, Robert A. 2002. *Master of the Senate*. New York: Vintage Books.

Democratic Policy Committee. 1960. "Minutes," 1953–1960. Provided by the Senate Historian's Office.

Drury, Allen. 1959. "Senate Rejects Strauss, 49-46, at Night Session." *New York Times*, June 19, 1.

Epstein, Edward. 2010. "Dusting Off Deliberation." *Congressional Quarterly Weekly Report*, June 14, 1436–1442.

Frymer, Paul. 1999. *Uneasy Alliances: Race and Party Competition in America*. Princeton, N.J.: Princeton University Press.

Hulse, Carl, and Adam Nagourney. 2010. "Senate G.O.P. Leader Finds Weapon in Unity." *New York Times*, March 17, A13.

Koger, Gregory. 2010. *Filibustering: A Political History of Obstruction in the House and Senate*. Chicago: University of Chicago Press.

Krock, Arthur. 1959. "Strauss Case Raises Issues for Election." *New York Times*, June 21, E3.

Lee, Frances E. 2009. *Beyond Ideology: Politics, Principles, and Partisanship in the U.S. Senate*. Chicago: University of Chicago Press.

Lynch, Megan Suzanne. 2009. "Unanimous Consent Agreements Establishing a 60-Vote Threshold for Passage of Legislation in the Senate." Congressional Research Service RL3449. Washington, D.C.: Government Printing Office.

Mann, Robert. 1996. *The Walls of Jericho: Lyndon Johnson, Hubert Humphrey, Richard Russell, and the Struggle for Civil Rights*. New York: Harcourt Brace and Co.

Mattingly, Phil, and Kate Davidson. 2009. "Financial Overhaul Wins First Test in House." *CQ Weekly*, December 14, 2878–2882.

McGrane, Victoria. 2010. "Beat the Clock with Bank Reform." *Politico*, March 11. http://www.politico.com/news/stories/0310/34298.html. Accessed June 10, 2010.

McGrane, Victoria, and Lisa Lerer. 2010. "GOP Senators: Reg Reform Will Pass." *Politico*, March 25. http://www.politico.com/news/stories/0310/34981.html. Accessed June 10, 2010.

"Morton Rips Up Petition." 1960. *New York Times*, March 4, 1.

Packer, George. 2010. "The Empty Senate." *New Yorker*, August 9. http://www.newyorker.com/reporting/2010/08/09/100809fa_fact_packer. Accessed August 15, 2010.

Philips, Kate, and Jeff Zeleny. 2010. "White House Blasts Shelby Hold on Nominees." *New York Times*, February 5. http://thecaucus.blogs.nytimes.com/2010/02/05/white-house-blasts-shelby-hold-on-nominees/. Accessed February 5, 2010.

Schattschneider, E. E. 1960. *The Semisovereign People: A Realist's View of Democracy in America*. Fort Worth, Texas: Harcourt Brace Jovanovich.

"Senate Calls Off 24-Hour Sessions." 1960. *New York Times*, March 9, 1.

Shiner, Meredith. 2010. "Shelby Lifts Hold on Nominees." *Politico*, February 8. http://www.politico.com/news/stories/0210/32718.html. Accessed February 9, 2010.

Shiner, Meredith, and Carrie Budoff Brown. 2010. "Reid Picks Up Wall St. reform Pace." *Politico*, May 17. http://www.politico.com/news/stories/0510/37356.html. Accessed June 10, 2010.

Shiner, Meredith, and Manu Raju. 2010. "Shelby Puts Hold on Obama Noms." *Politico*, February 5. http://www.politico.com/news/stories/0210/32584.html. Accessed February 5, 2010.

Sinclair, Barbara. 2006. *Party Wars: Polarization and the Politics of National Policy Making*. Norman: University of Oklahoma Press.

Sloan, Steven. 2010. "Financial Overhaul's Extended Homestretch." *CQ Weekly*, July 5, 1624–1626.

Smith, Steven S., and Marcus Flathman. 1989. "Managing the Senate Floor: Complex Unanimous Consent Agreements since the 1950s." *Legislative Studies Quarterly* 14: 349–373.

"Statistical Summary." 1960. Mike Mansfield Archive, XXII, 28, 6.

Stern, Seth, and Kathleen Hunter. 2010. "Recess Appointment Threat Prompts Confirmation of Several Nominees." *CQ Weekly*, February 15, 401.

Theriault, Sean. 2008. *Party Polarization in Congress*. New York: Cambridge University Press.

"This Sad Episode." 1959. *Time*, June 29.

Valelly, Richard M. 2004. *The Two Reconstructions: The Struggle for Black Enfranchisement.* Chicago: University of Chicago Press.

Wilson, Scott, and Shailagh Murray. 2010. "Sen. Richard Shelby of Alabama Holding Up Obama Nominees for Home-State Pork." *Washington Post*, February 6, A3.

# 9

# Advice and Consent in the "Slow" Senate

Sarah Binder

> The judicial appointments process has become needlessly acrimonious.
>
> Senate Republican Communications Center (2009)

With a measure of understatement, thus intoned Senate Republicans in 2009—even as they reserved the right to filibuster any of President Barack Obama's judicial nominations deemed unacceptable by the Republican Conference. "Regretfully, if we are not consulted on, and approve of, a nominee from our states, the Republican Conference will be unable to support moving forward on that nominee." Putting the Obama administration and Senate Democrats on notice, Republican senators gave fair warning of the tenor of advice and consent in the 111th Congress. One year later, that course appears to continue, with the trends of recent years— senatorial foot-dragging, declining confirmation rates, and protestations by both political parties about the broken nature of advice and consent— remaining firmly on track.

In this chapter, I explore the politics of nomination and confirmation over the past forty years, a period of time that substantially overlaps the long Senate career of Robert Dole (R-Kan.). Assessing patterns over the past four decades and focusing on judicial nominations, I show broad trends in the Senate's treatment of court nominees and pinpoint developments that have fueled conflict over the make-up of the federal bench. In contrast to scholars who claim that the process of selecting federal judges has always been political, I argue that conflict over judicial appointees varied significantly over Senator Dole's tenure in the Senate and across the federal bench. I bring the history up to date by exploring emerging trends in the Senate's treatment of the Obama administration's judicial nominations—as well as the spillover of conflict into the realm of executive branch nominees. I conclude that the heat over selection and confirmation of presidential appointments remains high—and unlikely to subside soon.

## Competing Accounts of Judicial Selection

For better or worse, federal judges in the United States are often asked to resolve society's most important and contentious public policy issues. Although some hold onto the notion that the federal judiciary is simply a neutral arbiter of complex legal questions, the justices and judges who serve on the Supreme Court and the lower federal bench are in fact crafters of public law. In recent years, for example, the Supreme Court has endorsed the constitutionality of school vouchers, struck down Washington, D.C.'s ban on hand guns, and, most famously, determined the outcome of the 2000 presidential election. The judiciary clearly is an active partner in the making of public policy.

As the breadth and salience of federal court dockets has grown, the process of selecting federal judges has drawn increased attention. Judicial selection has been contentious at numerous junctures in American history, but seldom has it seemed more acrimonious and dysfunctional than in recent years. Fierce controversies such as the battles to confirm Robert Bork and Clarence Thomas to the Supreme Court are emblematic of an intensely divisive political climate in Washington. Alongside these high-profile disputes have been scores of less conspicuous confirmation cases held hostage in the Senate, resulting in declining confirmation rates and unprecedented delays in filling federal judgeships. As of March 2010, 12 percent of the federal trial bench and 11 percent of the federal appellate bench remained vacant. Although Senate parties reach periodic agreements to release their hostages, conflict over judicial selection continues to rise. All the while, the caseload of the federal judiciary is expanding to an exceptionally heavy level.

As the media have paid more attention to the difficulties faced by judicial nominees in securing confirmation to the bench, political science and legal scholars have offered diverging approaches to understanding recent conflict over the selection of federal judges. Legal scholars have questioned the growing salience of ideology in confirmation hearings, while judicial scholars have examined how presidential ambitions shape the selection of judges and how interest groups succeed in derailing nominees they oppose (see Burbank 2002; Goldman 1997; Bell 2002; Scherer 2005). Such studies provide excellent but partial portraits of the forces shaping the contemporary politics of advice and consent.

To the extent that scholars have attempted to provide a broader explanation of the crisis in judicial selection, they have proposed two alternative accounts—neither of which fully captures the political and institutional dynamics in the Senate that shape contemporary advice and consent. One account—call it the "Big Bang" theory of judicial selection—points to a breaking point in national politics, after which prevailing norms of deference and restraint in judicial selection fell apart. The result has been a sea change in appointment politics—evidenced by the lengthening of the confirmation process and the rise in confirmation failure. A strong alternative account—call it the "Nothing new under the sun" theory of judicial selection—suggests that ideological conflict over the make-up of the bench has been an ever present force in shaping the selection of federal judges and justices. Judicial selection has always been political and ideological as senators and presidents vie for influence over the bench.

Adherents of the Big Bang account typically point to a cataclysmic event in Congress or the courts that had an immediate and lasting impact on the process and politics of judicial selection thereafter. Most often, scholars point to the battle over Robert Bork's nomination to the Supreme Court in 1987 as the event that precipitated a new regime in the treatment of presidential appointments by the Senate. As John Maltese (2004) has argued about Supreme Court appointment politics,

> The defeat of Robert Bork's 1987 Supreme Court nomination was a watershed event that unleashed what Stephen Carter has called "the confirmation mess." There was no question that Bork was a highly qualified nominee. He was rejected not because of any lack of qualification, or any impropriety, but because of his stated judicial philosophy: how he would vote as a judge.

The president's willingness to nominate a strong conservative deemed outside the mainstream by the Democratic majority, and Senate Democrats' willingness to challenge a qualified nominee on grounds of how he would rule on the bench—together these developments are said to have radically altered the practice of advice and consent for judicial nominees. Adherents of the Big Bang account have also argued that the Bork debacle spilled over into the politics of lower court nominations, significantly increasing the politicization of selecting judges for the lower federal bench (see Martinek, Kemper, and Van Winkle 2002).

Other versions of the Big Bang theory point to alternative pivotal events, including the Supreme Court's 1954 *Brown v. Board of Education* decision. As Benjamin Wittes (2006) has argued, "We can reasonably describe the decline of the process as an institutional reaction by the Senate to the growth of judicial power that began with the Brown decision in 1954." Still other versions of the Big Bang point to the transformation of party activists (from seekers of material benefits to seekers of ideological or policy benefits) and the mobilization of political elites outside the Senate attempting to affect the make-up of the bench (see Scherer 2005; Bell 2002).

No doubt, the Bork debacle, the changing character of elite activists, and the emergence of the courts as key policymakers have all shaped to some degree the emergence of conflict over appointments in the postwar period. Still, these explanations do not help us to pinpoint the timing or location of conflict over judges. The increasing relevance of the Warren Court on a range of controversial issues certainly must have played a role in increasing the salience of judicial nominations to senators. Had the Court avoided engaging controversial social, economic, and political issues, senators would have had little incentive to try to influence the make-up of the bench. But neither do we see large changes in the dynamics of advice and consent until well after the 1954 decision and until well after the emergence of more ideological activists in the 1960s. And certainly the no-holds-barred battle over the Bork nomination may have shown both parties that concerted opposition to a presidential appointment was within the bounds of acceptable behavior after 1987. Still, isolating the impact of the Bork fight cannot help us to explain the significant variation in the Senate's treatment of judicial nominees before and after the 100th Congress (1989–90). It is also important to recall that executive branch appointments also experienced a sea change in the late 1980s and 1990s, taking much longer to secure confirmation (see Mackenzie 2001). Thus, evidence to support the Big Bang account is incomplete. More likely, episodes like the Bork confirmation battle are symptoms, rather than causes, of the more taxing road to confirmation in recent decades.

Lee Epstein and Jeffrey Segal's "Nothing new under the sun" alternative suggests instead that "the appointments process is and always has been political because federal judges and justices themselves are political" (Epstein and Segal 2005). As these scholars argue, presidents have always wanted to use the appointment power for ideological and partisan purposes, and senators have always treated appointees to "help further their own goals, primarily those that serve to advance their chances of reelection, their political party, or their policy interests" (Epstein and Segal 2005). These scholars' views of legislators, judges, and presidents as strategic, political actors are important. We should expect to see legislators and presidents engage in purposeful behavior shaped by their goals. But that is only a starting point in accounting for the dynamics of advice and consent. It is quite difficult to explain variation in the Senate's treatment of judicial appointments—both over time and across circuits—if we maintain that the process has always been politicized. I certainly recognize the political nature of advice and consent, but also seek to identify the ways in which politicians exploit Senate rules and practices to target appointees deemed most likely to shift the ideological tenor of the federal bench.

## Patterns in Judicial Selection

Numerous indicators suggest that something has gone awry in the process of advice and consent for selecting federal judges. The broad pattern can be

**Figure 9.1**    Confirmation Rates for Judicial Nominations, 1947–2008

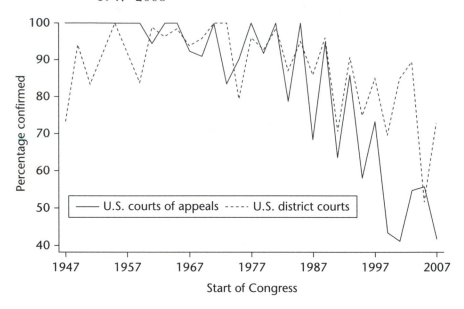

Source: Compiled by author from *Final Legislative and Executive Calendars*, U.S. Senate, Committee on the Judiciary, 80th–107th Congresses. Data for 108th–110th Congresses (through December 18, 2008) drawn from data compiled by the Department of Justice, Office of Legal Policy, at http://www.usdoj.gov/olp/ (accessed December 18, 2008).

seen in Figure 9.1, which shows confirmation rates for appointees to the U.S. district courts and courts of appeals between 1947 and 2008. The bottom has clearly fallen out of the confirmation process, with rates dipping below 50 percent in some recent Congresses. Moreover, perhaps most often missed in discussions of confirmation patterns is that conflict over the selection of federal judges has not extended equally across all twelve circuits.[1] As seen in Figure 9.2, nominations for some appellate vacancies attract reasonably little controversy, such as the Midwest's Seventh Circuit. Not so for the Court of Appeals for D.C. and for the Fourth, Fifth and Sixth Circuits, for which over half of the nominations have failed since 1992.

As the likelihood of confirmation has gone down, the length of time it takes for presidents to nominate and the Senate to confirm candidates for the bench has increased. At the end of the 1950s, it took on average about 200 days, or just over six months, for presidents to select a nominee once a

---

1. I exclude the Federal Circuit (created in 1982) from my purview, due to its fixed jurisdiction that focuses primarily on appeals arising under U.S. patent laws.

**Figure 9.2**    Failure Rates for Nominations Made to the Courts of Appeals, 1991–2008

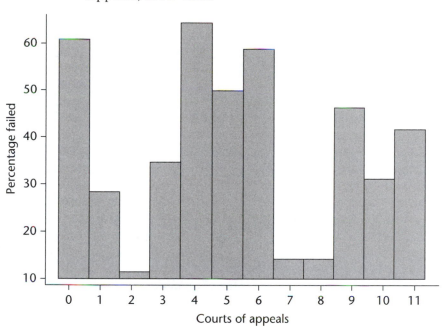

Note: Graph shows the percentage of nominations to each court of appeals that failed, averaged across all Congresses in the period; "0" court indicates Court of Appeals for the District of Columbia.

vacant judgeship occurred. By the end of the 1990s, it took an average of 600 days, roughly twenty months from vacancy to nomination.

As shown in Figures 9.3a and 9.3b, the length of time it takes for the Senate to act on nominees has also increased. Between the 1940s and 1980s, a typical appellate court judge was confirmed within two months of nomination. By the late 1990s, the wait for successful nominees had stretched to about six months. These average waits, however, pale in comparison to the experiences of nominees who failed to be confirmed during the Clinton and George W. Bush administrations. Since the mid-1990s, a typical appellate nominee who fails to secure confirmation lingers before the Senate for almost a year and a half. As the confirmation process has dragged out in recent years, some candidates have become increasingly reluctant to wait it out. As Miguel Estrada said in 2003 upon abandoning his two-year-long quest for confirmation, "I believe that the time has come to return my full attention to the practice of law and to regain the ability to make long-term plans for my family" (Hulse and Stout 2003).

Nominees for federal trial courts have also experienced delays, although to a somewhat lesser extent, as shown in Figure 9.3b. As I argue below, these

**Figure 9.3a**    Length of Confirmation Process for Successful Courts of Appeals Nominees, 1947–2008

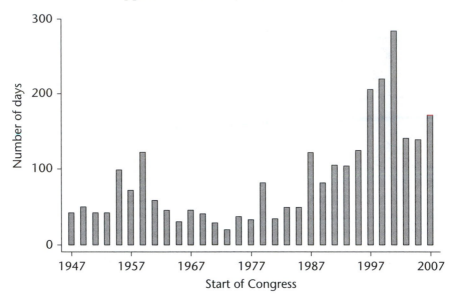

**Figure 9.3b**    Length of Confirmation Process for Successful District Courts Nominees, 1947–2008

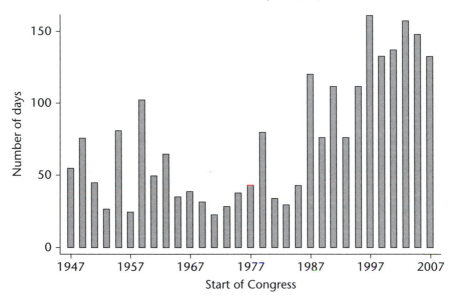

Source: Compiled by author from *Final Legislative and Executive Calendars*, U.S. Senate, Committee on the Judiciary, 102nd–107th Congresses. Data for 108th–110th Congresses drawn from data compiled by the Department of Justice, Office of Legal Policy, at http://www.usdoj.gov/olp/ (accessed September 24, 2008). Note the different scales on the y-axis.

multiple indicators of a judicial selection system potentially near its breaking point deserve attention and explanation. There is certainly something "new under the sun" when it comes to the state of advice and consent for candidates for the federal bench.

## The Politics of Advice and Consent

How do we account for the Senate's uneven performance in confirming federal judges? Why have confirmation rates slid downward over the past couple of decades, and why does it take so long for the Senate to render its decisions? Four forces shape the fate of nominations sent to the Senate. First and foremost are ideological forces: the array of policy views across the three branches affects the probability and speed of confirmation. Second, partisan forces matter: political contests between the president and the opposing Senate party help account for the Senate's treatment of judicial nominees. Third, institutional rules and practices in the Senate shape the likelihood of confirmation. Fourth, the electoral context matters.

### Partisan and Ideological Forces

Partisan and ideological forces are inextricably linked in the contemporary Congress as the two legislative parties have diverged ideologically in recent decades. Not surprisingly, Washington pundits assessing the state of judicial selection have often pinpointed poisoned relations between conservative Republicans and President Bill Clinton and between liberal Democrats and President George W. Bush as the proximate cause of the slowdown in advice and consent. They suggest that partisan and ideological antagonisms between Clinton and far-right conservatives led Republican senators to delay even the most highly qualified nominees. Democrats' foot-dragging on several of Bush's nominees in the 108th Congress (2003–04) was similarly attributed to ideological conflict and partisan pique, as liberal Democrats criticized Bush's tendency to nominate extremely conservative (and presumably Republican) judges. The rise of intense ideological differences between the two parties over the past two decades, in other words, may be directly affecting the pace and rate of confirming new federal judges.

Partisan politics may affect the process of advice and consent more broadly in the guise of divided party government. Because judges have lifetime tenure and the capacity to make lasting decisions on the shape of public law, senators have good cause to scrutinize the views of all potential federal judges. Because presidents overwhelmingly seek to appoint judges who hail from the president's party, Senate scrutiny of judicial nominees should be particularly intense when two different parties control the White House and the Senate. It is not a surprise then that nominees considered during a period of divided control take significantly longer to be confirmed than those nominated during a period of unified control. Judicial nominees are also less likely to be confirmed during divided government: between 1961 and 2008, the Senate confirmed on average 84 percent of appellate court nominees during periods of unified control, but only 66 percent of nominees under divided government.

Partisan control of the branches is particularly likely to affect nominations when presidents seek to fill vacancies on appellate circuits whose judges are evenly balanced between the two parties. Because most appellate court cases are heard by randomly generated three-judge panels, nominations to courts that are evenly divided are likely to have a more significant impact on the law's development, as compared to appointments to courts that lean decidedly in one ideological direction or the other. Senate majorities appear especially reluctant to confirm nominees to such courts when the appointment would tip the court balance in the favor of a president from the opposing party.

One of the hardest hit courts is the Sixth Circuit Court of Appeals, straddling populous midwestern states such as Michigan and Ohio. In recent years, a quarter of the bench has been vacant, including one seat declared a judicial emergency after sitting empty for five years. Moreover, the Sixth Circuit has recently been precariously balanced between the parties. The Senate slowdown on appointments to the circuit during the Clinton and Bush administrations was likely motivated by the strategic importance of the circuit. Blocking Clinton's Democratic nominees allowed Senate Republicans to prevent the Democrats from transforming the party-balanced court into a Democratic-dominated bench. Similarly, once Bush took office, the two Michigan senators (both Democrats) went to great lengths to prevent the Senate from taking action on Bush's conservative nominees for that court. In short, partisan dynamics—fueled in part by ideological conflict—strongly shape the Senate's conduct of advice and consent, making it difficult for presidents to stack the federal courts as they see fit.

## Institutional Forces

Partisan and ideological forces likely provide senators with an incentive to probe the opposition party's judicial nominees. But the capacity to derail nominees depends on the rules and practices of advice and consent—a set of institutional tools that distributes power across the institution. Thus, to explain the fate of the president's judicial nominees, we need to know something about the institutional context of the confirmation process.

Senators can exploit multiple potential vetoes when they seek to affect the fate of a nominee and have at their disposal an array of Senate rules and practices wielded in committee and on the floor by individual senators and the two political parties (Primo, Binder, and Maltzman 2008).

In theory, nominees only have to secure the consent of a floor majority, as nominations are considered for an up-or-down vote in the Senate's executive session. In practice, nominees must secure the support of several pivotal Senate players— meaning that more than a simple majority may be needed for confirmation.

The initial institutional hurdle for any nominee is securing approval from the Senate Judiciary Committee. By tradition senators from the home state of each judicial nominee take the lead on casting first judgment on potential appointees. The veto power of home state senators is institutionalized in judiciary panel procedures. Both of the home state senators are asked their views about judicial nominees from their home state pending before the committee. Senators can return the "blue slip" demarking their support or objection to the nominee, or they can refuse to return the blue slip altogether—an action signaling the senator's opposition to the nominee. One negative blue slip from a home state senator traditionally was sufficient to block further action on a nominee. As the process has become more polarized in recent years, committee chairs have been tempted to ignore objections from minority party senators. Indeed, the equivocation of Judiciary Committee chair Patrick Leahy (D-Vt.) at the start of the 111th Congress over how he would treat blue slips from Republican senators lies at the heart of the warning sent by Republican senators that they would filibuster nominees from states with Republican senators if their prior consent was not secured. At a minimum, blue slips today weigh heavily in the committee chair's assessment of whether, when, and how to proceed with a nominee; however, senators' objections do not carry any formal power over the committee's choice of whether or when to proceed.

Historically, greater policy differences between the president and the home state senator for appellate nominees have led to longer confirmation proceedings, suggesting the power of home state senators to affect panel proceedings. Conversely, the strong support of one's home state senator is essential in navigating the committee successfully. Given the often fractured attention of the Senate and the willingness of senators to heed the preferences of the home state senator, having a strong advocate in the Senate with an interest in seeing the nomination proceed is critical in smoothing the way for nominees.

Once approved by committee, a nomination has a second institutional hurdle to clear: making it onto the Senate's crowded agenda. By rule and precedent, both majority and minority party coalitions can delay nominations after they clear committee. Because the presiding officer of the chamber gives the majority leader priority in being recognized to speak on the Senate floor, the majority leader has the upper hand in setting the chamber's agenda. When the president's party controls the Senate, this means that nominations are usually confirmed more quickly; under divided control, nominations can be kept off the floor by the majority leader—who wields the right to make a non-debatable motion to call the Senate into executive session to consider nominees. That procedural advantage for the majority party enhances the importance of support from the majority leader—and the majority party caucus by extension—in shaping the fate of presidential appointees.

The majority leader's discretion over the executive session agenda is not wielded without challenge, however, as nominations can be filibustered once called up in executive session. The chance that a nomination might be filibustered typically motivates the majority leader to seek unanimous consent of the full chamber before bringing a nomination before the Senate. Such consultation between the two parties means that nominations are unlikely to clear the Senate without the endorsement of the minority party.

The de facto requirement of minority party assent grants the party opposing the president significant power to affect the fate of nominees, even if that party does not control the Senate. As policy differences increase between the president and the opposing party, that party is more likely to exercise its power to delay nominees. Given the high degree of polarization between the two parties today and the centrality of federal courts in shaping public law, it is not surprising that judicial nominations have become such a flash point for the parties. Indeed, when Democrats lost control of the Senate after the 2002 elections, they turned to new tactics to block nominees they disliked: the filibuster. To be sure, some contentious nominations have in the past been subject to cloture votes. But all of those lower court nominees were eventually confirmed. In 2003, however, numerous judicial filibusters were successful. Use of such tactics likely flowed from the increased polarization of the two parties and from the rising salience of the federal courts across the interest group community—as well as from the growing willingness of senators to exploit Rule 22 on policy matters before the Senate. The spillover from policy to confirmations should not be a surprise, not least on account of the life tenure of federal judges and the relatively low public salience of most nominees for the bench. Much of the recent variation in the fate of judicial nominees before the Senate is thus likely driven by ideologically motivated players and parties in both the executive and legislative branches exploiting the rules of the game in an effort to shape the make-up of the federal bench.

## Temporal Forces

Finally, it is important to consider how secular or cyclical elements of the political calendar may shape the fate of judicial nominees. Delays encountered by judicial nominees may be a natural consequence of an approaching presidential election (Binder and Maltzman 2009). Decades ago, the opposition party in the Senate might have wanted to save vacancies purely as a matter of patronage: foot-dragging on nominations would boost the number of positions the party would have to fill if it won the White House. More recently, opposition senators might want to save vacancies so that a president of their own party could fill the vacancies with judges more in tune with the party's policy priorities.

There is ample evidence of "vacancy hoarding" in presidential election years in the recent past. For example, with control of both the Senate and the White House up for grabs in November 2008, Democrats had by the fall confirmed only ten of the twenty-four nominations to the federal courts of appeals made by President Bush during the 110th Congress. Nominees for the less controversial federal trial courts did not fare much better, with just over 60 percent confirmed before the fall of 2008. More generally, over the past forty years the Senate has treated judicial nominations submitted or pending during a presidential election year significantly differently than other judicial nominations. First, the Senate has historically taken longer to confirm nominees pending in a presidential election than those submitted earlier in a president's term. Second, and more notably, these presidential-election-year nominees are significantly less likely to be confirmed. For all judicial nominations submitted between 1961 and 2008, appointees for the courts of appeals pending in the Senate in a presidential election year were over 40 percent less likely to be confirmed than nominees pending in other years.

Finally, the confirmation process has become more protracted over time. Figures 9.3a and 9.3b show the increase in how long it takes the Senate on average to confirm lower court nominations. Granted, it is difficult to separate the effects of a secular slowdown in the confirmation process from a concurrent rise in partisan polarization. But it is important to keep in mind that ideological disagreement between the parties should only affect advice and consent if the parties hold different views about the courts and their impact on public policy. The rising importance of the federal courts since the 1950s, as interest groups and politicians have used them as a venue for resolving intractable policy disputes, may well have encouraged both parties to take a more aggressive stance in reviewing nominations made by the opposition party's president (see Kagan 2001; Shapiro 2008; Silverstein 2009). As the federal courts become more central to the making of public policy, we should expect to find broader and heightened concern among politicians and political parties about the make-up of the bench.

## Explaining Trends in Advice and Consent

How do we account more systematically for variation in the degree of conflict over judicial nominees? The multiple forces outlined above are clearly at play. For social scientists investigating patterns over time, this raises a key question. Taking each of these forces together, how well do the trends noted here hold up? Once subjected to multivariate controls, what can we conclude about the relative impact of partisan, ideological, and institutional forces on the pace and rate of judicial confirmations? Answers to these questions are consequential as they help us to evaluate how well the president and the Senate discharge their constitutional duties of advice and consent.

To explain variation in conflict over judicial nominees, I track the fate of all nominations to the lower federal courts, focusing here on the courts of appeals between 1961 and 2006.[2] I use these data to estimate a model of the likelihood of confirmation for appellate court nominees, controlling for the forces noted above. The results shown in Table 9.1 can help us to disentangle the forces that shape the Senate's treatment of presidential appointees to the bench.[3] First, the degree of partisan polarization matters strongly. As the two parties diverge ideologically, the likelihood of confirmation goes down. The magnitude of the effect is substantial. During the least polarized Senate since the early 1960s (the 92nd Congress, 1971–72), the likelihood of confirmation was 99 percent, estimated by holding all the other variables at their mean values. During the most polarized Congress (the 109th, 2005–06), nominees had an estimated 33 percent chance of being confirmed. As the degree of difference between the two parties on major policy issues increases the less and less likely are the parties to give the other party's nominees an easy path to the bench. That effect is much stronger than the impact of divided party control. Nominations are less likely to be confirmed in periods of divided government. The magnitude of the effect, however, is less than 10 percent when we control for the other forces at their mean values.

Ideologically distant home state senators also appear to shape nominees' chances of confirmation. When the more distant home state senator

---

2. I compile data on judicial nominations from the *Final Calendars* printed each Congress by the Senate Committee on the Judiciary. Nominations data for the 108th and 109th Congresses (2003–2006) are drawn from the Department of Justice's Office of Legal Policy website: http:// www.usdoj.gov/olp/. I include the Court of Appeals for the District of Columbia, but exclude the appellate court for the Federal Circuit on account of its limited jurisdiction.

3. The independent variables are determined as follows. Polarization is measured as the difference in the mean ideology for each Senate party (as measured by DW-Nominate scores available at http://www.voteview.com). The partisan balance of each circuit in each Congress is measured as the proportion of active courts of appeals judges appointed by Democratic presidents and serving during the Congress. I determine whether the nominee's home state senator is ideologically distant from the president by selecting those home state senators for the nomination who are equal to or greater than one standard deviation of the mean DW-Nominate distance between the president and the more distant home state senator. Nominee quality is rated by the Standing Committee on the Federal Judiciary of the American Bar Association and are available for the 101st–109th Congresses here: http://www .abanet.org/scfedjud/ratings.html. I thank Sheldon Goldman for ABA ratings for the previous congresses.

**Table 9.1**   Determinants of Senate Confirmation of Nominations to the U.S. Courts of Appeals, 1961–2006

| Variable | Coefficient (robust SE) |
| --- | --- |
| Divided government | −1.11(.330)*** |
| Balanced bench | −.478(.284)* |
| Degree of partisan polarization | −8.884(1.202)*** |
| Ideologically distant home state senator | −.711(.310)** |
| Nomination pending during a presidential election year | −2.221(2.87)*** |
| Well-qualified nominee | .429(.293) |
| Constant | 9.312(1.002)*** |
| N | 470 |
| Log pseudo likelihood | −160.716 |
| Prob. Chi2 | .000*** |

Note: Parameter estimates are logit coefficients generated by the *logit* routine in Stata 9.0. *** $p < .001$, **$p < .01$, *$p < .05$ (all one-tailed tests). The dependent variable is coded 1 if nominee confirmed in the Congress in which s/he was nominated, 0 otherwise. Independent variables described in text.

for a nomination is still reasonably close to the president, the chance of confirmation is over 90 percent; the chance of confirmation slips 6 percent when one of the home state senators is ideologically distant from the president (and presumably then from the nominee). Lodging an objection through the blue slip—perhaps because the senator's objection may be backed up by the threat of a party filibuster—confers leverage on a senator seeking to derail a president's pick for a judgeship in his or her home state. We also see a noticeable impact in the case of an approaching presidential election, as confirmation is nearly 30 percent less likely when control of the White House—and hence the power to select judicial nominees—is at stake.

The partisan balance of the circuit also seems to affect the chances of confirmation. The likelihood of confirmation drops 7 percent when senators consider a nomination for a balanced circuit (assuming all other variables are set at their mean values). That finding puts into perspective debates in the late 1990s over the make-up of the Sixth Circuit. In 1997 and 1998, the circuit was nearly evenly balanced between Democrats and Republicans, as Democrats made up roughly 45 percent of the bench. That tight ideological balance led the parties to stalemate over additional appointments to that circuit, even though nearly a quarter of the bench was vacant during that period. Michigan's lone Republican senator blocked Clinton's nominees by exploiting the blue slip in the late 1990s, and the Republican chair of the judiciary panel recognized his objections. Michigan's two Democratic senators after the 2000 elections then objected to Bush's appointments to the Sixth Circuit. General disagreement over the policy views of the nominees certainly fueled these senators, but their opposition was particularly intense given the stakes of filling the judgeships for the ideological balance of the regional bench.

We find only weak evidence that the quality of the nominees, as signaled by the American Bar Association, has much bearing on the likelihood of confirmation. One possibility is that the ABA might not be seen as a neutral evaluator of judicial nominees, and thus senators may systematically ignore the association's recommendations. Alternatively, judicial qualifications may not be terribly important for most nominees. Very few nominees are actually rated "unqualified," and senators may not perceive much of a difference between a nominee deemed "well qualified" and one rated "qualified." Thus, senators' calculations about whether to confirm would be influenced more heavily by other considerations.

Collectively, these institutional and electoral forces matter quite a bit. Imagine a period of unified party control in which the two Senate parties are reasonably close ideologically. If the home state senator is fairly compatible in ideological terms with the president, and if the vacant judgeship occurred on a court of appeals firmly in one partisan camp or the other, then confirmation is all but guaranteed. In contrast, imagine a nomination submitted to the Senate in a period of unified government that featured ideologically polarized parties—as seems to be the case today with the return of unified Democratic control under President Obama. If that nomination is slotted for a judgeship on a roughly balanced court and the home state senator has strong policy disagreements with the president, then the chance of confirmation drops by twenty points.[4] This all assumes, of course, that the nominee's policy views more closely resemble those of the president rather than the views of the home state senator. To the extent that President Obama can select nominees who are perceived to be moderate, if not right of center, the prospects for confirmation improve. That said, even a moderate nominee like David Hamilton (selected by Obama and endorsed by the Republican home state senator Richard Lugar) endured dilatory tactics that concluded in a cloture vote some eight months after his nomination in March 2009.

## The New Wars of Judicial Selection

Statistical analysis suggests the enduring impact of partisan, institutional, and temporal forces on the fate of presidential appointments to the federal bench. Still, the fall-off in confirmation rates leaves no doubt that advice and consent has changed markedly in recent years. The media pay far more attention to these confirmation battles, and interest in the fate of presidential

---

4. Both simulations assume that the nominee has been rated highly by the ABA and is not pending before the Senate in a presidential election year.

appointees now extends beyond the home state senators. Both parties—often fueled by supportive groups outside the chamber—have made the plight of potential judges central to their campaigns for the White House and Congress (see Caldeira and Wright 1995; Flemming, MacLeod, and Talbert 1998; Bell 2002).[5] The salience of judicial nominations to the two political parties—inside and outside of the halls of the Senate— is prima facie evidence that there is definitely something "new under the sun" when it comes to the selection of federal judges. To be sure, not every nominee experiences intense opposition, as Democrats acquiesced to over three hundred of President George W. Bush's judicial nominees just as Republicans supported scores of Clinton nominees. But the salience of the process seems to have increased sharply starting in the early 1980s and continued with full force under the presidencies of Clinton and Bush.

The rising salience of federal judgeships is visible on several fronts. First, intense interest in the selection of federal judges is no longer limited to the home state senators for the nomination. Second, negative blue slips from home state senators no longer automatically kill a nomination, as recent judiciary panel chairs have been hesitant to accord such influence to their minority party colleagues. Third, recorded floor votes are now the norm for confirmation of appellate court judges, as nominations are of increased importance to groups outside the institution. And fourth, nominations now draw the attention of strategists within both political parties—as evidenced by President Bush's focus on judicial nominations in stumping for Republican Senate candidates throughout his tenure in office.

How do we account for the rising salience of federal judgeships to actors in and out of the Senate? It is tempting to claim that the activities of organized interests after the 1987 Supreme Court confirmation battle over Robert Bork are responsible. But interest groups have kept a close eye on judicial selection for quite some time. Both liberal and conservative groups were involved periodically from the late 1960s into the 1980s. And in 1984, liberal groups under the umbrella of the Alliance for Justice commenced systematic monitoring of judicial appointments, as had the conservative Judicial Reform Project of the Free Congress Foundation earlier in the decade. Although interest group tactics may have fanned the fires over judicial selection in recent years, the introduction of new blocking tactics in the Senate developed long after groups had become active in the judicial selection process (Davis and Greenberger 2004). Outside groups may encourage senators to take more aggressive stands against judicial nominees, but by and large Senate opposition reflects senators' concerns about the policy impact of judges on the federal bench.

---

5. Involvement of interest groups in lower court judicial selection reaches back decades, but a marked increase in their organized involvement occurred in the early 1980s.

Rather than attribute the state of judicial selection to the lobbying of outside groups, I see two concurrent trends indelibly shaping the politics of judicial selection. First, Democrats and Republicans are more ideologically opposed today than they have been for the past few decades. The empirical analysis above strongly suggests that ideological differences between the parties encourage senators to exploit the rules of the game to their party's advantage in filling vacant judgeships or blocking new nominees.

Second, if the courts were of little importance to the two parties, then polarized relations would matter little to senators and presidents in conducting advice and consent. However, the federal courts today are integral to the interpretation and enforcement of federal law. That means that the parties today are acutely sensitive to the ideological balance of the federal courts, since the policy views of judges may affect their rulings on the bench. Notably, when Democrats lost control of the Senate after the 2002 elections, the federal courts were nearly evenly balanced between Democratic and Republican appointees: the active judiciary was composed of 380 judges appointed by Republican presidents and 389 judges appointed by Democratic presidents (Alliance for Justice Judicial Selection Project 2002). Across the twelve appellate courts, seventy-five judges had been appointed by Republican presidents and sixty-seven by Democratic presidents.

Having lost control of the Senate, distrusting the ideological orientation of Bush appointees, and finding the courts on the edge of partisan balance, it is no surprise that Democrats made scrutiny of judicial nominees a caucus priority starting in 2003 and achieved remarkable unity in blocking nominees they deemed particularly egregious. No small wonder that Republicans responded in 2005 by threatening recalcitrant Democrats with the "nuclear option" (Binder, Madonna, and Smith 2007). Intense ideological disagreement coupled with the rising importance of a closely balanced federal bench has brought combatants in the wars of advice and consent to new tactics and new crises as the two parties struggle to shape the future of the courts. Of course, eight years of Republican rule under the Bush administration still left an imprint on the bench: roughly 60 percent of the appellate court judges had been appointed by Republican presidents by the end of 2009, up from 49 percent six years earlier.

## Advice and Consent during the Obama Administration

The return of unified party control increased Democrats' hopes of a smoother path to confirmation for Obama appointees. One year after taking office, Democrats' hopes were fading. Some of their concerns stemmed from a sluggish White House; others, from the persistence of Republican intransigence over confirming a Democratic president's nominees. Perhaps most interesting about the first year of the Obama administration was that conflict over advice and consent was no longer limited to nominations for the courts of appeals. Instead, the minority party sought to exercise their blocking powers over both appellate and trial courts, as well as over high profile (and not so high profile) executive branch nominees.

Confirmation statistics for the first year of the Obama administration typified the eventual record of the 111th Congress. One year into Obama's term, just six of twelve appellate court nominees and just eleven of thirty-three district court nominees had been confirmed. Two of those appellate court nominees—David Hamilton and Barbara Keenan—faced cloture votes after the majority leader was unable to secure unanimous consent for their floor consideration. Both of these cases merit a closer look. When nominated for a judgeship on the Seventh Circuit, Hamilton (who had served for fourteen years on the federal district court for Southern Indiana) had the support of his home state senators—including Republican Richard Lugar. Even the president of the conservative Indiana Federalist Society endorsed Hamilton, noting that he was an "excellent jurist with a first-rate intellect" (Richey 2009). Nevertheless, it took eight months for Hamilton to be confirmed, with 59 votes for confirmation after opponents mustered only 29 votes to maintain a filibuster.

Keenan, nominated for the Fourth Circuit, waited five months for a cloture vote, even though the Senate Judiciary Committee had unanimously approved her nomination months before. Reporters never seem to have figured out which senator or senators had placed a hold on her appointment, but she was confirmed unanimously, 99–0. Nor were trial court nominees immune from Republican blocking techniques. Although every district court nominee who made it to an up-or-down confirmation vote was confirmed unanimously, the path was a bit rocky for seven nominees whose nominations were returned to the president when Republicans refused to grant consent to waive the Senate's Rule 31 (that returns nominations to the president when the Senate adjourns or recesses for more than thirty days). Delaying district court nominations is not without precedent, as only roughly half of President Bush's trial court nominees were confirmed in the 109th Congress (2005–06). Once the precedent is set that district court nominees are fair game for close scrutiny and foot-dragging, however, it is tough to put the genie back in the bottle.

Partisan conflict also appears to have spilled over to infect advice and consent for Obama's executive branch nominees. Some were held up *en masse* when Sen. Richard Shelby of Alabama in early 2010 placed a blanket hold on roughly seventy nominees to protest two federal agency actions related to Alabama. Other nominees—including Obama's appointee to lead the General Services Administration—were stalled for nine months before receiving a unanimous cloture vote; Sen. Kit Bond (R-Mo.) had placed a hold on Johnson's nomination to force the GSA to relocate workers from a federal complex in Kansas City to a new building. Sen. Arlen Specter (D-Penn.) did the math in February 2010 and found that Republican holds had delayed the confirmation of forty-six executive branch nominations for at least three months and forty-five for at least four months. And nine nominees took six or more months after committee consideration before making it to floor consideration. As Specter noted, were the majority leader to file cloture on the several dozen nominations pending on the Senate's Executive Calendar, "it would take most of the year to deal with nominations" (Keen 2010).

The sparse record of the 111th Congress likely reflects a few trends. First, the pace of nominations from the White House was quite slow for much of 2009, perhaps as a result of the White House's preoccupation with health care and other administration priorities. Second, the polarization of the parties seems not to have abated. Deliberate foot-dragging by the Senate Republican Conference on David Hamilton's elevation to the appellate court—even given Senator Lugar's support— suggests that conservative Republicans are unwilling to defer to Republican home state senators. Instead, policy and political/partisan ambition seems to shape Republican strategy on nominations. Third, the persistence of Republican holds—which delay confirmation votes for nominees who are eventually confirmed unanimously—suggests that a parliamentary tit-for-tat is under way in the Senate. Republicans have not forgotten Democratic filibusters of Bush's nominees, and seem intent on repaying their adversaries. Obama's professed commitment to bipartisanship is one likely casualty of these developments.

## Conclusions

In the run-up to the 2008 presidential elections, nomination and confirmation of judges for the lower federal courts ground to a halt. Reflecting on the impasse, Texas Republican senator John Cornyn observed that Democrats were playing "a short-sighted game, because around here what goes around comes around. . . . When the shoe is on the other foot, there is going to be a temptation to respond in kind" (Rowley 2007). The senator's point was certainly on the mark. Each party's intolerance of the other party's nominees has recently been reciprocated when the parties swap positions in the Senate. Such behavior by both political parties—and the breach of Senate trust that appears to accompany it—does not bode well for lifting the Senate out of its confirmation morass.

Why should we care about the state of the confirmation process— especially if it brings to light the array of legal philosophies and policy views that potential judges would bring to the bench? Elsewhere, I explore the potentially harmful consequences of confirmation conflict for the performance of the courts and the public's views of judges and their decisions (Binder and Maltzman 2009). Here, I conclude with a brief thought about the impact of confirmation conflict on judicial legitimacy. As Fifth Circuit Court of Appeals judge Carolyn King has observed, "Judicial independence is undermined . . . by the high degree of political partisanship and ideology that currently characterizes the process by which the President nominates and the Senate confirms federal judges." Such a process, King continues, "conveys the notion to the electorate that judges are simply another breed of political agents, that judicial decisions should be in accord with political ideology, all of which tends to undermine public confidence in the legitimacy of the court" (King 2007). Equally troubling, King suggests that the polarization of the appointments process may be undermining the very act of judging, as judges on the right or the left may produce opinions not "true to the rule of law" (King 2007).

How widely Judge King's sentiment is shared within and beyond the Fifth Circuit is difficult to assess. But her vantage point as former chief judge of the circuit and her three decades on the appellate bench should encourage students of the Senate to take note of her warning and concerns. Unfortunately, there are few signs that the wars of advice and consent will abate anytime soon. More likely, they will intensify, especially when the next vacancy on the Supreme Court occurs. Unless the president selects someone with moderate ideological stripes—and even if he does—past battles over confirming judges could pale in comparison. The stakes of who sits on the federal bench are simply too high for combatants in the wars of advice and consent, inside and outside the Senate, to view the contest from the sidelines.

# References

Alliance for Justice Judicial Selection Project. 2002. *2001–2 Biennial Report*. Appendix 3.

Bell, Lauren Cohen. 2002. *Warring Factions: Interest Groups, Money, and the New Politics of Senate Confirmation*. Columbus: Ohio State University Press.

Binder, Sarah A., and Forrest Maltzman. 2009. *Advice and Dissent: The Struggle to Shape the Federal Judiciary*. Washington, D.C.: Brookings Institution.

Binder, Sarah A., Anthony Madonna, and Steven S. Smith. 2007. "Going Nuclear, Senate Style." *Perspectives on Politics* 5 (December).

Burbank, Stephen B. 2002. "Politics, Privilege, and Power: The Senate's Role in the Appointment of Federal Judges." *Judicature* 86:1 (July–August).

Caldeira, Gregory A., and John R. Wright. 1995. "Lobbying for Justice: The Rise of Organized Conflict in the Politics of Federal Judgeships." In Lee Epstein, ed., *Contemplating Courts*. Washington, D.C.: CQ Press.

Davis, Bob, and Robert S. Greenberger. 2004. "Two Old Foes Plot Tactics in Battle over Judgeships." *Wall Street Journal*, March 2.

Epstein, Lee, and Jeffrey Segal. 2005. *Advice and Consent: The Politics of Judicial Appointments*. New York: Oxford University Press.

Flemming, Roy B., Michael B. MacLeod, and Jeffery Talbert. 1998. "Witnesses at the Confirmations? The Appearances of Organized Interests at Senate Hearings of Federal Judicial Appointments, 1945–1992." *Political Research Quarterly* 51:3 (September).

Goldman, Sheldon. 1997. *Picking Federal Judges*. New Haven, Conn.: Yale University Press.

Hulse, Carl, and David Stout. 2003. "Embattled Estrada Withdraws as Nominee for Federal Bench." *New York Times*, September 4.

Kagan, Robert. 2001. *Adversarial Legalism*. Cambridge, Mass.: Harvard University Press.

Keen, Lisa. 2010. "Feldblum on Hold." *Metroweekly*, March 2. http://www.metroweekly.com/news/?ak=4939. Accessed March 12, 2010.

King, Carolyn Dineen. 2007. "Challenges to Judicial Independence and the Rule of Law: A Perspective from the Circuit Courts." Hallows Lecture, Marquette University Law School, February 20. http://law.marquette.edu/s3/site/images/alumni/Hallows Lecture2007.pdf. Accessed March 12, 2010.

Mackenzie, G. Calvin. 2001. *Innocent until Nominated: The Breakdown of the Presidential Appointments Process*. Washington, D.C.: Brookings Institution.

Maltese, John Anthony. 2004. "Anatomy of a Confirmation Mess: Recent Trends in the Federal Judicial Selection Process." A JURIST Online Symposium. http://jurist.law.pitt.edu/forum/Symposium-jc/Maltese.php#2.

Martinek, Wendy L., Mark Kemper, and Steven R. Van Winkle. 2002. "To Advise and Consent: The Senate and Lower Federal Court Nominations, 1977–1998." *Journal of Politics* 64.

Primo, David M., Sarah A. Binder, and Forrest Maltzman. 2008. "Who Consents? Competing Pivots in Federal Judicial Selection." *American Journal of Political Science* 52:3.

Richey, Warren. 2009. "Senate OK's David Hamilton to be US Appeals Court Judge." *Christian Science Monitor*, November 19. http://www.csmonitor.com/USA/Politics/2009/1119/senate-oks-david-hamilton-to-be-us-appeals-court-judge. Accessed March 12, 2010.

Rowley, James. 2007. "Senate Standstill to Let Obama or McCain Tip Balance on Courts." Bloomberg News, August 7. http://www.bloomberg.com/apps/news?pid=washingtonstory&sid=aPaxOvQrYI7k. Accessed March 12, 2010.

Scherer, Nancy. 2005. *Scoring Points*. Palo Alto, Calif.: Stanford University Press.

Senate Republican Communications Center. 2009. "Letter to the President on Judges." The Leader Board, March 2. http://republican.senate.gov/public/index.cfm?FuseAction=Blogs.View&Blog_ID=3c522434-76e5-448e-9ead-1ec214b881ac&Month=3&Year=2009. Accessed March 12, 2010.

Shapiro, Martin. 2008. "Comment." In Pietro S. Nivola and David W. Brady, ed., *Red and Blue Nation? Consequences and Correction of America's Polarized Politics*. Washington, D.C.: Brookings Institution.

Silverstein, Gordon. 2009. *Law's Allure: How Law Shapes, Constrains, Saves and Kills Politics*. New York: Cambridge University Press.

Wittes, Benjamin. 2006. *Confirmation Wars*. Palo Alto, Calif.: Hoover Institution.

# 10

# Congress and Energy Policy, 1960–2010:
# A Long-Term Evaluation

Bruce I. Oppenheimer

This chapter examines how effectively American political institutions, especially the U.S. Congress, have been in developing energy policies over the past half century. I think of the essay as an analysis of institutional political accountability. Although political accountability in American politics may occur in a variety of ways, the study of it is normally linked to elections. After all, elections offer the clearest opportunities for citizens to register their approval or disapproval of those with responsibility for governing.

American constitutional design provides different electoral time frames for House members, senators, and presidents, but all federal elected officials (and their political parties) get some feedback every two years whether or not they are required to run for reelection. So U.S. senators with six-year terms get electoral information every two years, even the two-thirds of them who do not face the voters. As I will argue in the conclusion of this chapter, ironically it may be the Senate, not the House, that in recent decades has become more sensitive to the short-term electoral ramifications of its policy decisions. This short electoral time frame allows voters frequent opportunities to reward or punish those with governing responsibility, and thus provides an incentive for officeholders and parties to be responsive to public preferences. It also means that those governing are not entrusted with extended time periods in which to produce policy results. True, individual officeholders may survive elections when their fellow party members fare badly. But they face a decline in governing influence, especially when their party loses the presidency or majority control in the Congress. Not surprisingly, officeholders and political parties are very sensitive to the cycles of elections and the significance of election outcomes.

Because of the importance and frequency of U.S. elections, prominent political scientists have written extensively on the impact of elections on the behaviors of officeholders, on the working of political institutions, and on the way public policies are designed (Mayhew 1974; Sundquist 1968; Arnold 1990). But rarely, if ever, have we endeavored to examine accountability from a different perspective. Instead of using the voters' approval or disapproval of a particular set of elected officials and the perceived effectiveness of policies that they have put in place between elections, might we instead ask whether American political institutions have been successful in addressing a major policy concern or issue area over the longer term? Unlike the voters who hold elected officials and political parties accountable primarily in the short term, my concern lies with questions about institutional accountability in the long term. Collectively, how effective have twenty-five Congresses and the ten presidential administrations been in developing a national energy policy over the past half century? And to what degree can we link the relative level of policy success or failure to the requirement that officeholders be particularly responsive to short-term accountability that is built into the constitutional system with frequent elections? Does this help us understand why other major issues have seemingly been left unresolved for long periods of time? And how do these issues differ from ones that Congress has found easier to resolve in ways that seem to meet public expectations?

## Energy Policy in Five Periods, 1960–2010

Conveniently, I have engaged in the study of Congress' ability to enact various aspects of energy legislation at regular intervals over the course of my professional career. Beginning with my Ph.D. dissertation research, in which I examined why the oil and gas industry employed different strategies to influence environmental legislation from those it used in tax legislation during the 1950s and 1960s, to analysis of the politics of energy legislation in the 1970s in the aftermath of the oil embargo, to more recent work on struggles in Congresses to respond to many of the issues that have persisted over the past decade because of reliance on fossil fuels and increased dependence on foreign sources of oil, I have focused on the impact of process on the capacity of Congress to develop public policy (see Oppenheimer 2009). In each instance my primary focus was on how certain aspects of the congressional process facilitated or deterred efforts to enact substantive policy change. Only recently has my attention turned to analyzing institutional response to energy policy problems from a longer-term perspective. As I examine those efforts, it strikes me that the past half century of congressional response to the needs for energy policy can be divided into five periods. The first of these in the 1960s occurs in the final decade of the era of committee government in Congress. Although both the House and the Senate were beginning to undergo the initial stages of major change, certain features persisted. Committee chairs were relatively strong, and committees retained a good deal of autonomy. Specialization was still given deference, and legislators valued comity. Thus, committees and committee loyalty often trumped party and party loyalty. In this context energy legislation was parceled out to committees with jurisdiction over various producing segments. Rarely did Congress think about those segments or try to legislate on them as part of a broader energy policy. Instead, oil and gas, coal, nuclear, and hydroelectric were addressed separately.

The second phase began in the 1970s as the 1973 OPEC oil embargo led to price increases and energy shortages. Congress was in the midst of evolving away from a committee-dominated decision structure to a transitional phase of subcommittee government in the House and a more individualistic Senate. In this context, initiation of new energy policy proposals was quite easy but the jurisdictional nightmare of overlapping committees and subcommittees, especially in the House, made the mobilization of sufficient majorities to resolve policy issues initially very difficult, even with unified party control of government and extraordinarily large majority party numbers in the House and the Senate. Only when party leaders were able to employ what then seemed like extraordinary means were they barely able to overcome deadlocks.

This was followed by the longest of the periods, lasting for nearly twenty years from shortly after the start of the Reagan administration until near the end of the Clinton years. With a return to relatively cheap energy, general economic prosperity, ongoing federal budget constraints, and an ideology favoring economic deregulation, there was little incentive for officeholders, regardless of ideology, to push for new energy legislation. Indeed, a number of existing government initiatives from the 1970s were discarded. With the public relatively quiescent on energy matters, Congress was largely unwilling to deal with an issue that closely divided its members, and energy policy was placed on the back burner for most of those three presidential administrations.

The return of sharp energy price increases, especially for oil and gas, beginning in 2000 stimulated a new period of government legislative initiate on energy policy. Many of the issues were the same as in the 1970s. The jurisdictional obstacles from the subcommittee government period were no longer a hindrance in the House as parties and party leaders now had the resources to mobilize majorities in that chamber. The Republican-controlled House could pass legislation that was at the median position of the chamber's majority party, fitting with the template that "conditional party government" theorists had modeled (see Chapter 12 in this volume). But the same was not true of the Senate, where more polarized and cohesive parties, the prerequisites of conditional party government, became obstacles to the passage of major legislation. Unlike the House, a cohesive minority party could employ the cloture requirements and block the legislative preferences of a cohesive majority. Thus, even with unified control of government for most of 2001–2006, Republicans were unable to invoke cloture on party-backed energy bills through two Congresses. Finally,

Republican congressional leaders and the Bush administration settled for a more modest and consensual piece of legislation in the 109th Congress, which enjoyed strong support from a majority of Senate Democrats as well as from Republicans.

With another round of energy price increases and the return of Democrats to majority status in Congress in the 2006 elections, we may have entered a fifth congressional period. Like the 1970s it involves another round of government activism in energy matters with renewed attention to conservation, new incentives for renewable and alternative sources of energy, and reduced reliance on fossil fuels. The first of these non-incremental policy changes occurred during the 110th Congress with passage of legislation that included marked higher CAFE standard requirements for motor vehicles to 35 mpg by 2020 (the first increase since the mid 1970s), with the Bush administration's tepid acceptance. In one of the most significant policy achievements of his administration to date, in May 2009 President Barack Obama announced that an agreement had been reached among a broad range of those involved in the struggle over motor vehicle mileage and emissions regulation to meet standards by 2016. The Senate, however, limited other Obama energy initiatives in the 111th Congress. It blocked legislation dealing with carbon dioxide emissions and fuel requirements for electricity generation and industrial production even after it appeared that the administration was willing to allow more offshore exploration as a trade off in an effort to win the additional support needed to get the bill through the Senate. (This occurred prior to the explosion on the BP platform in the Gulf of Mexico and the resulting catastrophic flow of oil.)

From the following analysis of activity during each of these five periods, we will be able to draw a set of conclusions about Congress' effectiveness in developing energy policy over the past half century. In general, those conclusions will not provide a positive picture of long-term accountability. In fact, if there is a major overall theme, it is that the successful short-term accountability provided by the American electoral system has undermined Congress's capabilities to develop effective long term-policy solutions (or, at least, policy resolutions) to the energy issues that face the country.

## Period 1. Committee Government and Energy Policy in the 1960s

It is a misnomer to label legislation dealing with various energy sources in the 1960s as "energy policy." Except for important overriding national security concerns, congressional decision making on oil and gas, coal, nuclear, hydroelectric, and so forth was done largely in an uncoordinated fashion. Jurisdiction affecting policies for different energy sources often resided in different committees. Coal and hydroelectric were in the domain of the Interior and Insular Affairs Committee. Electric utilities and oil and gas pipelines were the responsibility of the Interstate and Foreign Commerce Committee. Public Works had other areas of water power. And the Joint Committee on Atomic Energy was responsible for legislation on the development, use, and control of atomic energy. Further complicating the situation was the fact that key issues affecting oil and gas were as likely to be in the tax arena and thus under the jurisdiction of Ways and Means in the House and the Finance Committee in the Senate while coal pricing and supply were often more determined in decisions of the labor committees in the two chamber because of the heavy labor component to industry costs.

Not only was the locus of decision making for each energy source likely to be in a different committee, but in this era of committee dominance jurisdictional autonomy prevailed. Those House members and senators who were not members of the committee that reported legislation were reluctant to offer amendments or otherwise be active players during floor consideration. Moreover, given the emphasis on specialization, members in the 1960s, having considerably fewer staff resources than in later congresses, were unlikely to have sufficient expertise to make meaningful contributions to legislation outside the jurisdictions of the committees on which they served. Accordingly, there was little in the way of integrative energy policy. Instead legislation affecting each energy source was handled separately, not from some broader perspective of overall energy policy. The question that Congress addressed was: Did it make sense for natural gas, or for coal, or for atomic power?

Fitting with this jurisdictional separation and committee autonomy was a tendency of members from producing constituencies to be overrepresented on the committees with authority over legislation affecting their home energy-producing source. Nowhere was this concern more obvious than in the attention Speaker Sam Rayburn and Senate Majority Leader Lyndon Johnson paid to appointing members to the Ways and Means and Finance committees, respectively. Although 30 percent of all senators represented states with significant oil production, the Senate Finance Committee with few exceptions saw more than 40 percent of its membership come from oil-producing states through the 1950s and 1960s, especially in the years following President Harry Truman's 1951 attack on the oil depletion allowance. Although members from oil-producing districts were slightly underrepresented on the Ways and Means Committee, it was well known that support for favorable tax treatment for oil and gas, particularly for continuation of the depletion allowance, was a prerequisite for getting Rayburn's backing to fill an open slot on the committee. As John Manley (1970) observed in his book on the Ways and Means Committee:

It is generally believed that Rayburn would not let anyone on Ways and Means who would vote to cut the 27 1/2 percent allowance given to the oil industry, a provision that has become the symbol of tax loopholes and the *cause celebre* of liberal tax reformers, but not one member who got on the Committee under Rayburn could recall be[ing] asked if he supported the oil depletion allowance. But if Rayburn did not normally interview the members on the oil question he did allow the perpetuation of the widespread belief that no depletion reformers need apply, and this was sufficient. One of his closest associates said unequivocally: "Rayburn had two things. One was trade. He was 100 percent for international trade. And the second was the depletion allowance for oil and gas. There were the two.

Although Johnson would become vice president in 1961 and Rayburn would die that same year, the legacy of their influence over the composition of the Finance and Ways and Means Committees persisted. Because closed rules were the norm on tax legislation in the House during this period, there were no floor amendments to cut the depletion allowance on tax bills that the committee reported. In the Senate, on the other hand, Paul Douglas (D-Ill.), a Finance Committee member, regularly offered an amendment to modify the depletion allowance during the 1950s and 1960s, but at most won the support of thirty-five senators. It was not until 1969 that the Senate Finance Committee reported legislation that contained a reduction in the depletion allowance for oil to 23 percent (although it increased the percentage net limitation from 50 to 65 percent), and the House Ways and Means Committee lowered it to 20 percent, both as part of the Tax Reform Act of 1969. Even then there was considerable speculation about whether this represented a true shift in the positions of these committees or was instead meant to short circuit efforts at bigger cuts on the floor. In the House, for example, some Ways and Means members concluded that the committee would not be able to obtain a closed rule on the bill without a cut in depletion (Oppenheimer 1974).

Two other observations regarding Congress and energy policy in the 1960s are worth noting. First, it was an era during which interest group activity was still largely focused around peak associations (Heinz et al. 1993). So producers within the energy industry domain were normally able to present a united front. Cuts in the depletion allowance would not have affected many smaller oil producers, for example. Small producers placed a bigger emphasis on other oil tax issues such as the deduction of intangible drilling costs. But they remained united with larger producers when it came to the depletion issue. More importantly, many of the struggles over various aspects of energy legislation across various industries were ones on which an opposition interest group was often not present. Especially on tax legislation, the nature of the conflict was very limited. Stanley Surrey, a Harvard

Law professor and assistant secretary of the Treasury for taxation (1961–1968), argued that because of tax legislation's complexity and the focus of many interests on provisions that directly affect them, the Treasury department was often left standing alone in opposition to special provisions in the tax code, and it would not win all of the battles (Surrey 1957).

Second, the overall effect of the uncoordinated treatment of the variety of energy industries in the 1960s was a public policy result that won broad public approval. Energy supplies were plentiful and cheap. Undoubtedly, this helped fuel U.S. industrial growth and prosperity in the 1950s and 1960s. In this context legislating for energy was neither conflicted nor integrative. Members from producing constituencies, especially in the Senate where they were proportionately a larger share of the membership, were normally successful in meeting the demands of affected interests, and the broader public was generally satisfied with the policies that Congress enacted. Not only were the benefits of policy decisions concentrated, but the costs were also largely invisible to the public. The net effect of energy policy was to maintain prices at artificially low levels.

## Period 2. Reacting to the OPEC Embargo in a Democratized Congress

With the onset of the OPEC embargo in October 1973 came the quick realization of how dependent the United States had become on foreign energy sources and the effects that a cutback in supply and marked increase in the price of oil and gas could have on the country's economy, not to mention military and security concerns. No longer could Congress simply deal with each energy source separately. Instead, many legislators recognized the need for a more broadly integrative and longer-term approach to issues of energy sources, supply, conservation, and pricing. Yet in the context of this major threat to the long-term economic prosperity of the United States, it took until 1980 to resolve many of the most vexing issues.

There were a number of reasons for the slow response. First, political officeholders and the public at large were closely split between competing approaches regarding the appropriate solutions to the energy crisis. It is only a slight simplification to say that there were two broad and relatively evenly balanced camps. One side preferred solutions built on increasing domestic supplies of oil and gas through what it contended were free market approaches. Its adherents argued that price controls should be lifted so that incentives would exist for private companies to explore and develop new sources of fossil fuels and that other energy sources would come on line once they became price competitive. The other side emphasized a more conservation and renewable energy source approach focused on decreasing dependence on fossil fuels. Although the former claimed to be for free markets instead of government intervention, many of its adherents favored various incentives to encourage exploration for costly but potentially large new oil and gas reserves and government assistance when energy prices plummeted. Meanwhile, those who insisted on energy conservation efforts wanted to limit the impact of higher energy prices to the public, thus undercutting incentives for consumers to reduce energy consumption.

Second, the structure of decision making in both the House and Senate had changed from the committee- and committee chair–dominated practices of the post–World War II era. No longer would either the House or Senate rank-and-file members be expected simply to defer to the key committee chairs and their brokered solutions. Subcommittee government and a less hierarchical decision-making structure in the House not only established a new veto layer, but it also provided more vehicles for those who wished to delay or obstruct. During the 94th Congress in particular, those resisting compromises on major energy legislation worked to unravel major bills by taking advantage of the tensions  produced by overlapping committee and subcommittee jurisdictions, which resulted in duplication and turf protection. Even with the majority party Democrats holding two-thirds of the House seats, party and committee leaders appeared relatively powerless to produce majorities. Only in the 95th Congress, with newly elected Speaker Thomas "Tip" O'Neill taking the extraordinary step of creating the Ad Hoc Select Committee on Energy, was the House able to overcome the chaos of subcommittee government and pass a more comprehensive energy package, albeit considerably stripped down from the proposal that President Jimmy Carter had requested (see Oppenheimer 1981).

Although the Senate's jurisdictional concerns were not as problematic, changing behavioral patterns in that chamber also affected its capacity to pass energy legislation in the 1970s. Notably, the movement away from the "folkway" norms of the 1950s and early 1960s to an institution in which individualism prevailed also constrained the ability to mobilize majorities (Sinclair 1989). In addition, by 1970 the gradually increasing workload of the Senate had transformed the institution from one that had often finished sessions by the summer months to one that worked year-round. The increasing individualism of the Senate and the January-through-December work schedule combined to make the use or threat of filibusters more prevalent, eventually resulting in the modification of the cloture rule in 1975. In a time-constrained environment the filibuster and other weapons of delay became far more effective. A classic example of this occurred in September 1977 when the Senate was considering President Carter's energy package. Once the Senate had voted cloture on an amendment to gradually deregulate the price of new natural gas, Howard Metzenbaum (D-Ohio) and James Abourezk (D-S.D.) proceeded with a post-cloture filibuster, calling up the many amendments that they had pending as a means of delaying passage. Only after several day and night sessions did Majority Leader Robert Byrd proceed to have Vice President Walter Mondale, who was presiding, rule each amendment out of order because of its dilatory nature. Although this ended the filibuster, Byrd and Mondale were roundly criticized for their actions. Still, it symbolized the problems that major legislation was beginning to face.

Ironically, the gas deregulation provision was one that the Carter administration opposed. But recognizing that it would not win that battle in the Senate, the administration wanted the legislation to proceed. By contrast, Democrats Metzenbaum and Abourezk, although supportive of the president's initial opposition to the deregulation of natural gas, were holding to a more extreme position; they would defeat the entire package if the alternative were a compromise to allow natural gas price deregulation. This illustrates another dilemma that confronted those trying to enact major energy legislation during the 1970s. Unlike in recent years, when coalition building occurs on a more strictly partisan or ideological basis, the struggles of the 1970s more frequently featured the extremes against the middle. The coalition that formed in the Senate on a final effort by Metzenbaum to derail the Carter energy package is illustrative. When the conference report was considered on the Senate floor, Metzenbaum moved to recommit it with instructions to remove the natural gas pricing sections. Although his motion failed, eighteen Democrats and twenty-one Republicans, of profoundly different ideological stripes, supported it. Democrats voting for the motion included the Senate's most liberal members—Gaylord Nelson and William Proxmire of Wisconsin, Abourezk and George McGovern of South Dakota, Paul Sarbanes of Maryland, Don Riegle of Michigan, and Ted Kennedy of Massachusetts—as well as energy state conservatives—Lloyd Bentsen of Texas and Russell Long and Bennett Johnston of Louisiana. Similarly, Republican supporters included Dewey Bartlett and Henry Bellmon of Oklahoma, Clifford Hansen and Malcolm Wallop of Wyoming, Robert Dole of Kansas, and Barry Goldwater of Arizona as well as the liberal maverick Lowell Weicker of Connecticut. A similar split occurred on the crucial House vote to adopt the rule for considering the conference report; seventy-nine Democrats joined with Republicans in an unsuccessful attempt to defeat the rule. Many were relatively conservative Democrats from the energy-producing states of Texas, Louisiana, and Oklahoma. But they were joined by liberal Democrats from energy-consuming districts, including six northern Californians, six New Yorkers, five from Minnesota and Wisconsin, and even five from Speaker O'Neill's home state of Massachusetts.

By the end of the second Carter congress, many of the key energy issues were finally resolved and something resembling a package that could collectively be labeled as energy policy was in place. CAFE standards for automobiles had been raised. New appliance efficiency standards were encouraged. Prices of new natural gas would gradually be deregulated. And oil price decontrol coupled with a windfall profits tax was in place. Tax credits were available for business and residential improvements in energy conservation. Loan and purchase guarantees for synthetic fuels were available. And coal was to replace oil and gas as burner fuel in electric utility generation. In sum, Congress had adopted a mix of proposals designed to encourage production of oil and gas, to develop new domestic energy sources, to improve motor vehicle efficiency, and to encourage energy conservation. But in dealing with the "moral equivalent of war," it had still taken nearly seven years to enact policies largely formulated during the Nixon and Ford presidencies. The new structure of congressional decision making had given those on both sides of energy issues the means to delay and defeat proposed compromises.

Compared to the first period, the making of energy policy had changed in significant ways. It had moved from a back-burner issue to a front-burner one. It had gone from a relatively low-conflict arena largely in the hands of producing interests and the members of Congress from those constituencies to a high-conflict arena in which producing and consuming energy interests and the members representing those constituencies were active players with opposing conceptions of the appropriate policy solutions. But in the context of OPEC-induced supply shortages and marked increases in energy prices, stalemate was not an acceptable long-term alternative, even if resolving policy differences was difficult and time consuming. Ironically, shortly after this full array of energy policies was finally in place after nearly a decade of struggle, the issue and political contexts changed.

## Period 3. Oversupply, Low Energy Prices, and a Return to Market Solutions for Energy, 1981–2000

The incentives for Congress to undertake additional government programs toward longer-term solutions to the dependence of the United States on foreign energy supplies diminished significantly in the early 1980s and remained dormant for most of two decades. The election of Ronald Reagan and a Republican Senate strengthened the coalition that preferred private, market-based solutions to energy issues. Although Reagan never succeeded in fulfilling his campaign commitment to abolish the Department of Energy, support for ongoing programs, such as synthetic fuels, was non-existent, and efforts were instead geared at removing government involvement from energy markets. For example, the administration successfully proposed the repeal of the phase-out of natural gas as fuel in electric utility generation as part of the 1981 reconciliation package. Efforts failed to immediately decontrol natural gas prices, another Reagan initiative, as the anti-decontrol forces still had sufficient numbers to block that proposal, although they clearly lacked enough support to re-control prices.

Perhaps more important than the change in partisan control of the presidency and the Senate were external factors that affected energy prices and supply. With a recession in the early 1980s came a cut in energy demand, an oil glut, and a resulting squabble within OPEC. OPEC members were no longer willing to abide by agreements to restrict production. Thus, the expected price increases for gasoline due to oil price deregulation (and later for natural gas) were minimal. The public demand to do something about the longer-term problem of energy dependence disappeared in an environment of plentiful supply and low prices. Given that energy issues still closely divided the opposite sides in Congress, and were partly constituency based, and not just party based, congressional leaders had little incentive to take up energy issues. In addition, with overriding concerns about budgetary shortfalls, support for new authorizations of any kind was limited.

Occasionally, a minor piece of energy legislation would pass. The 99th Congress, for example, enacted the first bill to promote the use of ethanol as motor vehicle fuel. More often, however, major energy legislation failed to reach the House or Senate floor or faced defeat if it did. In 1990 Senators Richard Bryan (D-Nev.) and Slade Gorton (R-Wash.) tried to resurrect legislation to raise CAFE standards in the aftermath of the Iraq invasion of Kuwait. But with the Bush administration and the auto industry opposed to the provision, it fell three votes short on a cloture motion. Even if it had passed the Senate, the stronger presence of automobile industry and labor constituencies among House Democrats would have likely meant defeat in that chamber.

The only major energy legislation enacted during the 1980s and 1990s occurred in the 102nd Congress, and only because the spike in oil prices in response to the Persian Gulf War made that possible. As prices eased, however, many of the more controversial and most important elements of the bill were dropped. Unlike in the 1970s when power in the House was so dispersed, the Democratic Party leadership took control in melding together pieces of the legislation, which fell under the jurisdictions of eight separate standing committees, and used procedures designed in the Rules Committee to prevent the offering of controversial amendments. Such procedures were no longer viewed as unusual in a chamber where members had ceded considerably greater authority to their party leadership than in the 1970s. In the Senate, when combining the various pieces of the bill within the package, Bennett Johnston (D-La.), the Energy Committee chair, relied on one-on-one negotiations with individual senators to work out compromises on tax provisions, coal sections, and nuclear waste depository issues that were outside the jurisdiction of the committee. Although the bill dealt with some key issues—deregulation of electric power markets, simplification of licensing procedures for nuclear power plants, and establishment of Department of Energy research and development projects—most of the provisions were incremental in nature, such as demonstration projects for renewable energy, government purchase of alternative fuel vehicle fleets on a phase-in basis, and tax deductions for the purchase of alternative fuel vehicles. Other issues were left unresolved. Disagreement among three groups of senators over whether to require or allow the president to increase CAFE standards, and by how much, meant that no change was included. And deal-killing proposals to allow drilling in the Alaska National Wildlife Refuge (ANWR) were also dropped.

Without the threat of supply shortages or higher energy prices, efforts to make major longer-term policy changes on either the production or conservation side of the equation were not politically feasible. Except for the brief period around the first Gulf War, energy prices remained stable in real-dollar terms and even declined somewhat in the late 1990s. Although parties in Congress became more unified during the 1980s on many policies, energy issues still cut across party lines, at least until after the 1994 election. Even though party leaders had the resources to mobilize their members to support or oppose bills and amendments on many issues, energy legislation was not yet a party issue. As in the 1970s, Republicans fell mainly on the production solution side and Democrats mainly on the conservation and alternative fuels side, but the two parties were considerably short of internal unity on energy issues. With a number of Democratic House members and senators from oil-producing constituencies, not to mention those from districts with substantial auto industry presence, party leaders could not produce majorities relying solely on their own members. Even with the election of Bill Clinton, a Democratic president who might be more willing than Reagan or Bush had been to involve government in energy matters, there were few new initiatives. During the 103rd Congress, Clinton proposed broad increases in federal energy taxes, but these were as much sources of additional revenues as they were a means of encouraging energy conservation. Leading the opposition to Clinton's proposals were energy state Democrats, Johnston and David Boren (D-Okla.). The Republican House and Senate majorities in the final six years of the Clinton administration limited attention to energy issues, and oil prices remained at the same level in constant dollars as prior to the OPEC embargo.

Without public pressure, political leaders both in Congress and the executive branch were unwilling to make energy policy a front burner item. Energy policy was rarely an issue in elections, so inaction produced no fear of immediate political accountability from the electorate.

## Period 4. Partisan Initiative in the Wake of a New Energy Crisis: Overcoming Senate Obstacles, 2001–2006

After two decades of relative government inaction on energy policy, and with few market incentives to conserve or to develop new domestic energy sources, the United States found itself at the start of the new century as dependent on foreign energy supplies as it had been in the 1970s. With the sudden upward spiral of energy prices in response to increasing worldwide demand, and with greater concerns about the reliability of supply—especially in the aftermath of the 9/11 and other terrorist attacks, and the subsequent Iraq War—the public renewed expectations for government action to address energy supply and price concerns during the 107th Congress. Although faced with the same basic energy problem of over-dependence on foreign sources as in the 1970s, the structure of political decision making in Congress had changed. Congressional parties and party leaders were far stronger than in the 1970s, and the constituency-based cleavages on energy issues largely reinforced those party cleavages rather than muting them. Instead of building cross-party coalitions or cleavages where the extremes coalesced against the middle with policy outcomes at median chamber positions as in the 1970s, majority party leaders employed a more partisan form of coalition building based on holding party members to median party positions. This conditional party government approach was successful in fostering the passage of Republican energy policy prefer-ences in the House of Representative on three separate occasions between 2001 and 2005. With party leaders in greater control of the selection of committee chairs, with chairs term-limited, and with an ideologically more cohesive membership, working out differences among committee bills was far easier than it had been in the 1970s. If committees would not settle their differences, the party leaders would settle them. It was no longer controversial for the Rules Committee not only to limit the amendments the majority party would allow to be offered, but also to restrict the time for debate, making floor action more predictable. There was no need of an ad hoc committee similar to the one that Speaker O'Neill had employed.

The constituency bases of the two parties had changed as well. Those members from energy-producing districts, who were at one time somewhat evenly divided between the two parties, now resided far more heavily in the Republican Party. There were fewer than half as many House Democrats from Texas, Louisiana, and Oklahoma as there had been in the 1970s, and fewer Republicans from the energy-consuming districts in the Northeast. On each of the three major bills considered during the 2001–2005 period, House decision making fell largely along party lines. At the same time, Republican leaders could allow some Northeast moderates to defect, know-ing that with the support of remaining Democrats from energy-producing states they could still construct majorities on key amendments. So the House no longer encountered problems in enacting non-incremental energy legislation. With Republicans in the majority, the House passed three suc-cessive bills that emphasized incentives and opportunities to increase fossil fuel production, including opening ANWR to oil and gas exploration. By comparison, provisions supporting alternative fuels primarily focused on modest ethanol requirements.

The problem with this conditional party government approach to energy legislation during this period was that using median party positions was effective in building cohesion within the majority party, but it also guaranteed a cohesive opposition to the legislation by the minority. Although not a problem in the House, where almost all votes required only simple majority, the Senate's sixty-vote cloture rule gave the minority party substantial leverage (see Sinclair 2007; Binder and Smith 1997; Warwo and Schickler 2006; Koger 2010). In 2002, when the Democrats were briefly the majority party in the Senate, Republican efforts to invoke cloture on an amendment introduced by Frank Murkowski (R-Alaska) to allow exploration in ANWR, a provision already in the House bill, was defeated 46–54 a largely party line vote. Only the least conservative Republicans from states with the lowest energy production voted against cloture, and only the most conservative Democrats from high energy-producing states voted in favor of it.

A year later, with Republicans holding a Senate majority, House Republican conferees recognized the need to attract enough Democratic votes for cloture and made some concessions. Most notably, in an attempt to win over farm state Democratic senators they accepted a Senate provision to double the use of ethanol by 2012, as well as dropping the provision allowing exploration in ANWR. But House Republicans insisted on preserving a liability waiver for MTBE producers that was in the House bill.[1] Eight Democratic senators who had opposed cloture in 2002 voted for cloture in 2003, including seven from major corn-producing states. Unlike the House, however, where the party leaders have more effective resources to hold their members in support of party legislative position, the Senate leadership lacked the equivalent tools in dealing with a membership that prides itself on individualism. Five Republican senators from low corn- and low energy-producing states voted against cloture. House Republicans and the Bush administration were unwilling to move farther from the median party position in order to pass a bill, and efforts to persuade any of the Republican senators who opposed cloture to change their votes failed.

Another two years would go by before energy legislation would be enacted. With a steep rise in gasoline prices by 2005, House Republicans and the Bush administration were forced to move away from median party positions on energy legislation in order to ensure the passage of some legislation. Although the House again passed a bill that was similar to the ones in the two preceding congresses, the Senate, by comparison, pursued a more bipartisan package that contained no ANWR provision, no liability

---

1. MTBE, methyl *tert*-butyl ether, is a gasoline additive designed to prevent engine knocking. It was found, however, to be a significant groundwater contaminant, especially with leakage from underground storage tanks.

protection for MTBE producers, a larger ethanol requirement, more favorable treatment of renewable energy sources, and less favorable treatment of fossil fuels. This movement to a position more palatable to Senate Democrats did not mean that the Democrats got the non-incremental changes in energy policy that they would have preferred. Their efforts to increase CAFE standards and to include a provision on global warning were rejected. In the end, the final bill contained provisions much closer to the Senate version than the House. The Senate adopted the conference report overwhelmingly and without a cloture vote. But the provisions in the 2005 bill, with the exception of those for ethanol use and purchase, were largely incremental in nature. The political context and concerns with short-term electoral accountability required that some bill be passed, but on major issues of energy production and conservation to address the continuing problem of dependence on foreign sources the status quo persisted.

## Period 5. 2007 and Beyond: Motor Vehicles—Yes, Power Plants—?

With many of the longer-term energy issues still unresolved despite the 2005 legislation, and with high energy prices largely unabated, it was hardly surprising that the Democrats' agenda once winning back majority control of the House and Senate in the 2006 elections included energy legislation more geared toward conservation and production of alternative and renewable sources. Although the status quo might have been the preferred position of the Bush administration and congressional Republicans, the political context of public expectation of some action and the fact that Democrats would offer alternatives meant that some legislation was likely to pass. The potential for a Republican filibuster in the Senate or a Bush veto limited the ability of Democrats to pass legislation at a median party position, however. There were three major items in proposals Democrats sponsored: an increase in the CAFE standards, a repeal of the subsidies for fossil fuel production and the transfer of that money to renewable sources, and a requirement that a designated level of electric utility power generation be produced from renewable energy sources.

In the end, only a change in CAFE standards was enacted, increasing the requirement to 35 mpg for cars, trucks, and SUVs by 2020. Senate Republicans had sufficient votes to block cloture on a requirement for the use of renewable sources in the generation of electricity (insisting, among other things, that nuclear power be included in the definition of renewable sources), just as Senate Democrats had been able to block key Republican provisions from 2001–2005. In addition, the Bush administration threatened to veto a bill that transferred incentives for fossil fuel production to other energy sources. Nevertheless, the increase in CAFE standards was perhaps the most significant piece of energy legislation adopted since the 1970s. Its immediate effect, however, was delayed because the Bush administration chose not to implement a timetable for the increases.

The Obama election removed some of the barriers that Democrats had faced in pursuing major energy policy changes, but the problems associated with achieving cloture in the Senate persisted, even though the Democrats' Senate membership reached sixty for much of 2009. The major policy changes occurred through presidential action, although media attention focused on whether the Senate would pass a version of the energy bill that had already cleared the House but contained controversial provisions on "cap and trade" and requirements for the use of renewables for electric utility generation. First, the Obama administration set in motion the timetable for increasing CAFE standards. But second, and more importantly, in May 2009 the president announced a major agreement among a broad range of interests on fuel efficiency and emission standards. Included among those supporting the agreement were not only environmental groups but also motor vehicle manufacturers and the UAW. A key part of the agreement came in a commitment to reaching the CAFE standards of 35 mpg by 2016 instead of 2020. Given that less than two years earlier many of these interests had argued that they could not meet those levels even by 2020 and had lobbied against passage of the legislation, this represented a huge change both in terms of energy policy and the reduced level of conflict on motor vehicle efficiency and emission standards.

If motor vehicles represent one of the two major prongs on the usage side of the energy policy equations, the remaining one includes industrial fuel use and electricity generation. Whether, in fact, non-incremental policy change would occur on this prong depended much on the capacity of Senate leadership to cobble together a coalition of sixty votes to act on legislation that had passed the House in 2009. Efforts of Senate advocates to revive the bill in the aftermath of the BP well explosion in the Gulf of Mexico were not successful as concern with the electoral implications of voting for the bill held sway with some senators. And the subsequent loss of Democratic Senate seats in the 2010 midterm elections, as well as Republicans winning a House majority, made the outlook for resolving the issue in the 112th Congress bleak.

## Discussion

The foregoing analysis presents Congress and most presidents as reluctant to pursue major energy policy changes during the past half century unless there has been a crisis and significant public demand for such change. And even in those instances—following the OPEC embargo of the 1970s and the gasoline price hikes more recently—Congress did not produce policy change immediately. In other potential energy crises, such as during the first Gulf War, the crisis abated, and Congress jettisoned proposals for major policy change in favor of more incremental ones. When Congress did act, as in the aftermath of the OPEC embargo, many of the longer-term policy mechanisms were abandoned once lower prices and plentiful supplies resumed in the early 1980s. Major internal alterations in the way Congress operated—moving from committee government to subcommittee government in the House and to individualism in the Senate and later to conditional party government—did not alleviate the ability to block action on or even consideration of major energy policy changes. In part, this is because the active players in the energy policy debates have been closely divided, and those players have held strongly opposing views on the appropriate direction of policy resolution, especially since the 1970s. Until recent years these cleavages cut across the political parties. Consistent with cartel theory, party leaders were reluctant to have Congress consider legislation that divided their party members (see Cox and McCubbins 2007). They were mindful of the potential electoral costs that might ensue. With the majority party more unified in its energy policy preferences in recent years, the minority party has been equally cohesive in blocking energy legislation in the Senate.

Underlying many of the shortcomings of energy policymaking over the past half century has been the consistent need of political officeholders to be sensitive to short-term accountability that is built into the system of U.S. federal elections. Except in times of crisis, the emphasis has been on policies that front-load benefits, defer costs, or make costs hard to trace in cases where concentrating benefits and dispersing costs were not available options. As Douglas Arnold (1990) has so thoughtfully theorized and empirically documented, members will either get electoral rewards because attentive constituent interests reap the concentrated benefits or they will not have to fear retribution from inattentive publics because the policy avoids immediate traceable costs on which challengers can mount effective campaigns. But the strong focus of national policymakers on short-term electoral accountability has not been without public policy consequences with longer-term policy costs. Thus, I reach a far less optimistic conclusion about the capacity of Congress and the president to resolve major policy issues in an effective manner than Arnold did both in his overall theory of congressional policymaking and his specific analysis of energy policy decision making of the 1970s. Although we agree that Congress is able to resolve energy issues when it can "deliver group and geographic benefits while imposing only the most general costs," Arnold reaches a more positive view about institutional capacity, stressing the ability of coalition leaders to structure choices in ways that allowed members to support sound policy resolution of both the natural gas and oil pricing issues by minimizing the potential negative electoral consequences

(Arnold 1990). Having examined energy policy over a far longer time span, however, I come away with a different conclusion. True, coalition leaders have been able to resolve major energy policy issues through the skillful structuring of alternatives. Thus, they packaged the gradual deregulation of natural gas with other, more popular energy proposals, minimized the immediate impact of price increases, and linked the decontrol of oil price to the adoption of a windfall profits tax in the 1970s. Likewise, they raised CAFE standards legislatively in 2007 and speeded up their implementation in 2009. But these non-incremental policy changes were only achieved when energy crises became so visible to the electorate that retention of the policy status quo was potentially more costly politically than imposing on voters the immediate costs of policy change. Accordingly, in 2007 the Bush administration and many congressional Republicans, as well as some Democrats representing motor vehicle production constituencies, would have preferred the status quo to an increase in CAFE standards. But with growing concerns about increasing gasoline prices, the electoral costs of supporting the status quo were unacceptable for many of them, resulting in passage of the requirement to meet the 35 mpg standard by 2020. And yes, as with Arnold's analysis of energy legislation in the 1970s, the skill of coalition leaders played an important role. Speaker Nancy Pelosi's decision not to have the House vote on the CAFE standards issue in its initial passage of the energy bill was crucial in keeping House Democrats unified. She did not want her members, especially those with strong organized labor constituencies, to have to choose between supporting the UAW or environmental groups—both interests strongly linked to the Democratic Party. Later, they could overwhelmingly support a final package that included the CAFE standard increase.[2]

Lacking a crisis environment for most of the two decades from 1980–2000, public policy on energy moved to a back burner. Some of the policy decisions of the 1970s that imposed visible short-term costs in the pursuit of longer-term benefits were scrapped. The active political agenda did not include efforts to address the domestic energy supply side through increased production of fossil fuels (offshore or in Alaska, for example), the development of safer nuclear power plants (and the issues surrounding the production and storage of nuclear waste), or the encouragement of a range of renewable energy sources. Similarly, strategies designed to encourage greater energy conservation by increasing

---

2. Before action on the legislation was complete, John Dingell (D-Mich.), the longtime senior member of the Energy and Commerce Committee and the key advocate of UAW and automobile interests in Congress, stood with his party's leadership in supporting CAFE standard increases.

motor vehicle efficiency standards, requiring greater efficiency in industrial and electric utilities, and/or increasing the price of energy to reflect
true replacement costs and thus achieve voluntary conservation were not
actively pursued. Had one been a Rip Van Winkle and begun a twenty-year
sleep in 1980, little would have changed in terms of the underlying energy
policy problem when one awoke in 2000. Dependence on oil and gas and
on non-domestic supplies would be largely the same. The focus on short-
term electoral accountability has been a major impediment to effectively
addressing longer-term dependence, either through the development of
increased domestic energy supplies (fossil fuels, nuclear, renewables, or
some combination) or reducing consumption through higher efficiency
standards, price incentives and disincentives, or some mix.

For eighteen of the twenty years between 1981 and 2000 party control
of American national government was divided. And divided party control
may have inhibited the enactment of major energy policy changes, although
research on its effect on the enactment of major policies is far from conclu-
sive (Mayhew 1991; Binder 2003). Even during the 103rd Congress, however, with Democrats in control of the presidency and both legislative
chambers, a modest effort at increasing energy taxes was significantly
diluted before enactment, and that effort was directed more at increasing
federal revenues than at encouraging energy conservation. In an era of relatively cheap energy and ample supplies, there were few incentives for presidents and congressional party leaders of either party to take the electoral
risks of pushing production or conservation solutions to resolving the
longer-term issue of energy dependence. The costs of most solutions would
be near term and traceable, with benefits to come largely in the future. In
contrast, there were few short-term policy or political costs from maintaining the status quo.

I would contend that this scenario is not just limited to energy policy.
The same might be said about health care, Social Security, long-term deficit
reduction, and immigration reform, although more detailed analyses of
those issues would be needed to test that argument. Unless there is a
visible crisis or the costs can be widely dispersed, deferred, or remain non-
traceable, significant policy change rarely occurs in the contemporary
context. The focus on electoral costs is too great in a system with frequent
opportunities for voters to hold officeholders accountable.

Ironically, in recent years it has been the U.S. Senate rather than the
House of Representatives that seems to be more responsive to short-term
partisan impulses. One would assume that with their longer, six-year terms
senators would be more willing to adopt policies that might confer short-
term, traceable costs on the electorate to achieve long-term policy benefits. But that has not been the case for a number of reasons. Obviously, the

cloture rule has been a major cause, not only giving the minority the ability to block legislation, but also serving as a rallying point for minority party supporters in the electorate on a broad range of issues. Because of the frequency of efforts to block cloture on major legislation over the past two decades and the growth of party cohesion in the Senate, the ability of one party to win sixty Senate seats was seen as paramount—a sort of electoral Holy Grail. In the 2008 election, focus on whether the Democrats could win a mislabeled, filibuster-proof, sixty-member majority became a major media concern. And the outcome of a special election to fill the vacancy created by the death of Ted Kennedy took on major proportions in perceived consequence for the outcome of legislation, most notably the Obama health care bill but also energy legislation.

In addition, it has been party control of the Senate, not the House, that has proved more volatile, despite the fact that only a third of its seats are contested every two years. Over the past half century, majority control of the House has only shifted three times—after the 1994, 2006, and 2010 elections—while it has changed in the Senate following the 1980, 1986, 1994, 2002, and 2006 elections and in 2001 when Jim Jeffords (Vt.), elected as a Republican, became an independent and organized with the Democrats. Although longer terms mean that senators individually may not have to be as concerned with the ebbs and flows of public opinion as House members, the national parties and party leaders know that party control is more fragile in the Senate. With a greater percentage of its seats electorally competitive, with the roll call votes of senators more visible to the electorate, and with voters more likely to hold senators accountable for policy decisions, the Senate, not the House, has arguably become the institution more sensitive to transitory shifts in public preferences and less able to pursue policies that have potential electoral costs in the short term. The Senate of the past half-century has grown increasingly divorced from its traditional role. Its unique ability within the institutional framework of American democracy to pursue the country's longer-term policy interests rather than being responsive to the whims of the electorate has eroded.

It may be undemocratic to argue that the United States has too much electoral accountability for its own good. But when national decision makers, especially in the Congress, focus so heavily on how their policy choices affect the outcome of an election every two years they become overly reluctant to pursue policy options that impose short-term cost on the electorate to achieve long-term benefits. The country thus often delays resolving those issues until there is a crisis. And then the cost of corrective action is often much greater. The politics of energy policy since 1960 offers visible examples of this increased emphasis on short-term accountability.

# References

Arnold, Douglas. 1990. *The Logic of Congressional Action*. New Haven, Conn.: Yale University Press.

Binder, Sarah. 2003. *Stalemate: Causes and Consequences of Legislative Gridlock*. Washington, D.C.: Brookings Institution.

Binder, Sarah, and Steven S. Smith. 1997. *Politics or Principle: Filibustering in the United States Senate*. Washington, D.C.: Brookings Institution.

Cox, Gary, and Matthew D. McCubbins. 2007. *Legislative Leviathan: Party Government in the House*, 2nd ed. New York: Cambridge University Press.

Heinz, John, Edward O. Laumann, Robert L. Nelson, and Robert H. Salisbury. 1993. *The Hollow Core: Private Interests in National Policy Making*. Cambridge, Mass.: Harvard University Press.

Koger, Gregory. 2010. *Filibustering: A Political History of Obstruction in the House and Senate*. Chicago: University of Chicago Press.

Manley, John. 1970. *The Politics of Finance*. Boston: Little Brown.

Mayhew, David. 1974. *Congress: The Electoral Connection*. New Haven, Conn.: Yale University Press.

———. 1991. *Divided We Govern*. New Haven, Conn.: Yale University Press.

Oppenheimer, Bruce. 1974. *Oil and the Congressional Process: The Limits of Symbolic Politics*. Lexington, Mass.: Lexington Books.

———. 1981. "Congress and the New Obstructionism: Developing an Energy Program." In Lawrence C. Dodd and Bruce I. Oppenheimer, eds., *Congress Reconsidered*, 2nd ed. Washington, D.C.: Congressional Quarterly Press.

———. 2009. "The Process Hurdles: Energy Legislation from the OPEC Embargo to 2008." In Lawrence C. Dodd and Bruce I. Oppenheimer, eds., *Congress Reconsidered*, 9th ed. Washington, D.C.: CQ Press.

Sinclair, Barbara. 1989. *The Transformation of the U.S. Senate*. Baltimore: Johns Hopkins University Press.

———. 2007. *Unorthodox Lawmaking: New Legislative Processes in the U.S. Congress*, 3rd ed. Washington, D.C.: CQ Press.

Sundquist, James L. 1968. *Politics and Policy*. Washington, D.C.: Brookings Institution.

Surrey, Stanley. 1957. "The Congress and the Tax Lobbyist—How Special Tax Provisions Get Enacted." *Harvard Law Review* (May).

Warwo, Gregory, and Eric Schickler. 2006. *Filibustering: Obstruction and Lawmaking in the U.S. Senate*. Princeton, N.J.: Princeton University Press.

# 11

## The Senate and Foreign Policy

### James M. Lindsay

Thomas Shannon had every reason to expect quick and favorable Senate action on his nomination in spring 2009 to be the U.S. ambassador to Brazil. The 51-year-old foreign service officer had impeccable credentials. A graduate of the College of William and Mary, he had earned a doctorate from Oxford University. As a junior foreign service officer he had spent three years in Brasilia. He later served two stints handling Latin America affairs on the staff of the National Security Council, first under Bill Clinton and then under George W. Bush. After leaving the Bush White House in 2005 and until his nomination to be ambassador, he was assistant secretary of state for Western Hemisphere Affairs. The fact that a Bush appointee could find favor in the new Obama administration attested to his expertise and bipartisan appeal.

And yet, Shannon's nomination ran into trouble. In July, Jim DeMint, a first-term Republican senator from South Carolina, invoked an informal Senate practice and placed a "hold" on his nomination, thereby preventing it from coming to a vote (see Rosen 2009; Sheridan 2009; Stockman 2009). DeMint did not object to Shannon's credentials or to U.S. policy toward Brazil. Instead, he was angry over U.S. policy toward Honduras. The Obama administration, at the behest of virtually all the countries of Latin America, was insisting that Honduras's president, who had been ousted in a coup a month earlier, be restored to office. DeMint insisted to the contrary that the ouster of the Honduran president had been both legal and justified. While the White House and DeMint bickered over U.S. policy toward Honduras, Shannon had no choice but to watch as the Senate confirmed other ambassadorial nominees over the summer of 2009.

DeMint's tenacity eventually paid off. In early November, the White House dropped its insistence that Honduras's president be restored to power. Instead, the administration announced that it would accept the outcome of new elections in Honduras. The shift in position angered many Latin American capitals, but it satisfied DeMint. He lifted the hold. After other Republican senators briefly placed a hold on the nomination to protest the administration's policy toward Cuba, a vote finally went through and Shannon was duly confirmed.

The Shannon confirmation battle provides a glimpse of how foreign policy is handled in the modern Senate and a reminder of how much it has changed over the past half century. In the days when J. William Fulbright and Richard Russell dominated the Senate it would not only have been unthinkable for a senator to use a hold to contest a president's foreign policy choice, it would have been unimaginable for a first-term senator to have done so. The 1950s and 1960s were instead a time of "consent without advice" as a Senate largely followed the president on foreign policy and junior senators deferred to senior ones. That changed in the 1970s and 1980s as the Senate struggled to take back the authority it had previously surrendered, even as the two parties bickered between and among themselves over the substance of foreign policy. The trend toward contention and partisanship accelerated in the 1990s and 2000s, except for a brief time after the attacks of September 11, 2001. The genteel, "Marquis of Queensbury" norms that once governed the Senate gave way to, as DeMint's hold suggests, an attitude of "all is fair in love and war."

The change in Senate behavior on foreign policy from 1960 to 2010 stemmed from many of the same developments that reshaped Senate decision making more generally over that half century. But it also reflected the erosion of the liberal internationalist consensus on the direction and practice of U.S. actions overseas. By 1960 containment had been accepted on both sides of the aisle as the cornerstone of U.S. foreign policy. The Soviet Union was seen as presenting a clear and present danger, and the nuclear balance of terror made roll-back policies impractical. The perception of mortal danger began to crumble after Vietnam, a process that intensified after the fall of the Berlin Wall, with only a brief respite immediately following September 11. With growing disagreements over what threats (if any) the United States faced and what strategies would best serve U.S. national interests, more contentious Senate debates on foreign policy were inevitable.

The merits (or demerits) of the modern Senate's often fractious handling of foreign policy lie in the eye of the beholder. Democrats liked it when the Senate constrained George W. Bush but not when it hampered Barack Obama. Republicans felt the opposite. And despite the longings frequently expressed in Washington for a return to the bipartisanship that characterized the consent without advice Senate, politics is not likely to stop at the water's edge any time soon. Partisanship in foreign policy has been more the norm than the exception in U.S. history, and the two parties' deep divisions on America's interests in the world and how to pursue them ensures that it will continue.

## Framers' Intent

The Senate shares with the House numerous constitutionally assigned powers in foreign policy. Together they have the powers to declare war, provide for the common defense, and regulate trade among other authorities.

But the Senate has two additional responsibilities: the power to confirm presidential nominees and the power to provide "advice and consent" to treaties. Of the two, the advice and consent power is the more significant for the conduct of foreign policy.

The Framers' decision to restrict the congressional role in treaty making to the Senate reflected their assessment of the House's likely weaknesses. In their view, representatives would be too numerous and, by virtue of being elected every two years, too likely to lack the political maturity needed to pass considered judgment on the grave matters of state that treaties were presumed to entail. As John Jay put it in *Federalist* No. 64: "They who wish to commit the [treaty] power under consideration to a popular assembly, composed of members constantly coming and going in quick succession, seem not to recollect that such a body must necessarily be inadequate to the attainment of those great objects, which require to be steadily contemplated in all their relations and circumstances" (Wills 1982). By contrast, senators would be older, indirectly elected, and fewer in number, making it less likely that they would be moved by popular passions rather than the national interest and more likely that they could act with "secrecy and dispatch" (Wills 1982). (Whatever virtues the Senate possessed as a result of indirect election evaporated with the passage of the Seventeenth Amendment in 1913 mandating direct election of senators.) In excluding the House from treaty making, the Framers elevated the Senate in prestige and sowed the seeds for an institutional rivalry that continues to this day.

In assigning the advice and consent power to the Senate the Framers consciously sought to check presidential power. Their experiences with King George III and overall disdain for monarchical rule had left them wary of an unfettered executive. This was true even for Alexander Hamilton, possibly the most enthusiastic proponent of presidential power among the Framers. As he wrote in *Federalist* No. 75, "[I]t would be utterly unsafe and improper to trust that [treaty] power to an elective magistrate of four years duration. . . . The history of human conduct does not warrant that exalted opinion of human virtue which would make it wise in a nation to commit interests of so delicate and momentous a kind as those which concern its intercourse with the rest of the world to the sole disposal of a magistrate, created and circumstanced, as would be a president of the United States" (Wills 1982). The Senate, with it talents and experience, would make it less likely that a president would enter into treaties rashly or unwisely.

In assigning the treaty power to the Senate, the Framers anticipated that the president would consult closely with senators as treaties were being proposed and negotiated. George Washington tried to bring that vision to life. Four months after assuming the presidency, he went to the Senate's chambers to solicit advice on the terms of a treaty with the Cherokee Indians. The discussion did not go as he had hoped. At first several senators complained that the noise of passing carriages on the street outside was drowning out Washington's remarks. Then several senators asked that documents mentioned by Washington be read aloud. This request triggered a confused discussion that culminated in senators fervently debating a motion that had already been postponed. Once the dust settled on the wrangle over the rules of procedure, senators who worried that Washington's presence was inhibiting a frank discussion on the substance of the treaty successfully moved to table the matter. Angered by the Senate's reluctance to discuss the treaty with him, Washington bellowed: "This defeats every purpose of my coming here." As he left the Senate's chambers he vowed that "he would be damned if he ever went there again" (see Haynes 1960; Hayden 1920; Tansill 1924).

The Senate's reluctance to move quickly should not have surprised, let alone angered, Washington. In a famous exchange with Thomas Jefferson shortly after the Constitutional Convention, he had defended the decision to establish the Senate rather than create a unicameral Congress by making an analogy to pouring hot coffee into a saucer: "We pour legislation into the senatorial saucer to cool it" (Mann and Ornstein 2006). And the senators who questioned Washington's plans for dealing with the Cherokee believed they had good reason to cool his rush to a new treaty. As one complained: "The President wishes to tread on the neck of the Senate. . . . He wishes us to see with the eyes and hear with the ears of his Secretary only. The Secretary to advance the premises, the President to draw the conclusions, and to bear down our deliberations with his personal authority and presence. Form only will be left to us. This will not do with Americans" (Haynes 1960).

Washington, of course, was neither the first nor the last person to laud a process in the abstract only to be frustrated by it in practice. Indeed, his experience with the senatorial "saucer" would become the enduring lesson of the next two hundred years: presidents want the Senate to provide quick consent on their terms, and senators frequently decline to provide it.

## "Consent without Advice" (1950s–1960s)

President Washington would have found much to like in the Senate's handling of foreign policy in the 1950s and 1960s. These two decades, which marked the height (or depth) of the Cold War, were a time of extensive senatorial deference to presidential power. In the face of the rise of the "imperial presidency," brought about as successive presidents asserted greater constitutional authority to act abroad, the Senate was far more eager to pass the legislation the president requested and to consent to treaties than to insist that its advice be heard (Schlesinger 1973). Just as remarkable in hindsight was the fact that the Senate's deference on foreign policy was bipartisan. Both parties saw the virtue of strong presidential leadership, and to the extent they complained it was that the occupant of the White House was not assertive enough.

The Senate's preference for consent without advice hardly seemed inevitable at the beginning of the 1950s. Although the Senate rallied around President Harry Truman's decision in June 1950 to send U.S. troops to defend South Korea against North Korea—the Senate majority leader even urged Truman not to seek formal congressional support for his decision—that goodwill faltered once the fighting began to go badly (see Acheson 1969). Truman and his secretary of state, Dean Acheson, became the targets of bitter attacks by Senate Republicans. The so-called Great Debate of 1951 produced a sense-of-the-Senate resolution asserting that the president could send troops abroad only with congressional approval. The resolution was non-binding, and Truman and his successors proceeded to ignore it (see Acheson 1969). Two years later, Sen. John Bricker (R-Ohio) led an effort to amend the Constitution to restrict the use of executive agreements. One version of the so-called Bricker Amendment came within one vote of passage in a Republican-controlled Senate, despite the fervent opposition of President Dwight Eisenhower (see Tananbaum 1988).

The defeat of the Bricker Amendment signaled the end of senatorial assertiveness in foreign policy for more than a decade. Clashes between the White House and the Senate over foreign policy became more and more infrequent and would remain so until after the Tet Offensive of 1968. This is not to say that the Senate slavishly followed the White House's lead. Senators could be counted on to quibble with the details of the annual foreign aid budget, and from time to time they demanded that more be spent on defense. But attempts to challenge the president on foreign policy became rare, with much of the Senate's activity addressing marginal issues. As Sen. Gaylord Nelson (D-Wis.) put it in 1965, senators generally responded to even the most far-reaching presidential initiatives by "stumbling over each other to see who can say 'yea' the quickest and the loudest" (Sundquist 1981). This was especially true with the respect to the war power, where the Senate (and the House as well) seldom challenged the White House except, as Arthur Schlesinger (1973) stated, "when national security zealots on the Hill condemned the executive branch for inadequate bellicosity."

Aggressive executive efforts to expand presidential power partly explain senatorial deference. Just as important, however, senators were eager to surrender their powers. Fearful of the communist threat, many if not most senators believed as a matter of principle that senatorial second-guessing would endanger national security. They even worried that the president was not powerful enough. Sen. J. William Fulbright (D-Ark.), chair of the Senate Foreign Relations Committee, spoke for many of his colleagues in 1961 when he complained that America's eighteenth-century Constitution had "hobbled the president by too niggardly a grant of power"

(Fulbright 1961). Political incentives reinforced principled arguments for senatorial deference. Voters were not demanding Senate activism on foreign policy; like many lawmakers, they too worried that vigorous debate would weaken the country and embolden its critics. In such a political climate, senators were reluctant to challenge the president; those who believed he was being too muscular risked being accused of being unpatriotic. Few wanted to run that risk, especially since they knew that in terms of changing presidential policy their efforts would likely be, as Senator Fulbright described it, "useless and utterly futile" (Yarmolinsky 1971).

Although the era of consent without advice marked a low point in Senate influence on foreign policy, it marked the high point in the prestige of the Senate Foreign Relations Committee (Fransworth 1961; Jewell 1962). As opposed to subsequent decades, Foreign Relations had no difficulty attracting or retaining prominent members—many of whom chaired other committees. In 1960, for example, its roster included such lions of the Senate as Fulbright, Hubert Humphrey (D-Minn.), and Mike Mansfield (D-Mont.), as well as the man who would soon be president, John F. Kennedy (D-Mass.). More generally, senators gave up seats on other committees, including prestigious committees such as Appropriations and Finance, to join Foreign Relations; they did not leave Foreign Relations in search of other committee assignments (see Matthews 1960). Membership on Foreign Relations also tilted heavily in the direction of seniority. In 1960 ten of the sixteen committee members had completed at least two full terms in the Senate; only two members were in their first term in office.

Foreign Relations' ability to attract prominent members reflected the salience of foreign policy and national security issues in the 1950s and 1960s. Senators, like most people, gravitate toward issues in the news, and demonstrated expertise in foreign affairs would be essential to any senator thinking of higher office. As Donald Matthews (1960) described it at the time in his classic examination of the Senate, "Service on Foreign Relations, for example, does not help many senators back home in their states—indeed, in most cases, it is a distinct liability—but it provides the best committee position from which to build a national reputation and launch an assault on the presidency." The Senate Foreign Relations Committee in the 1950s and 1960s, then, embodied the virtues of experience that the Framers had envisioned would characterize the Senate. The problem was that they seldom put those virtues to work. That was soon to change.

## "Reclaiming Advice" (1970s–1980s)

The Vietnam War, itself a product of the Senate's willingness to follow the White House's lead, brought the era of consent without advice to an end. (When a senator said during the debate over the 1964 Gulf of Tonkin

Resolution that he hoped it would not mean "the landing of large American armies in Vietnam," Senator Fulbright, the bill's floor manager agreed, but added that the resolution would authorize "whatever the Commander in Chief feels is necessary." See Ely 1993.) As U.S. casualties mounted, senators, as well as representatives and the broader public, saw more virtue in an eighteenth-century Constitution and less in an imperial presidency. Foreign policy activism in the Senate spiked as a result; senators sought to reclaim their ability to shape the direction of U.S. foreign policy.

The Senate's new activism manifested itself in new legislation, of which the War Powers Resolution may be the best-remembered example, and increased oversight, perhaps best exemplified by the work of the Church Committee on intelligence matters. Senate activism increased on treaty making as well. Whereas President Richard Nixon had handled SALT I as an executive agreement, the Senate was able to compel the consideration of SALT II as a treaty. The prospects for passage of that agreement were always questionable, and Jimmy Carter was forced to withdraw it from Senate consideration without a vote after the Soviet Union invaded Afghanistan in 1979. Carter succeeded in persuading the Senate to consent to the ratification of the Panama Canal Treaties, but that victory came only after a prolonged and politically costly White House campaign.

The Senate's new found activism, however, did not translate into commensurate influence over foreign policy. Senators discovered that powers easily surrendered are not easily recaptured. Successive presidents from both parties declined to relinquish powers their predecessors had claimed. In the case of the War Power Resolution, for example, presidents largely ignored its provisions, reducing it to, in the words of Arthur Schlesinger (1973), a "toy handcuff." At the same time, the recognition that events overseas could change rapidly and in ways that legislators could not predict meant that senators had to insert waivers and other "escape hatches" into foreign affairs legislation. Presidents could, and did, exploit these openings to push their own preferred policies. And in *Goldwater v. Carter* (1979), *I.N.S. v. Chadha* (1983), and other rulings the Supreme Court made it more difficult for the Senate (and the House) to put its imprint on foreign policy (see Franck and Bob 1985; Gibson 1992; Silverstein 1997).[1]

The era of reclaiming advice was marked by significant changes in how the Senate approached foreign policy issues. Prodded by Vietnam, Watergate, and the election of new, more individualistic members, the Senate adopted internal reforms that reduced the power of committee

---

1. In *Goldwater v. Carter* (1979), the Supreme Court declined to bar President Carter from unilaterally abrogating the Mutual Defense Treaty with Taiwan. In *I.N.S. v. Chadha* (1983) the Court sharply limited the use of legislative vetoes, a procedure that allowed Congress to overrule presidential decisions.

chairs. As was the case with other Senate committees, Foreign Relations created new subcommittees with permanent jurisdictions and staff. More equitable rules for assigning committee slots meant that junior members had greater access to seats on Foreign Relations. In 1980, for example, fewer than half the seats on the fifteen-member committee were held by senators who had served two full terms; six of the committee members were in their first term. And with a broader trend toward decentralization of power in the Senate, senators found it less costly to influence committee decisions from within and far easier to influence them from without.

At the same time, the Senate witnessed growing divisions between as well as within the Democratic and Republican Parties. The bipartisan foreign consensus that had made the era of consent without advice possible eroded as partisanship increased. But consensus within the two parties was often missing as well. Many Democrats soured on the merits of an interventionist foreign policy, while others, led by Sen. Henry "Scoop" Jackson (D-Wash.), favored it. Conversely, Republican senators fractured between those who favored the Nixon-Kissinger school of realism and those who preferred the muscular idealism of Ronald Reagan.

These changes cut both ways in terms of the Senate's ability to shape policy. The divisions and disagreements that arose virtually guaranteed that presidents would hear contrary voices in the Senate on almost any step they took in foreign policy. By the same token, the divisions provided potential sources of support for the White House as well. Presidents sought, and often succeeded, in attracting senators in the opposing party. Jimmy Carter secured passage of the Panama Canal Treaty with sixteen Republican votes, while Ronald Reagan prevailed on issues ranging from support for the Nicaraguan contras to adoption of the Strategic Defense Initiative by securing the votes of conservative Democrats.

## "Advice but not Necessarily Consent" (1990s–2000s)

The end of the Cold War accelerated the trends that had begun in the 1970s and 1980s. With the Soviet threat no longer serving to orient American foreign policy, senators enjoyed even greater freedom to challenge the White House. As senators offered advice but not necessarily consent, the traditional norms that had limited what was permissible—the Senate's version of the "Marquis of Queensbury Rules"—eroded further, and in some cases gave way completely. As a result, foreign policy increasingly became, to paraphrase Clausewitz, the continuation of domestic politics by other means.

Bill Clinton felt the brunt of the surge in senatorial (and more broadly, congressional) activism. On issues ranging from China to the Balkans to trade to climate change to aid for Mexico, he found his policy choices questioned, revised, and challenged on Capitol Hill. Not surprisingly, Clinton

(1995) accused lawmakers of launching "nothing less than a frontal assault on the authority of the president to conduct the foreign policy of the United States." He gained support for his charge from many Republican foreign policy professionals. Lawrence Eagleburger, secretary of state under the elder George Bush, warned that the restrictions that the House and Senate were seeking to place on the president "are an absolute attack on the separation of powers" (Lewis 1995).

Emblematic of the Senate's willingness to challenge the White House on foreign policy was the 1999 defeat of the Comprehensive Test Ban Treaty (CTBT) (see Diebel 2002). Although the United States had observed a unilateral moratorium on nuclear testing since 1992 and the U.S. Joint Chiefs of Staff had endorsed the treaty, only forty-eight senators voted to provide consent—far short of the two-thirds required for approval. All but four of the Senate's fifty-five Republican senators voted no. The CTBT's defeat marked only the eighteenth time in U.S. history that the Senate had voted down a treaty, and the first time it had done so on a national security matter since the rejection of the Treaty of Versailles eighty years earlier (see Collier 1987). The CTBT defeat also marked the first time since one of the three votes on the Treaty of Versailles that the "nay" votes outnumbered the "yea" votes.

More remarkable than the outcome of the CTBT vote, however, was the fact that it was held in the first place. When Clinton realized that the treaty was doomed, he asked the Senate's Republican leadership to withdraw it from consideration. He was joined in his request by sixty-two senators. In the past, the Senate leadership would have complied on the grounds that publicly rebuffing the president would have damaged the national interest—as it did in 1980 when President Carter requested that the Senate shelve consideration of SALT II. Not this time. A group of Republicans led by Sen. Jon Kyl (R-Ariz.) pressed Majority Leader Trent Lott (R-Miss.) to hold the vote. Their zeal—and the prospect that they would make Lott's life miserable if he agreed to Clinton's request—more than outweighed the fact that twenty-four Republican senators had publicly joined with their Democratic colleagues to ask that the treaty be withdrawn. Moreover, unlike past executive-legislative confrontations over issues such as Vietnam, the MX missile, or aid to the Nicaraguan contras, anti-CTBT Republicans were not reflecting broad-based public opposition to the White House's policies. Polls showed that upward of 70 percent of Americans favored passage of CTBT (Diebel 2002).

When George W. Bush took the oath of office in January 2001, many Senate Democrats intended to be just as vigorous in challenging his foreign policies as their Republican colleagues had been in challenging Bill Clinton's. Indeed, as the spring and summer of 2001 progressed Washington prepared for a showdown over Bush's expected decision to withdraw the

United States from the ABM Treaty. That confrontation never occurred. In the wake of the September 11 attacks, Bush's public approval ratings soared to 90 percent—a figure seen only once before, when his father waged the Gulf War, and even then only briefly. The sense of threat reached a level not seen since the 1950s and the era of consent without advice. Not surprisingly, senators (and representatives) quickly saw virtue once again in following the president's lead. When Bush asked Congress to give him authority to wage war on Iraq, senators quibbled with some of the language of the draft resolution but ultimately passed it overwhelmingly. When asked why Senate Democrats had not done more to oppose a resolution that so many of them said privately was unwise or premature, Senate Majority Leader Tom Daschle (D-S.D.) replied, "The bottom line is . . . we want to move on" (Rich 2002).

Many senators soon came to regret their deference. As dissatisfaction with the U.S. occupation of Iraq grew, Senate Democrats in particular recovered their willingness to challenge the White House on foreign policy. In 2005, for instance, Senate Democrats filibustered the nomination of John Bolton to be U.S. ambassador to the United Nations, a maneuver Bush sidestepped by making Bolton a recess appointment. In challenging Bush over Iraq, Senate Democrats discovered what their predecessors had discovered during Vietnam: it is easy to criticize a president's handling of the war but difficult for both political and policy reasons to change it. That lesson is especially true when, as with Bush, a president is willing to pay a high political price to follow his policy preferences (see Lindsay 1995, 2000a). Thus, even as senators from both parties pushed Bush to reduce U.S. forces in Iraq, he eventually opted to increase them. At the same time, because Bush preferred to maximize freedom of action for the United States rather than enter into treaties that might constrain its room for maneuver, senators found fewer opportunities to block presidential action.

Potential Senate opposition was a more significant burden for President Barack Obama. He took office with an ambitious foreign policy agenda that required the Senate's cooperation on issues such as climate change and nuclear nonproliferation. He frequently found that senators had different ideas. In 2010 Senate Majority Leader Harry Reid (D-Nev.) admitted that Obama's plans to establish a cap-and-trade system to limit greenhouse gas emissions—a plan the House had endorsed a year earlier—was dead in the Senate. Obama's efforts to win speedy Senate approval in 2010 for the New START Treaty with Russia turned into a pitched battle. Although the treaty was endorsed by Republican foreign policy luminaries such as former secretaries of state Henry Kissinger and James Baker and former national security advisers such as Brent Scowcroft and Stephen Hadley, leading Republican senators argued that the treaty jeopardized U.S. security. Quite tellingly, these critics challenged treaty provisions that they had embraced seven years earlier when the Senate voted 95–0 to approve the Moscow Treaty, a similar arms reduction pact negotiated by George W. Bush (see Pincus 2010).

At the same time the Obama White House was struggling with the Senate over high profile issues such as climate change and arms control, it also found itself embroiled in spats with senators over more obscure foreign policy issues. As in the case of Senator DeMint and Honduras, the weapon of choice for many senators was the hold, which spiked in popularity.[2] Because both sides of the aisle were willing to honor the informal practice, senators found it a useful lever to extract information and policy concessions from the administration. They also found it useful to secure parochial benefits. In 2009, for instance, Sen. Jim Bunning (R-Ky.) blocked Senate consideration of a nominee to be U.S. trade representative for eight months to protest Canada's ban on flavored cigarettes and small cigars—not coincidentally an export of his home state of Kentucky (see Cohn 2010; Cooper 2009; Marcus 2009; Phillips 2009). Not to be outdone, in 2010 Sen. Richard Shelby (R-Ala.) placed holds on seventy presidential nominations because of "unaddressed national security concerns" (Wilson and Murray 2010). These concerns turned out to be his displeasure that two government programs that provided jobs in Alabama had been cut.

The willingness of Senate Republicans to obstruct Obama's foreign policy agenda had collateral consequences that went beyond the specific issues being contested. In a classic example of anticipated reactions, administration officials assessed their nomination and legislative decisions with an eye toward reducing the chances of provoking confrontations with senators. The most visible casualty was CTBT. Halting nuclear proliferation was one of Obama's signature foreign policy initiatives. He had given a major speech in Prague in April 2009 pledging to work for a world without nuclear weapons, he had hoped to strengthen the Nuclear Nonproliferation Treaty, and he was working to keep Iran from going nuclear. Administration officials calculated that persuading the Senate to bless CTBT, which by 2010 had been ratified by more than 150 countries, would advance all three goals. But by 2010 it was also clear that even a Senate dominated by Democrats was not prepared to move swiftly on CTBT. White House officials also recognized that Republican criticism of New START had as much if not more to do with dissuading the administration from undertaking further arms reductions negotiations. And to find ways to win over Republican critics of New START, the White House promised to spend more aggressively on the modernization of the U.S. nuclear forces.

---

2. A review of the indices of eight books published between 1989 and 2000 on Congress's handling of foreign policy found no mention of the use of holds (see Blechman 1990; Crabb, Antizzo, and Sarieddine 2000; Crabb and Dunbar 1992; Henehan 2000; Hinkley 1994; Lindsay 1994; Warburg 1989; Weissman 1995).

The Senate's increased ability in the advice-but-not-necessarily-consent era to frustrate the White House did not mean, however, that the Senate Foreign Relations Committee had regained the prominence it had held a half century earlier. To the contrary, the Senate's activism largely bypassed the committee, which continued its decades-long decline (see Fowler and Law 2008). By 2010 it had been a quarter of a century since the committee had managed to push through Congress what had once been its signature piece of legislation, the foreign aid authorization bill. The growing role of the military in U.S. foreign policy meant that the locus of key committee debates had shifted to the Armed Services Committee. And membership on Foreign Relations was not necessary to drive the foreign policy debate. Senator Kyl was a first-term senator with seats on the Appropriations, Judiciary, and Intelligence committees when he orchestrated the defeat of CTBT. Eleven years later, Foreign Relation's chair and ranking minority member were supplicants seeking to persuade Kyl to endorse New START. (He eventually came out in opposition to the treaty.) Exactly who held the balance of power was evident in Kyl's comment: "Until I'm satisfied about some of these things, I will not be willing to allow the treaty to come up [for a vote]" (Baker 2010).

## An Eroded Internationalist Consensus

The Senate's handling of foreign policy issues in 2010 looked much different than it had a half century earlier. A committee-centered process dominated by senior senators and that deferred considerably to presidential leadership gave way over time to a more decentralized and partisan brand of decision making. Behavior that once was unthinkable, such as forcing a treaty vote over the president's objections or blocking nominations in order to steer more parochial benefits back home, became part of the standard retinue of options open to all senators.

The changes in the Senate's behavior on foreign policy reflect many of the same factors that reshaped its behavior more broadly (see Mann and Ornstein 2006; Packer 2010; Sinclair 1989). The changing social bases of the Democratic and Republican Parties, changes in the media and communication technologies, and the tremendous expansion in lobbies all reshaped who came to the Senate and what they did once they arrived. Likewise, the rules changes that the Senate adopted in the 1970s in response to Vietnam, Watergate, and the election of new, more individualist members reduced the power of committee chairs and distributed influence more broadly within the institution (see Smith and Deering 1990; Fowler and Law 2008).

But the changes in Senate behavior on foreign policy also reflect a change peculiar to this sector, namely, the erosion of the internationalist consensus forged after (and by) World War II on the nature of the threats facing the United States and how to address them (see Beinart 2008; Kupchan and Trubowitz 2007, 2010; Wiarda and Skelly 2006; Chaudoin, Milner, Tingley 2010; Busby and Monten 2008; Lindsay 2000b). By the mid-1950s, containment (as opposed to rollback) of the Soviet Union had become a core principle of U.S. foreign policy. The country saw itself as gravely at risk, and this sense of peril both encouraged deference to presidential leadership and discouraged anything that could be viewed as playing politics with national security. If there was any tendency in the Senate to criticize the president, the bias was toward arguing that he was doing too little rather than too much.

Vietnam created a fissure in the internationalist consensus that the demise of the Soviet Union broke wide open. The battles in the Senate during the 1970s and 1980s over issues such as the Panama Canal, arms control with the Soviet Union, and aid to the Nicaraguan contras reflected deep-seated disagreements about the nature of the threats and opportunities facing the United States and what should be done about them. With the fall of the Berlin Wall, containment could no longer serve as the orienting principle for U.S. foreign policy, and no other concept arose to replace it. Instead, there is considerable disagreement within the Senate—and just as important, outside it—on the nature of the threats and opportunities facing the country and what can or should be done about them. It is hardly surprising that Senate debate on foreign policy became more contentious in the face of such disagreement.

Just as important, ideological disagreements on foreign policy increasingly came to fall along party lines rather than cut across them. By the late 1990s, the foreign policy splits that had developed within the Democratic and Republican Parties as a result of Vietnam had largely closed. Conservative Democrats typified by Scoop Jackson, John Stennis, and Ernest Hollings and liberal internationalist Republicans typified by Jacob Javits, Clifford Case, Charles Mathias, and John Chafee had all but become extinct. The greater degree of ideological homogeneity within each party in turn made it easier for party leaders to enforce party discipline and harder for presidents to pick up support from across the aisle.

But the advice-but-not-necessarily-consent Senate cannot be explained solely by ideological disagreement. Politics too played a role. The roots of modern partisanship are complex and not easily explained (see Chapters 5 and 6 in this volume). But in the area of foreign policy the demise of the Soviet Union was critical. The fall of the Berlin Wall created a widespread sense among Americans that foreign threats to the United States were low. Foreign policy issues tumbled in importance. September 11 reversed that perception but only for a time. One consequence of the sense that the threats to U.S. interests are low is that inhibitions over using foreign policy issues to score political points flagged as well. After all, it is easy to indulge your passions when your interests are not at risk. So holds on the president's ambassadorial nominations to keep federal jobs at home were no longer unthinkable. Likewise, filibustering a defense appropriations bill became an acceptable tactic to delay action on an unrelated health care bill, as Republicans did briefly in December 2009 (see Kane and Montgomery 2009).

The composition of the Senate Foreign Relations Committee in 2010 illustrated how political incentives changed. The committee offered no particular advantage to any senator seeking to establish a national reputation, which could be done with any set of committee assignments. To be sure, Barack Obama came to national prominence while sitting on Foreign Relations, but that was hardly the reason for his ascent. Meanwhile, Foreign Relations remained a post that, as Donald Matthews noted a half century earlier, could be a distinct liability with voters. It was a liability not just because it frequently dealt with matters irrelevant to the immediate concerns of most Americans, but also because, as Sen. Chuck Hagel (R-Neb.), who served on the committee for two terms, noted, "it is not a particularly strong committee to fundraise from" (Lindsay 2000b.) Not surprisingly, thirteen of the committee's eighteen members in 2010 were first-term senators. Although Senator Hagel's description of the committee during his service as a "kind of a wasteland" perhaps overstated things, the committee hardly embodied the deep reservoir of experience on foreign affairs that the Framers had envisioned or that the Senate of the 1950s and 1960s had produced.

## Consequences

Is it a problem that Senate action today on foreign policy—like many areas of domestic policy—is fractious, contentious, and frequently gridlocked? The answer to that question is inherently subjective. Where you stand depends on what you want. The president's backers bemoan gridlock; his critics applaud it. As former secretary of the navy John Lehman once put it: "I have been a 'strong president man' when in the executive branch and a 'strong Congress man' when out of the government in political opposition" (Lehman 1992).

Have gridlock and increased partisanship diminished the Senate's oversight of foreign policy? Passionate arguments certainly have been made that oversight has atrophied (see Deering 2001, 2005; Fisher 2005; Mann and Ornstein 2006; Smock and Bruns 2010). But the evidence is at best mixed. For every frustrated Senate staffer who complains that the golden age of oversight has passed there is a harried executive branch official who complains about being micromanaged by Congress. The traditional quantitative indicators used to measure oversight—committee hearings, report requests, and floor amendments—may reveal little about whether effective oversight is being conducted. Senators may miss committee hearings or fail to pay attention when they are there, and demands for reports and floor amendments may be intended more as a sop for interest groups than an effort to oversee the executive branch. The implicit assumption that oversight means systematic reviews of an administration's policies also misunderstands how oversight is done. Rather than operating as "police patrols," Senate (and congressional) oversight more often than not entails responding to "fire alarms" as consistuents, the media, or some other aggrieved party warns of a problem (see McCubbins and Schwartz 1984). And when compared to the consent-without-advice Senate of the 1950s and 1960s, the modern Senate stands as a bastion of oversight.

So what can be said of the modern Senate's handling of foreign policy? Four points are worth making. First, the Senate's behavior today has ample precedent. The latter half of the nineteenth century has for good reason been called the era of "senatorial domination." Between 1871 and 1898 the Senate refused to approve every major treaty put before it, with the votes often falling along party lines (see Cheever and Haviland 1952; Holt 1933; Warburg 1989). This assertiveness prompted one nineteenth-century scholar to complain that the Senate had transformed its treaty-making power into a "treaty-marring power" (Wilson 1956). Three decades later, scholar-turned-president Woodrow Wilson saw that treaty-marring power used to doom his great achievement, the Treaty of Versailles. In the two decades after Wilson's death, isolationist senators dealt successive presidents foreign policy defeats. In that respect, then, the idea that "politics stops at the water's edge" has been more the exception than the norm in U.S. foreign policy.

Second, the fact that the modern Senate is more inclined to challenge the White House does not mean that presidents always lose. Far from it. Presidents can prevail over even stiff Senate opposition. Bill Clinton persuaded a Republican-controlled Senate to enlarge NATO and to approve the Chemical Weapons Convention. George W. Bush carried the day on the decision to surge U.S. forces in Iraq. Barack Obama did likewise in Afghanistan, and he won Senate approval of the New START Treaty despite being opposed by the two top ranking Senate Republicans.

The president's ability to override Senate opposition depends to a great extent on what law or custom requires. Presidents face a higher burden when they need Senate (or congressional) approval to act, as in the case of treaties, than when they are free to act unless the Congress stops them, which would certainly entail overriding a veto. Bush's ability to proceed with the Iraq surge in the face of strong bipartisan opposition was simply a newer version of a truth that Teddy Roosevelt demonstrated a century earlier. Roosevelt responded to the threat made by the chair of the Senate

Naval Appropriations Committee to block funding for the Great White Fleet's famed trip around the world by daring him to "try and get it back" (Kinzer 2006). The power that the Senate or Congress wields in practice may fall far short of the power they wield in theory. And some presidential powers in foreign policy, such as whether and what to negotiate about, whether to grant diplomatic recognition, and whether to withdraw from or end a treaty, lie beyond the Senate's (and Congress's) purview entirely. Even where Senate consent is needed presidents can prevail by committing the full power of their office to building bipartisan coalitions and taking their case to the American public. Clinton overcame fierce conservative resistance to the Chemical Weapons Convention by putting his White House staff on "war room" footing and painstakingly negotiating almost two dozen conditions to the resolution of advice and consent to satisfy wavering senators and assemble a winning coalition. Obama did much the same to secure passage of the New START Treaty.

Third, the dangers of a contentious and fractious Senate are easily overstated. To be sure, the practices of the modern Senate are at times unsightly. The Framers' probably did not envision senators holding presidential nominations hostage as a way to steer federal jobs into their states. And hindsight provides many examples in which Senate opposition to presidential initiatives looks wrongheaded. The defeat of the Treaty of Versailles and the various neutrality acts of the 1930s come readily to mind. But there are also great costs to a compliant Senate, witness the Gulf of Tonkin Resolution and the 2002 debate over authorizing the Iraq War. And while presidents seldom like an assertive Senate because it generally means they will accomplish less, having to work to secure Senate support often means that what they do accomplish will likely be better policy.

Fourth, procedural reforms will not produce more orderly or "better" Senate decision making on foreign policy. Because the Senate's assertiveness (or obstructionism) is rooted in disagreements over the nature of the threats and opportunities facing the United States as well as in a partisanship that has deep structural roots, committee realignments and limits on holds are unlikely to spur greater deliberation or more collaborative decision making. Whatever the rules, partisans committed to blocking presidential action in foreign policy will search for ways to use them to their advantage. In that respect, the Senate's rules have been less the cause of the senatorial "misbheavior" in recent years than a symptom. The Senate of Fulbright, Mansfield, and Kennedy was governed by norms that greatly limited what senators could do, regardless of what the rules entitled them to do. Those norms have crumbled, and no rules changes will restore them.

The truth be told, the modern Senate's handling of foreign policy is in keeping with the Framers' vision. They did not labor under the illusion that legislative decision making would be all sweetness and light. To the contrary. Their own experiences and disagreements made them realists about human nature. As James Madison famously put it in *Federalist* No. 51, "If men were angels, no government would be necessary." And since they weren't, "ambition must be made to combat ambition" (Wills 1982). The Framers anticipated that senators would wrangle, even if they didn't like the idea of political parties (or "factions") or complained when their favored ideals fell victim to the Senate's cooling saucer. Their intuition was not that giving the Senate a say would guarantee that the country would always choose wisely. It was instead that it would decrease the chances that the country would choose unwisely. They have yet to be proven wrong.

# References

Acheson, Dean. 1969. *Present at the Creation: My Years in the State Department*. New York: W.W. Norton.

Baker, Peter. 2010. "White House Presses Republicans on Arms Treaty." *New York Times*, July 22.

Beinart, Peter. 2008. "When Politics No Longer Stops at the Water's Edge: Partisan Polarization and Foreign Policy." In Pietro S. Nivola and David W. Brady, eds., *Red and Blue Nation?* Vol. 2: *Consequences and Correction of America's Polarized Politics*. Washington, D.C.: Brookings Institution.

Blechman, Barry M. 1990. *The Politics of National Security: Congress and U.S. Defense Policy*. New York: Oxford University Press.

Busby, Joshua W., and Jonathan Monten. 2008. "Without Heirs? Assessing the Decline of Establishment Internationalism in U.S. Foreign Policy." *Perspectives on Politics* 6 (September).

Chaudoin, Stephen, Helen V. Milner, and Dustin H. Tingley. 2010. "The Center Still Holds." *International Security* 35 (Summer).

Cheever, Daniel S., and H. Field Haviland Jr. 1952. *American Foreign Policy and the Separation of Powers*. Cambridge, Mass.: Harvard University Press.

Clinton, William J. 1995. "Presidential Statement to the Press Pool." The White House. May 23. Available at http://archives.clintonpresidentialcenter.org/?u=052395-presidential-statement-to-the-press-pool.htm. Accessed

Cohn, Peter. 2010. "Senator Blocks Treasury Nominees." *Congress Daily*, January 7.

Collier, Ellen C. 1987. "U.S. Senate Rejection of Treaties: A Brief Survey of Past Instances." Congressional Research Service, Report no. 87-305F, March 30.

Cooper, Helene. 2009. "Legislative Limbo Strands Many of Obama's Nominees." *New York Times*, December 27.

Crabb, Cecil V., Jr., and Robin Dunbar. 1992. *Invitation to Struggle: Congress, the President, and Foreign Policy*, 4th ed. Washington, D.C.: CQ Press.

Crabb, Cecil V., Jr., Glenn J. Antizzo, and Leila E. Sarieddine. 2000. *Congress and the Foreign Policy Process: Modes of Legislative Behavior*. Baton Rouge: Louisiana State University Press.

Deering, Christopher J. 2001. "Principle or Party? Foreign and National Security Policymaking in the Senate." In Colton C. Campbell and Nicol Rae, eds., *The Contentious Senate*. Lanham, Md.: Rowman and Littlefield.

———. 2005. "Foreign Affairs and War." In Paul J. Quirk and Sarah A. Binder, eds., *The Legislative Branch*. New York: Oxford University Press.

Diebel, Terry L. 2002. "The Death of a Treaty." *Foreign Affairs* 81 (September/October).

Ely, John Hart. 1993. *War and Responsibility: Constitutional Lesson of Vietnam and Its Aftermath.* Princeton, N.J.: Princeton University Press.

Fisher, Louis. 2005. "Deciding on War against Iraq: Institutional Failures." In Robert Y. Shapiro, ed., *The Meaning of American Democracy*. New York: Academy of Political Science.

Fowler, Linda L., and R. Brian Law. 2008. "Make Way for the Party: The Rise and Fall of the Senate National Security Committees, 1947–2006." In Nathan W. Monroe, Jason M. Roberts, and David W. Rohde, eds., *Why Not Parties? Party Effects in the United States Senate*. Chicago: University of Chicago Press.

Franck, Thomas M., and Clifford A. Bob. 1985. "The Return of Humpty Dumpty: Foreign Relations Law after the Chadha Case." *American Journal of International Law* 79 (October).

Fransworth, David N. 1961. *The Senate Committee on Foreign Relations*. Urbana: University of Illinois Press.

Fulbright, J. William. 1961. "American Foreign Policy in the 20th Century under an 18th Century Constitution." *Cornell Law Quarterly* 47 (Fall).

Gibson, Martha Liebler. 1992. *Weapons of Influence: The Legislative Veto, American Foreign Policy, and the Irony of Reform*. Boulder, Colo.: Westview Press.

Hayden, Ralston. 1920. *The Senate and Treaties, 1789–1817*. London: Macmillan.

Haynes, George H. 1960. *The Senate of the United States: Its History and Practice*, Vol. I. New York: Russell and Russell.

Henehan, Marie T. 2000. *Foreign Policy and Congress: An International Relations Perspective*. Ann Arbor: University of Michigan Press.

Hinckley, Barbara. 1994. *Less than Meets the Eye: Foreign Policy Making and the Myth of the Assertive Congress*. Chicago: University of Chicago Press.

Holt, W. Stull. 1933. *Treaties Defeated in the Senate*. Baltimore: Johns Hopkins Press.

Jewell, Malcolm E. 1962. *Senatorial Politics and Foreign Policy*. Lexington: University of Kentucky Press.

Kane, Paul, and Lori Montgomery. 2009. "Senate Democrats Block GOP Filibuster." *Washington Post*, December 18.

Kinzer, Stephen. 2006. *Overthrow: America's Century of Regime Change from Hawaii to Iraq*. New York: Times Books.

Kupchan, Charles A., and Peter L. Trubowitz. 2007. "Dead Center: The Demise of Liberal Internationalism in the United States." *International Security* 32 (Fall).

———. 2010. "The Illusion of Liberal Internationalism's Revival." *International Security* 35 (Summer).

Lehman, John. 1992. *Making War: The 200-Year-Old Battle between the President and Congress over How America Goes to War*. New York: Scribner's.

Lewis, Anthony. 1995. "Capitol Power Grab." *New York Times*, May 26.

Lindsay, James M. 1994. *Congress and the Politics of Foreign Policy*. Baltimore: Johns Hopkins University Press.

———. 1995. "Congress and the Use of Force in the Post-Cold War Era." In Bruce D. Berkowitz, ed., *The United States and the Use of Force in the Post–Cold War Era*. Washington, D.C.: Brookings Institution and the Aspen Strategy Group.

———. 2000a. "Cowards, Beliefs, and Structures: Congress and the Use of Force." In H. W. Brands, ed., *The Use of Force after the Cold War*. College Station: Texas A&M University Press.

———. 2000b. "The New Apathy: How an Uninterested Public Is Reshaping Foreign Policy." *Foreign Affairs* 79 (September/October).

Mann, Thomas E., and Norman J. Ornstein. 2006. *The Broken Branch: How Congress Is Failing America and How to Get It Back on Track.* New York: Oxford University Press.

Marcus, Ruth. 2009. "Advise and Stall." *Washington Post,* October 7.

Matthews, Donald R. 1960. *U.S. Senators and Their World.* Chapel Hill: University of North Carolina Press.

McCubbins, Mathew D., and Thomas Schwartz. 1984. "Congressional Oversight Overlooked: Police Patrols versus Fire Alarms." *American Journal of Political Science* 28 (February).

Packer, George. 2010. "The Empty Chamber." *New Yorker,* August 9.

Phillips, Kate. 2009. "Senate Leader Blasts Holdup on Obama's Nominees." *New York Times,* October 29.

Pincus, Walter. 2010. "New START: A Similar Arms Reduction Pace but a Different Republican Reaction." *Washington Post,* August 10.

Rich, Frank. 2002. "It's the War, Stupid." *New York Times,* October 12.

Rosen, James. 2009. "SC Senator Forces U.S. Change on Honduras." McClatchy Newspapers, November 14.

Schlesinger, Arthur, Jr. 1973. *The Imperial Presidency.* Boston: Houghton Mifflin.

Sheridan, Mary Beth. 2009. "Kerry's Attempt to Block DeMint's Honduras Trip Reveals Policy Feud." *Washington Post,* October 2.

Silverstein, Gordon. 1997. *Imbalance of Powers: Constitutional Interpretation and the Making of American Foreign Policy.* New York: Oxford University Press.

Sinclair, Barbara. 1989. *The Transformation of the U.S. Senate.* Baltimore: Johns Hopkins University Press.

Smith, Stephen S., and Christopher J. Deering. 1990. *Committees in Congress,* 2nd ed. Washington, D.C.: CQ Press, 1990.

Smock, Raymond, and Roger Bruns. 2010. "Contract Fraud? CIA Abuses? Financial Crisis? Congress Used to Investigate." *Washington Post,* August 8.

Stockman, Farah. 2009. "Kerry, GOP Senator Tussle over Honduran Trip." *Boston Globe,* October 3.

Sundquist, James L. 1981. *The Decline and Resurgence of Congress.* Washington, D.C.: Brookings Institution.

Tananbaum, Duane. 1988. *The Bricker Amendment Controversy: A Test of Eisenhower's Political Leadership.* Ithaca, N.Y.: Cornell University Press.

Tansill, Charles C. 1924. "The Treaty-Making Powers of the Senate." *American Journal of International Law* 18 (July).

Warburg, Gerald Felix. 1989. *Conflict and Consensus: The Struggle between Congress and the President over Foreign Policymaking.* New York: Harper and Row.

Weissman, Stephen R. 1995. *A Culture of Deference: Congress' Failure of Leadership in Foreign Policy.* New York: Basic Books.

Wiarda, Howard, and Esther M. Skelly. 2006. *The Crisis of American Foreign Policy: The Effects of a Divided America.* Lanham, Md.: Rowman and Littlefield.

Wills, Gary, ed. 1982. *The Federalist Papers,* by Alexander Hamilton, James Madison, and John Jay. New York: Bantam.

Wilson, Scott, and Shailagh Murray. 2010. "Senator Richard Shelby of Alabama Holding Up Obama Nominees for Home-State Pork." *Washington Post,* February 6.

Wilson, Woodrow. 1956. *Congressional Government: A Study in American Politics.* Cleveland, Ohio: Meridian Books.

Yarmolinsky, Adam. 1971. *The Military Establishment: Its Impact on American Society.* New York: Harper and Row.

# 12

## Looking Back to See Ahead:
## The Senate in the Twenty-First Century

David W. Rohde

To talk of the twenty-first century Senate is to consider the present and future Senate. That discussion, to be more than speculation or guesswork, must build on our understanding of the Senate over the past half century. Some might think that to claim that we can anticipate how the Senate will work over the next few decades is hubris. But if we have a theory or set of theories that offer solid explanations of current legislative organization (and I believe that we do), then those theories should provide us with dependable expectations about the Senate and its operations in the near future. I do not imply that our foresight will be perfect, but we can expect that the causal forces that have shaped the current Senate—the forces that our theories focus on—will shape future patterns.

### Major Causal Forces

First we will consider the major causal forces that our theories tell us have been important in shaping the operation of the current Senate and transforming it from the very different institution described by Eric Schickler and others (see Chapter 1 in this volume). Principal among these, I would argue, was the political realignment, first in the South and later in other regions, that reshaped American politics. Southern loyalty to the Democratic Party was one of the most significant and enduring political legacies of the Civil War and Reconstruction, but it began to break down after World War II. Dwight Eisenhower made the initial southern breakthrough for the Republicans in presidential politics, followed by the increased successes of the Goldwater and Nixon candidacies in the region. Barry Goldwater's candidacy also fostered the first GOP victories in congressional races in the deep South in 1964, and over ensuing decades the party's rate of success in House races in the region grew. In 1994 Republicans finally won a majority

I want to express my thanks to Aaron Houck, Aaron King, and Frank Orlando—graduate students in the Political Institutions and Public Choice Program at Duke University—for their research assistance in the preparation of this paper.

of southern seats in the House and Senate, helping them to gain majorities in both chambers for the first time in forty years.

One significant consequence of these changes was the transformation of the ideological make-up of the congressional delegations of both parties. During the New Deal, southern Democrats had become more conservative than their northern counterparts on the main political issues of the day, and the degree of divergence continued to increase through the 1970s (see Rohde 1991; Poole and Rosenthal 2007). However, due to a number of factors, including the enfranchisement of black southerners with passage of the Voting Rights Act of 1965 and the gradual egress of white southern conservatives from the Democratic Party, the Democrats began nominating and electing senators (and representatives) in the South who were more similar ideologically to northern Democrats. On the other hand, the southern Republicans who were being elected in increasing numbers were mostly extremely conservative, which moved the GOP Senate contingent sharply to the right.

That evolution in the GOP, in turn, affected the political reputation of the Republican Party in the rest of the country, presenting a more conservative image to the electorate. Along with other developments discussed below, this made GOP candidates in the north less attractive to moderate voters, which increased the success of Democratic Senate candidates. Some data will illustrate the trends. After the 1952 elections 100 percent of the senators from the South were Democrats (and again, most of them were conservatives), while in the Northeast and Midwest the Democratic percentages were 25 and 12 percent, respectively. After 2008, only 27 percent of southern senators were Democrats, none of whom were conservative by current standards, and the party's northeastern and midwestern percentages were 81 and 56, respectively (for more on this, see Chapter 2).

As noted, one result of these trends was to make the Democratic and Republican contingents in both chambers of Congress more ideologically homogeneous within the parties and more divergent between them (see Chapter 2). For example, in 2009 a majority of Democrats opposed a majority of Republicans on 72 percent of all roll calls (these are termed "party unity votes"), a post–World War II record by a considerable margin. The average party unity score (i.e., the proportion of party unity votes on which a member votes with her party) for Democrats was 91 percent while for Republicans it was 87 percent. It should be noted that as recently as 1976 the average unity score for both parties was below 63 percent (*CQ Weekly*, January 11, 2010).

This development is central to a theoretical argument about stronger parties within government developed by John H. Aldrich and myself that we term "conditional party government," or CPG for short (Rohde 1991; Aldrich 1995, 2000; Rohde and Aldrich 2010). The essential argument of

CPG is that when congressional parties are ideologically diverse internally and not very different from one another collectively, members will be reluctant to delegate substantial powers to parties and their leaders because they would be uncertain about the consequences of the use of those powers. Each member would fear that strong leaders could take actions that would be contrary to that member's policy or electoral interests.

When, however, each party's members are ideologically similar and the two party contingents are markedly different (as has been increasingly the case over the last twenty-five years), a party's members' interests are more similar, and so they will be less concerned about leaders' taking actions they would not like. Moreover, the increased divergence between the parties means that the opposite party's success, either in passing legislation or achieving electoral victory, would be more damaging to members' interests than in the past. The evidence of increasing delegation of power to parties and leaders is very strong in the House, where majorities can largely work their will unencumbered. In the Senate, with greater institutional leverage granted to minorities and individuals, the patterns are less clear, but considerable evidence has mounted in recent years of progressively greater coordinated partisan action over time and increasing strength for Senate parties (see Sinclair 2009).

A second causal force has been the transformation of primary electorates. Those electorates are not a random sample of the entire population or even of partisan identifiers. Primary voters tend to be stronger partisans, more policy-oriented, and more ideologically extreme than nonparticipants. Moreover, over time the number of people participating in primaries has been declining (even during the period since 1992 when turnout in general elections was increasing). In 1962, 19.9 percent of age-eligible persons voted in Democratic primaries, but in 2006 the percentage was only 8.4. The corresponding percentages for Republicans were 12.8 in 1962 and 7.2 in 2006 (Kiely 2010). This means that primary electorates have become even more "distilled" and less representative than they had been earlier, tilting further away from the center in opposite directions.

This, in turn, has given a greater competitive advantage to candidates who voice more extreme views, and it has undermined incumbents and other candidates who have displayed evidence of departure from orthodox party positions or a willingness to compromise with the opposition. In 2010, for example, Rep. Joe Sestak of Pennsylvania, campaigning as "a real Democrat" in the party primary, defeated Sen. Arlen Specter from the left. Specter had switched parties to avoid a right-wing opponent in the GOP primary who had attacked him for being too liberal. Sestak, in turn, linked Specter to former president George W. Bush in television ads. In Arkansas, Democratic senator Blanche Lincoln was challenged for renomination by Lt. Governor Bill Halter with support from many leaders of organized labor who were unhappy with her moderate record. They mounted the challenge in part to warn other moderates that labor support could not be taken for granted (see Rucker 2010). Halter forced Lincoln into a runoff, which she narrowly survived.

Ideological primary contests have become even more frequent and more intense among Republicans, as other 2010 contests illustrate. Sen. John McCain of Arizona, his party's 2008 nominee for president, received a primary challenge from former representative and recent conservative talk-radio host J. D. Hayworth. Another Republican senator, Robert Bennett of Utah, despite having a party support score of 83 percent in 2009 (*CQ Weekly*, January 11, 2010) and having served three previous terms, was attacked by conservatives for supporting President Bush's Troubled Assets Relief Program in 2008 and for working with Democrats to seek common ground on health care. He drew multiple GOP opponents and could not amass enough votes at the party convention to finish as one of the top two contenders. As a result, Bennett was not even eligible to participate in the party primary (Gardner 2010). Similar ideological contests have occurred in races without GOP incumbents, as in Kentucky, where Rand Paul beat the candidate favored by the national party apparatus with the support of conservative "Tea Party" activists.

Of course, not all primary contests center on ideological clashes, and when they do the more extreme candidate does not always win. That pattern, however, is not required for the changes in primaries to affect candidates' behavior. It is not necessary that the candidacies of members who stray from party orthodoxy be always contested or always lost—just that it happens sometimes, leaving candidates well aware of the threat. This awareness will affect the strategic calculations and positions of those already in office (like McCain and Lincoln). Similarly, it is not necessary that more extreme candidates be always victorious—just that it happens more often than in the past. Moreover, countervailing pressure is minimal in primaries. There are few if any instances in recent decades of candidates being challenged for being too loyal to the party. Therefore, candidates with moderate tendencies are now often led to jettison such positions, as when McCain withdrew his support for a proposal that he had sponsored to set up a special commission to tackle the national debt because conservatives claimed it was a vehicle to increase taxes (Philips 2010).

Since this process has occurred in both parties, general election voters have increasingly been presented with a choice between a Democrat who is substantially to the left of the median voter and a Republican who is substantially to the right. Under these circumstances, no matter which party does better or by how much in the aggregate election outcomes, the overall result will be partisan polarization in the chamber.

A third important force that has shaped the current Senate is related to the previous two; an increasing proportion of the Senate's membership has strong personal policy commitments. This is distinct from the increase in the proportion of members with relatively extreme positions (and thus of polarization), although the two appear to be related. Over time, a disproportionate share of the newer, more extreme members entering the Senate appear to care greatly about the nature of policy outcomes. Further, they seem to be less willing than earlier senators to depart from those preferred positions in reaching compromise solutions that can be adopted by the chamber; they are also more inclined to use the leverage that Senate rules give to every member to impede what they oppose. The result is the growth of ideological battles over legislation in which each side is passionately committed to resisting victory by their opponents.

This is a difficult development to demonstrate objectively, because we have no good systematic measures of senators' *private* political preferences. Some might argue that these senators are engaging in mere position-taking in order to appeal to their primary or general electorates (Mayhew 1974)—and certainly this is a factor. Yet I think most close observers of the Senate would agree with my contention, and there is both systematic and anecdotal evidence that is consistent with it. For example, Sean Theriault (2008) has shown that much of the increase in the Senate's polarization over the last thirty years results from the entrance into the chamber of Republican members who had served in the House with the highly partisan Newt Gingrich. Moreover, Theriault and David Rohde (2011) have shown that this pattern is not due simply to differences in the constituencies those members serve (such as the state's partisanship, its region, or its size), nor to electoral factors like the margins of victory in general elections or primaries.

The anecdotal evidence is more plentiful in the Senate of the 111th Congress (2009–11). Sen. Thomas Coburn (R-Okla.) has become famous (or infamous, depending on one's point of view) for his strong policy commitments and his willingness to exploit the Senate's rules in extreme ways to pursue them. Coburn recognizes that floor time is an essential commodity for those (particularly in the majority party) who want to pass legislation, and he employs devices that will consume time on legislation he opposes. For example, during the health care debate he took the unusual step of requiring the full text of a 767-page amendment to be read aloud, a move that was eventually short circuited by the withdrawal of the amendment (Pierce and Drucker 2009b). A month later Coburn sought to delay consideration of the bill to raise the limit on the national debt by using an arcane parliamentary device to split a proposed amendment into seventeen separate parts, each requiring a roll call (Stanton 2010a).

Actions like Coburn's are often endorsed, at least privately, by the leaders of the member's party because, as we will discuss below, the party sees electoral or policy benefits from them. In other instances, however, some members will employ procedural devices for policy purposes without their party's assent. For example, Jim Bunning (R-Ky.) conducted filibusters over the course of two weeks against a pair of bills designed to extend unemployment benefits for those whose time out of work had exceeded existing benefit limits. He continued his effort despite pressure from both Democrats and Republicans to relent. Moreover, his actions were clearly not rooted in reelection motives because he had already announced his decision not to seek another term (Stanton and Pierce 2010). Finally, Jim DeMint of South Carolina, another strong conservative popular with the Tea Party, has exerted substantial efforts in recent years to influence Senate GOP primaries in order to expand the number of like-minded Republicans, frequently in opposition to the candidates preferred by the national party. He has stated that he would "rather have 30 Republicans in the Senate who believe in the principles of freedom than 60 who don't believe in anything" (*National Journal* 2010).

Beyond these specific examples, there is plenty of testimonial evidence from participants and observers about these changes in the Senate. A salient example is the view expressed by Sen. Evan Bayh in February 2010 when he unexpectedly announced that he would not seek a third term. Bayh lamented, "There is too much partisanship and not enough progress— too much narrow ideology and not enough practical problem solving" (Cillizza and Murray 2010). In an interview the following month, he articulated exactly the developments we have been discussing: "The most energetic elements of both parties sometimes frustrate the cause of progress by taking an all-or-nothing approach. . . . There's a tendency on the part of some to view any compromise as an act of weakness or immorality" (Rushing 2010).

## Intermediate Consequences

These primary causal forces lead to intermediate consequences that, in turn, reinforce the effects of the primary forces. One result of increasing party homogeneity is the lack of opposite-party ideological allies.

*The lack of opposite-party ideological allies.* In the mid-twentieth century Senate, no matter where a senator stood on the ideological spectrum, he or she had allies with similar positions in the other party (Sinclair 2006; see also Chapter 1 in this volume). That is no longer true, and for the members who tilt toward the extremes there is no one across the aisle whose views are even remotely close. It is no wonder that today the kind of easy, close personal relationships between members of different parties that were common fifty, or even twenty-five, years ago are rare. Increasingly, senators see their opposite numbers less as individual human beings and more as political platforms, which they are likely to find unattractive. This makes it more difficult to bridge policy differences and find common ground, and has the increasing tendency to transform policy disagreements into personal dislike.

*The uncertainty of majority control.* A second consequence is the uncertainty of majority control. Until 1980 there was little doubt at the beginning of any Congress which party would be in the majority at the beginning of the next. The Democrats had held unbroken control of the chamber since 1955, but beginning with the surprise shift in control at the time of Ronald Reagan's initial election all that changed. From 1980 on changing party fortunes for the GOP in the South and of the Democrats elsewhere has made room for doubt about who will have control of the Senate. The majority party has changed six times between 1980 and 2009.

As a result of this development, members and leaders of both parties must constantly calculate the potential impact of every legislative act, not only on their own personal electoral survival, but also on the possibility of a shift in majority control. And that majority control is of great consequence to members, regardless of their political goals. For policy-motivated senators, whether or not their party is in the majority can mean the difference in whether their preferred policy is adopted by the Senate. For power-motivated members, majority status means control of committee and subcommittee chairs, all of which are denied to minority members. And for senators concerned about their own reelection, being in the majority provides greater access to campaign funds and other electorally relevant resources.

*Increased nationalization of elections.* A related electoral consequence has come in the increased nationalization of Senate elections, seen through a partisan prism. Since the 1970s, voters have had clearer and more divergent images of the two parties. Over that period they have increasingly perceived differences between Democrats and Republicans, with the GOP seen as the more conservative party (Aldrich 2011). Those developments have made the party label an easier and a more informative basis for voter choice, and this in turn has led voters increasingly to respond to elections in partisan terms, making the link between party identification and choice stronger than it has been for decades (Bartels 2000; Aldrich 2011; see also Chapter 2 in this volume). Of course, it has been known for a long time that party has had an impact on the outcome of congressional elections, both in individual races and in the aggregate, as in the well-established propensity of the president's party to lose House seats in midterms. But recent research shows that both the collective evaluation of Congress's performance and the degree of unity within each party have important consequences for individual and collective electoral success (Jones and McDermott 2009; Grynaviski 2010).

One manifestation of the increased consequence of party labels in Senate elections is the significant tendency since 1980 of close races to move in tandem in favor of one party at the end of the campaign in years when there is a "national tide" in favor of that party. Table 12.1 illustrates this

**Table 12.1**    Senate Elections in "National Tide" Years since 1980

| Year | Number of close races | Number won by advantaged party | Percentage won by advantaged party |
|---|---|---|---|
| 1980 | 16 | 13 | 81 |
| 1986 | 15 | 11 | 73 |
| 1994 | 17 | 11 | 65 |
| 2000 | 12 | 8 | 67 |
| 2004 | 9 | 8 | 89 |
| 2006 | 11 | 10 | 91 |
| 2008 | 11 | 7 | 64 |
| Total | 91 | 68 | 75 |

pattern. There have been seven election years from 1980 to the present in which one party gained four or more seats (and no other in which a party gained more than two seats). If we accept this as a rough indicator that a national trend favored that party, we can see what happened in close races in those years.[1] It is apparent that the nationally favored party took the lion's share of close races in each year. In every year the advantaged party won at least 64 percent of the close contests, and the overall average was 75 percent. This pattern offers potentially convincing evidence to members of a party that if they stick together, and if they are successful in helping to fashion a positive perception of their party, that can facilitate securing or expanding a Senate majority.

Moreover, parties have become more consequential as organizational actors in elections. Four or five decades ago the national parties played little role in the recruitment or funding of Senate candidates. In those days, candidates were largely self-starters who bore the responsibility of securing the resources to sustain their campaigns. More recently, national parties have become active in candidate selection, encouraging some to run and discouraging others, based largely on perceptions of likely success. In addition, the party campaign committees have become major players in raising and spending campaign funds. In 2008, for example, the Democratic Senate Campaign Committee spent over $3 million in each of eight contests and over $70 million in total. The corresponding GOP committee spent over $3 million in seven separate races, with total spending in excess of $36 million (Campaign Finance Institute 2008). The people who contribute the funds to these committees care a great deal about the *collective* actions of the parties in

---

1. Close races are those contests that *CQ Weekly* categorized as "no clear favorite" or only leaning toward a party in the last assessment before the election.

office, and about the policies they pursue. Thus all of these nationalizing electoral trends reinforce the internal homogeneity of the parties and the partisan polarization between them.

*Increased pressures for partisan conformity.* The growth of ideological homogeneity and interparty divergence, both within the Senate and among party identifiers and activists, has produced powerful pressures for partisan conformity among members. The exterior pressures are sometimes manifested in ideology-based primary challenges like those discussed above. In other cases, they take the form of criticism and attacks directed at "transgressors" (which, of course, carry the potential for future challenges). For example, Sen. Lindsey Graham (R-S.C.) was censured by two South Carolina county Republican committees for working with Democrats on a number of issues (see "S.C. Republicans" 2010). Similarly, the conservative website Redstate.com called Graham a "RINO (Republican in Name Only), and commentator Glenn Beck said: "You read his stuff. It's like reading Obama's campaign speech" (Milbank 2010).

Nor are more conventional GOP senators immune from such pressure. In December 2009, during the health care debate, Rush Limbaugh and The Gun Owners of America attacked Minority Leader Mitch McConnell (Ky.) for not being sufficiently aggressive in his opposition to the Democrats' bill (Bolton 2009b). Perhaps coincidentally (or perhaps not), shortly after the Limbaugh criticisms McConnell gave an interview assessing Barack Obama's first year in which he attacked the president's "hard left" agenda (Stanton 2009).

In addition to the outside pressures, and partly because of them, both Democratic and Republican members regularly face demands for partisan conformity from their colleagues. One example on the Democratic side involved efforts by Sen. Max Baucus of Montana, chair of the Finance Committee, to negotiate compromises with GOP members on the health care bill (see Pierce and Drucker 2009a). Liberals indicated that Baucus was entertaining options that they would not support, and Majority Leader Harry Reid of Nevada told Baucus that his bill had to include certain provisions backed by the White House despite Republican resistance. Many Democrats thought that Baucus was just being used by opponents of reform to delay final consideration of the bill. In response, some liberals floated the idea of a secret-ballot vote at the beginning of every Congress on whether a committee chair should continue in his or her position (Bolton 2009a).

Such pressures are even stronger in the GOP given Republicans' minority status, especially since the Democrats regained the White House. Minority Leader McConnell argued that a strategy of united resistance to the majority's proposals was the best avenue to pursue, and his colleagues overwhelmingly agreed. Pursuing this course, great efforts were made to keep members in line. Arlen Specter indicated that during the

2009 economic stimulus talks (before he switched parties) he experienced "tremendous" pressure from GOP leaders "not to participate." And Sen. Bob Corker (R-Tenn.), scarcely a moderate, acknowledged that his party leaders discouraged cooperation with Democrats on many issues (Newmyer and Pierce 2010).

Another target of Republican conservatives was Sen. Charles Grassley of Iowa, the ranking Republican on the Finance Committee. Grassley had often compromised with Democrats in the past, raising his colleagues' ire and angering conservatives back home in the process. In 2008 Grassley was passed over for appointment as a delegate to the party's national convention. In response to internal pressure over health care, Grassley pledged before a full meeting of the Senate Republican Conference that he would reveal the details of any potential deal before he made any commitments to Baucus and the Democrats (see Calmes 2009; Bolton 2009c).

The growth of these exterior and interior pressures does not mean that there is no cooperation on legislative matters between members across party lines. Indeed, a substantial majority of the legislative agenda is consensual (Klein 2009). It does mean, however, that on issues important to partisans, and especially on the most salient ones, inter-party cooperation and compromise is significantly less likely than it used to be, and that those members who deviate from the party line have more reason to anticipate threats and sanctions.

## Partisan Procedural Politics

The major causal forces we have discussed, reinforced by the intermediate consequences, have interacted to create a twenty-first century Senate context with incentives for members that are markedly altered compared to the past. These altered incentives have resulted in a final major change in the Senate: members of both parties now employ Senate rules differently in order to accomplish their political ends. As the essays by Frances Lee, Steven Smith, and Barbara Sinclair in this volume make clear, the Senate's procedural politics have changed profoundly over time. Consider one salient example. In December of 1964, Mike Manatos, Lyndon Johnson's Senate liaison, wrote the president to provide an assessment of the chances for his Medicare proposal in light of the outcomes of the November elections. Manatos said: "If all our supporters are present and voting we would win by a vote of 55 to 45" (Klein 2009). The key point is that Manatos never mentioned the possibility of a filibuster against the bill, even though the fifty-five votes of support would have been twelve short of the number needed to invoke cloture under the two-thirds standard then in effect. This was because none of the participants in the process at the time had any expectation that a filibuster would be used for that purpose, despite substantial opposition to the bill. In light of the situation in today's Senate, such restraint can only be called quaint.

Another unusual feature, by current standards, of the Senate's consideration of the Medicare bill in 1965 was its speed. The first roll call on an amendment to the bill was taken on July 8, initial passage of the bill occurred on July 9, and the conference report was adopted on July 28—three weeks from start to finish. These two aspects of the Senate's consideration of Medicare relate to what are, I believe, the two fundamental strategic aspects of the procedural transformation of the body: blocking and delay. And, as Steven Smith points out in Chapter 7, central to our understanding of procedural transformation is that it occurred in the context of the polarization of policy preferences by party—due to the causal forces we have discussed.

As preferences became more similar within parties, and more different between them, the majority party more often became the source of policy proposals that appealed to most of its members, especially when the party also held the presidency. For the same reasons, the majority's proposals became increasingly unattractive to the minority. With the increase in homogeneity in both parties, the minority became less and less able to secure majority party allies to prevent adoption of majority proposals. Thus, if minority members were to prevent adoption of the majority's agenda, they had to rely on their own resources. Simple arithmetic made it clear that this could not be done with just votes, so the minority turned increasingly to their only other feasible alternative: procedure.

*Minority moves.* The prototypical procedural device to employ was the filibuster. Eric Schickler notes in Chapter 1 that, based on research by Barbara Sinclair, in the period 1951–1960 there was an average of only one filibuster and two cloture votes per Congress. The number of filibusters began to increase in the 1970s, but as recently as Jimmy Carter's first Congress (1977–78) there were only thirteen cloture roll calls, accounting for just 1 percent of votes. In 110th Congress (2007–08), however, there were 112 roll calls on cloture, 17 percent of the total (see Figure 12.1). Figure 12.2 shows the increasing partisanship of roll calls on cloture. In 1977–78 (the 95th Congress), the average index of cohesion for both parties was below .6.[2] By 1995–96 (the 104th Congress), the average cohesion for both parties was close to .9, and it has remained near that level in most congresses since.

Thus the filibuster has become not just a weapon of assorted minorities in the Senate; it is a weapon of the minority *party*, and its use has expanded substantially. That expansion reflects the fact that the filibuster has also changed from a device primarily used to try to block the passage of

---

2. The index of cohesion is the absolute difference between the proportion of party members voting "aye" and the proportion voting "nay" on a roll call.

**Figure 12.1**    Roll Calls on Cloture as a Percentage of All Roll Calls,
95th–110th Senate (1977–2008)

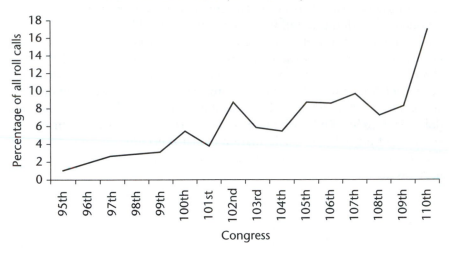

**Figure 12.2**    Index of Cohesion on Cloture Roll Calls, by Party,
95th–110th Senate (1977–2008)

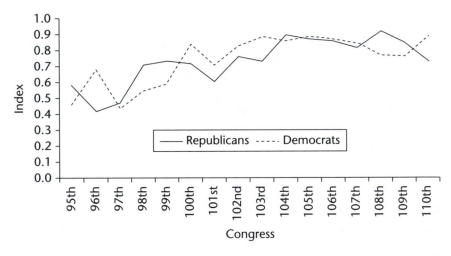

Note: Index of cohesion computes the absolute difference between the proportion of a party's members voting "aye" and the proportion voting "nay" on a given vote.

a few specific bills that an ad hoc minority strongly opposed to one that was used across a wide range of bills to drain legislative time in order to prevent the majority party from doing much at all. In the twenty-first century Senate, the operative word with regard to the use of "extended debate" (as the filibuster is known) is *extended*.

Moreover, the filibuster has become not just a legislative weapon for the minority party, but an electoral one as well. The watershed event for this development was the GOP success in taking control of the Senate in 1994. Leading up to the elections, Senate Republicans came to believe that if the Democrats could be prevented from passing their agenda, the public would blame the majority—due to their unified control of government—rather than the minority. As a consequence, they launched a series of filibusters against Democratic priorities late in 1994 and succeeded in blocking virtually all of them. When the elections gave the GOP majority control, many in both parties were convinced of the success of the Republicans' strategy. And while it is difficult to be certain of the role the strategy played in the GOP's electoral triumph, some evidence suggests that they were right (Abramson, Aldrich, and Rohde 1995).

In the context of this previous experience, after Obama's election and the Democrats' Senate gains in 2008 Minority Leader McConnell proposed a strategy of united resistance for his party conference. As a *New York Times* analysis put it, he wanted to "use his extensive knowledge of Senate procedure to slow things down, take advantage of the difficulties Democrats would have in governing, and deny Democrats any Republican support on big legislation" (Hulse and Nagourney 2010). He was almost completely successful in holding his members together, with few defections on major bills. And the strategy seemed to have its promised benefits, as the Democrats' difficulties in passing bills on health care, financial reform, and other matters were accompanied by declining approval numbers for Obama and congressional Democrats. As McConnell said in an interview about his strategy: "I think the reason my members are feeling really good . . . is they believe that the reward for playing team ball this year was the reversal of the political environment and the possibility that we will have a bigger team next year" (Hulse and Nagourney 2010).

The procedural strategies of Senate minorities include more than the just outright filibusters. Some devices, like "holds," are related to the filibuster. Holds are, as Smith describes in Chapter 7, requests by a member that a measure not be considered on the floor. The requests win compliance because they are backed by the implicit threat to object to a unanimous consent request and/or to launch a filibuster if they are not. Holds are used not just on legislation, but also to prevent votes on presidential nominations, as Sarah Binder illustrates in Chapter 9 (Pear and Herszenhorn 2009).[3]

Another delaying device is the amendment process. When the Senate began debate on the health care bill, Sen. Judd Gregg (R-N.H.) circulated

---

3. Additionally, she illustrates that holds on nominations are also sometimes used to extract executive compliance on matters that have nothing to do with the nominations per se.

a memo to his GOP colleagues entitled "minority rights." In it he reminded them that unless the Democrats successfully invoked cloture the minority had the right to offer an unlimited number of amendments "germane or nongermane—on any subject" (Pear and Herzenhorn 2009). (Non-germane amendments are those that deal with some other subject than what the bill under consideration addresses.)

The strategy of a deluge of amendments is often referred to as a "filibuster by amendment," and the Republican minority in the last two congresses has sought to use it extensively. Delay is not, however, the only potential benefit. Electoral payoffs may be targeted as well, as when majority senators are forced to vote on a non-germane issue that will cause them trouble back home. And often amendments that are technically germane will be used to the same purpose. For example, Coburn offered an amendment to the health care bill that would have prohibited subsidizing the purchase of erectile dysfunction medication by registered sex offenders (*CQ Weekly*, March 29, 2010). Coburn also made known early in 2010 that he was preparing a set of amendments on gun rights that he planned to offer to a variety of bills (Stanton 2010b).

I think that a key point to recognize is that given the homogeneous policy preferences within the minority and their divergence from the majority's preferences, most members of the minority see procedural exploitation as the only workable strategy open to them. For most, a compromise in the middle between the parties would be unacceptable if they are motivated by their own policy goals, and it would be unacceptable to their party base if they are not. Even worse, from either point of view, would be acceptance of the majority's proposals; that would be capitulation and betrayal. Thus, most members of the minority are left to embrace the options of resistance and delay through procedural devices. However, few minority senators find just saying no to be a desirable option. Most of them want to take positive legislative action, even if it is just to undo things the majority has done, and in almost all instances that would require majority control to switch. This provides strong incentives to support party strategies designed to undermine the majority's electoral fortunes.

*Majority responses.* Just as procedural strategies provide the only feasible options for the minority, the same is usually true for the majority as a consequence of the minority's actions. Those majority senators who care about policy want to accomplish things while they can, and the remainder will be concerned about their own electoral survival and the maintenance of their majority status. Short of having at least sixty votes, the majority cannot prevail by numbers alone, and even with sixty votes only perfect cohesion can accomplish that.

Of course a partial strategy in response is to maximize majority unity and impose cloture whenever possible. In most congresses, cloture votes have been successful less than half the time, although in the 111th Congress Reid's success rate was nearly 90 percent (see *CQ Weekly,* April 19, 2010). However, even when successful cloture as a strategy deals only with the minority's outright blocking power; the minority still has other procedural devices available.

Thus the majority party too must turn to parliamentary devices to move forward on the items on their agenda, and the impetus for doing so does not come solely from party leaders. The same goals mentioned above for minority members—achieving desired policies, personal reelection, majority status—motivate majority senators, and these concerns are especially prominent among more junior senators. In the spring of 2010, junior Democrats who were frustrated by Republican tactics pressed Harry Reid to become more aggressive in response. Sheldon Whitehouse (D-R.I.) said: "I think we've allowed the Republicans to get away with too much obstruction without using our prerogatives" (Stanton 2010c). One Democratic majority strategy is to compel minority senators to actually filibuster to block Democratic proposals rather than simply permit them to rely on secret holds or other tactics outside the public eye. The Bunning filibuster described above began with a hold, but when he was forced to act in the open he could not sustain the support of other Republicans.

Another majority strategy is to use procedural devices to exert some control over the amendment process. Without a unanimous consent agreement, the Senate's amendment process is usually open and unrestricted, as noted above, but there are some ways to counter the deluge. A tabling motion is one way. Instead of permitting the minority to put majority members on the record on the substance of a politically risky amendment, the majority can move to table it. Majority senators from constituencies that would favor the amendment may feel the leeway to oppose it on the procedural move when they would not feel safe voting against the substance. Because of this difference in context, tabling motions have become a prominent device for countering minority amendments. Those motions have the additional benefit to the majority of being non-debatable, permitting disposing of amendments without using up a lot of time (see Hartog and Monroe 2008; King, Orlando, and Rohde 2010).

An analogous device for preventing a substantive vote on an amendment is a motion that the amendment would violate some provision of budget rules governing the matter under debate. While the use of this procedure is thereby limited in scope, like the tabling motion it permits majority senators to avoid being put on the record on difficult substantive issues by disposing of an amendment on a procedural vote. Moreover, it has the additional advantage for the majority that in order for the minority to overcome the device they must secure the votes of sixty senators to waive the budget provisions. Obviously, overcoming this super-majority requirement would be very difficult for the minority when pursuing a partisan end (see Gold 2008).

Another procedural strategy offers an alternative means of overcoming the filibuster threat: reconciliation. A part of the budget reform process in the 1970s, reconciliation was originally designed to be a means for making spending align with revenues. In relatively short order, however, the device was also used to try to enact significant policy changes, including the overhaul of welfare programs in 1996, and both parties employed it when in the majority (see Mann et al. 2010). The principal attractions of reconciliation bills in this context are that they cannot be filibustered, and that all amendments must be germane. Of course most readers will already know that this process was used in 2010 to pass the Democrats' health care reform bill without any GOP support. Democratic moderates had voiced reluctance to use reconciliation to pass such a major program, but as it became clear that unified Republican resistance would make any alternative route impossible, most acquiesced. In the end, only three Democrats voted no.

Of course, even in combination these procedural devices do not make the Senate into a majority rule institution like the House. They do, however, permit a unified majority party to mitigate the minority's blocking and delaying tactics now so commonplace in the chamber. The partisan uses of procedure by the minority party are countered by the equally partisan use of procedures by the majority.

## Looking Ahead

With our discussion of the significant causal forces that research indicates have shaped the twenty-first-century Senate now complete, we can revisit those forces to assess the likely patterns of operation the Senate will display as the century moves forward. The first, and probably the most dependable, expectation is that the polarized political environment will persist. The political divisions that resulted from the realignment discussed above are likely to remain in effect until a major new issue emerges to alter them or until one of the parties becomes so persistently unsuccessful that it is forced to change its approach to the electorate. New presidents of both parties, including the two most recent ones, as well as congressional leaders of new majorities routinely promise to work in a bipartisan manner with their opposition. And the willingness to do so is sincere—each side would be happy to be part of bipartisan majorities, but not at the price of giving up their own policy priorities.

The rank-and-file voters of each party have different preferences, their activists have different preferences, and their officeholders have different preferences, and on most important issues those differences are very stark (at least for the latter two groups). Relatively few senators have either personal preferences or constituency-induced preferences for an outcome in the middle of the policy spectrum, and those that do are constrained from pursuing them by pressure from their electoral bases and their colleagues. It seems exceedingly unlikely that the current make-up of primary electorates that advantage more extreme candidates relative to centrist ones will undergo systematic change. It is also unlikely that we will see fewer senators with strong personal policy commitments. If that is true, then the internal pressures against moderation and compromise will persist along with the external ones.

This means that the incentives that have induced the parties to pursue partisan procedural politics will probably not diminish. As long as the senators of each party disagree about what policies are desirable and care about policy outcomes (either personally or because of their electorates), the use of procedure to advance their causes will seem advantageous, if not essential. The only ways I can see that this situation might change would be either if members develop a new sense of self-restraint regarding procedural strategies, or if the substantial procedural advantages granted to minorities by the rules of the Senate were significantly diminished. The first development is implausible. If one party were to change strategies unilaterally, the policy consequences would be severe, and the personal animosities between parties that the current situation has fostered undermine the trust that a joint bargain would require.

That leaves institutional reform. As noted above, the core of the current procedural situation rests on the filibuster rules. Some tinkering could be done with the rules on secret holds, but by itself that would make little difference. On the filibuster, it seems almost inconceivable that a significant change could muster the sixty-seven votes necessary to end debate on that move. So the only remaining option is some version of the "reform by ruling" scenario, discussed by Steven Smith in Chapter 7, in which the presiding officer rules that a simple majority of the Senate can change the rules (probably at the beginning of a Congress). Even if that scenario were feasible, it is not clear that fifty-one members of the majority would support it. Some majority senators may oppose such a device on principle, and others may be unwilling to sacrifice the weapons of minority status, especially as long as maintenance of majority status remains doubtful. Thus, absent some "nuclear option," it seems likely that the polarized and procedurally partisan Senate will be with us for a considerable time.

## References

Abramson, Paul R., John H. Aldrich, and David W. Rohde. 1995. *Change and Continuity in the 1992 Elections*, rev. ed. Washington, D.C.: CQ Press.

Aldrich, John H. 1995. *Why Parties? The Origin and Transformation of Political Parties in America*. Chicago: University of Chicago Press.

————. 2011. *Why Parties? A Second Look*. Chicago: University of Chicago Press.

Bartels, Larry M. 2000. "Partisanship and Voting Behavior, 1952–1996." *American Journal of Political Science* 44 (January).

Bolton, Alexander. 2009a. "Dems Warn Baucus with Gavel Threat." *The Hill*, July 3.

————. 2009b. "Limbaugh vs. McConnell as Conservative Groups Target GOP Leader on Amendments." *The Hill*, December 10.

————. 2009c. "Sen. Grassley Promises Not to Sell Out His Party." *The Hill*, July 31.

Calmes, Jackie. 2009. "G.O.P. Senator Draws Critics in Both Parties." *New York Times*, Sept. 23.

Campaign Finance Institute. 2008. "A First Look at Money in the House and Senate Elections." November 8.

Cillizza, Chris, and Shailagh Murray. 2010. "Bayh Announces He Won't Seek 3rd Senate Term." *Washington Post*, February 16.

*CQ Weekly*, January 11, 2010.

*CQ Weekly*, March 29, 2010.

*CQ Weekly*, April 19, 2010.

Gardner, Amy. 2010. "For Tea Party, Victory at Utah GOP Convention." *Washington Post*, May 9.

Gold, Martin B. 2008. *Senate Procedure and Practice*, 2nd ed. New York: Rowman & Littlefield.

Grynaviski, Jeffrey D. 2010. *Partisan Bonds*. Cambridge: Cambridge University Press.

Hartog, Chris Den, and Nathan W. Monroe. 2008. "Agenda Influence and Tabling Motions in the U. S. Senate." In Nathan Monroe, Jason M. Roberts, and David W. Rohde, eds., *Why Not Parties?* Chicago, University of Chicago Press.

Hulse, Carl, and Adam Nagourney. 2010. "G.O.P. Leader Finds Weapon in Party Unity." *New York Times*, March 17.

Jones, David R., and Monika L. McDermott. 2009. *Americans, Congress, and Democratic Responsiveness*. Ann Arbor: University of Michigan Press.

Kiely, Kathy. 2010. "Voter Turnouts for Primaries 'a Concern.'" *USA Today*, March 15.

King, Aaron S., Frank J. Orlando, and David W. Rohde. 2010. "Beyond Motions to Table: Exploring the Procedural Toolkit of the Majority Party in the United States Senate." Paper delivered at the annual meeting of the Midwest Political Science Association, Chicago.

Klein, Ezra. 2009. "After Health Care, We Need Senate Reform." *Washington Post*, December 27.

Mann, Thomas E., Norman J. Ornstein, Raffaela Wakeman, and Fogelson-Lubliner. 2010. "Reconciling with the Past" www.nytimes.com, March 6. Accessed on March 16, 2010.

Mayhew, David R. 1974. *Congress: The Electoral Connection*. New Haven, Conn.: Yale University Press.

Milbank, Dana. 2010. "Running Afoul of Purity Police." *Durham Herald-Sun*, March 16.

*National Journal*, June 19, 2010.

Newmyer, Tory, and Emily Pierce. 2010. "Bipartisanship Has Few Fans." *Roll Call*, February 1.

Pear, Robert, and David M Herszenhorn. 2009. "Senate Breaks Health Stalemate; First Votes Today." www.nytimes.com, December 2.

Philips, Michael M. 2010. "McCain Tested from Right Flank." online.wsj.com, February 4.

Pierce, Emily, and David M. Drucker. 2009a. "Baucus Presses for Health Deal." *Roll Call*, July 9.

———. 2009b. "Partisan Wars Erupt in Senate." *Roll Call*, December 17.

Poole, Keith T., and Howard Rosenthal. 2007. *Ideology and Congress*. New Brunswick, N.J.: Transaction Publishers.

Rohde, David W. 1991. *Parties and Leaders in the Postreform House*. Chicago: University of Chicago Press.

Rohde, David, and John Aldrich. 2010. "Consequences of Electoral and Institutional Change: The Evolution of Conditional Party Government in the United States." In Jeffrey M. Stonecash, ed., *New Directions in American Political Parties*. New York: Routledge.

Rucker, Philip. 2010. "Unions Turn against Sen. Lincoln in Ark. Democratic Primary." *Washington Post*, May 11.

Rushing, J. Taylor. 2010. "Senator Evan Bayh: News of My Retirement Got Ahead of Me." *The Hill*, March 16.

"S.C. Republicans Scold Graham Again." 2010. *USA Today*, January 6.

Sinclair, Barbara. 2006. *Party Wars*. Norman: University of Oklahoma Press.

———. 2009. "The New World of U.S. Senators." In Lawrence C. Dodd and Bruce I. Oppenheimer, eds., *Congress Reconsidered*, 9th ed. Washington, D.C.: CQ Press.

Stanton, John . 2009. "McConnell's Fighting Words." *Roll Call*, December 10.

———. 2010a. "Coburn Hijacks Debate on Debt Limit Hike." rollcall.com, January 26. Accessed February 11, 2010.

———. 2010b. "Coburn Takes Out the Guns." *Roll Call*, February 4.

———. 2010c. "Junior Democrats Want a Fight." *Roll Call*, March 4.

Stanton, John, and Emily Pierce. 2010. "GOP Sending Mixed Signals on Bunning Blockade." rollcall.com, March 2. Accessed March 16, 2010.

Theriault, Sean M. 2008. *Party Polarization in Congress*. New York: Cambridge University Press.

Theriault, Sean M., and David W. Rohde. 2011. "The Gingrich Senators and Party Polarization in the U.S. Senate." *Journal of Politics* 73 (forthcoming).

# Index